I0453512

Black Mecca Down: The Fall of the City Too Busy to Hate

Black Mecca Down

The Fall of the City Too Busy to Hate

By Paul Kersey

ANTELOPE HILL PUBLISHING

Copyright © 2012, 2023 Paul Kersey

First print edition published 2012. This second edition
published 2023 by Antelope Hill Publishing. Second printing.

This work is a compilation of articles originally
published on SBPDL Blog at *The Unz Review*,
except where otherwise noted, 2011 to 2012.

Cover art by Swifty.

Antelope Hill Publishing | antelopehillpublishing.com

Paperback ISBN-13: 979-8-89252-003-4
EPUB ISBN-13: 979-8-89252-004-1

Dedicated to the memory of Brittney Watts

Contents

Introduction

In the final days of 2012, only a few people are aware of the coming fury. American history—according to White liberals—goes something like this:

- Evil White people killed a bunch of Native Americans
- Evil White people exploited Black slaves in building a great nation
- Evil White people from the southern states tried to secede, so righteous White people (who would later be evil again) from the northern states waged war on them
- Evil White people in Europe had to be defeated by evil White people in America during World War II
- Evil White people in America, having defeated evil White people in Germany, were practicing racism by denying Black people freedom
- Holy Black people marched for their civil rights
- Evil White people in places like Little Rock, Oxford, and Birmingham fought holy Black people
- Civil rights became the law of the land; holy Black people took control of their own destiny

Well, the narrative of American history flows something like that in the history classrooms across the nation, with a good measure of blankets covered in small pox for Indians, ubiquitous lynchings for Black people, and the dastardly Jim Crow denying Blacks their freedom.

But one thing you don't get in American history is what comes after the Civil Rights movement in 1960s; what happened to cities like Little Rock and Birmingham? What hap-

1

pened to those cities, like Detroit, which saw its Black population explode from less than 1.2 percent in 1910 to more than 92
percent in 2012?

We aren't supposed to even consider this question, for history ends when evil White people were kicked out of power; history doesn't record what happened when those victorious in the
great battle to carry out the Civil Rights agenda took power,
because history is written by the winners.

Thus, Detroit's condition in 2012 after almost forty years of
uninterrupted Black political power is only something evil
White people would care about; after all, freedom for Black people was the ultimate aim of the Civil Rights movements. Who
cares what happened next?

In *Escape from Detroit: The Collapse of America's Black Metropolis*, I documented what happened to the city once known
as "the Arsenal of Democracy."

It's a book that has become an underground bestseller, allowing those individuals still capable of making up their
minds—free of prepackaged, government approved thoughts—
the chance of exploring the truth behind Detroit's demise.

And, yes, it's a story about race.

We live in a nation governed by an ideology, what I've
dubbed Black-Run America (BRA). Put simply, BRA doesn't
necessarily mean that America is run by Black people; it means
America—at every level of society—is run for the benefit of
Black people, to the detriment of everyone else.

Which brings us to the book in your hands. *Black Mecca
Down: The Fall of the City Too Busy to Hate* represents the
work of the past three years, collected from the pages of
SBPDL.com (Stuff Black People Don't Like). It is not a history
lesson of what happened in Atlanta prior to the passing of the
Civil Rights legislation and the dismantling of Jim Crow; it is,
however, a history lesson of the type of government those victorious implemented in cities and counties where they became
the demographic majority.

And, as you'll learn by the actions of people like Maynard Jackson, Victor Hill, Bill Campbell, and Andrew Young, it's a story of the type of retributive justice unleashed upon those vanquished.

But one question this book will address is one that cuts to the heart of the notion of equality: if Atlanta is such a "Black Mecca," why do Black people follow Whites wherever they flee, to whatever suburb they create?

Why can't Black people in Atlanta—who control the government—create an economy or a school system that will see Blacks flourish? Why must they follow White people to Cobb, Douglas, Fayette, Clayton, DeKalb, and Gwinnett County to experience a level of civilization devoid of the wanton violence and crime found in majority Black areas?

Worse, why did Clayton and DeKalb County—once they became majority Black—see the climate of the counties radically altered to become just another extension of the type of community White people initially fled: that being replete with wanton Black violence and crime, plus an unhealthy dose of business closings followed by property devaluations?

All of the below population figures for 1980 and 1997 population by racial groups for each metro Atlanta county is provided by "Sprawl City: Race, Politics, and Planning in Atlanta" (p.123), which help to debunk the idea of exclusively White suburbs that White people have fled to, in a racist attempt to escape Blacks in Atlanta. Of course, the data you are about to read does beg one question; if White people are so racist, why do Black people follow them wherever they go?

In 1980, DeKalb County was 71 percent White and 28 percent Black; by 1997, DeKalb County was 51.1 percent White and 48.9 percent Black. Today, DeKalb County is 30 percent White and 54 percent Black.

In 1980, Clayton County was 91 percent White and 8 percent Black; by 1997, Clayton County was 71 percent White and 28 percent Black. Today, Clayton County is 15 percent White and 66 percent Black.

In 1980, Gwinnett County was 96 percent White and 3 percent Black; by 1997, Gwinnett County was 90 percent White and 9 percent Black. Today, Gwinnett County is 43 percent White and 25 percent Black.

In 1980, Fayette County was 95 percent White and 5 percent Black; by 1997, Fayette County was 91 percent White and 8 percent Black. Today, Fayette County is 67 percent White and 20 percent Black.

In 1980, Rockdale County was 90 percent White and 9 percent Black; by 1997, Rockdale County was 89 percent White and 10 percent Black. Today, Rockdale County is 40 percent White and 46 percent Black.

In 1980, Cobb County was 94 percent White and 5 percent Black; by 1997, Cobb County was 86 percent White and 14 percent Black. Today, Cobb County is 56 percent White and 25 percent Black.

In 1980, Douglas County was 94 percent White and 5 percent Black; by 1997, Douglas County was 90 percent White and 9 percent Black. Today, Douglas County is 48 percent White and 40 percent Black.

In 1980 Cherokee County was 97 percent White and 3 percent Black; by 1997, Cherokee County was 96 percent White and 4 percent Black. Today, Cherokee County is 80 percent White and 6 percent Black.

•   •   •

Maybe it's fate that the city Sherman famously burnt in his march to the sea is on the verge of supplying the entire nation with a glimpse of the future of politics in the United States of America, for in the soil that the entire metro Atlanta area has sprung from resides the blood of those who died defending the idea of self-government and self-determination. "Black Mecca Down" offers a journey into why White people decided to create communities of their own, far from downtown Atlanta and, for a small period of time, devoid of Black residents.

With the fall of Jim Crow, the White middle class fled Atlanta for the suburban counties surrounding Fulton County (home to Atlanta). Places like DeKalb, Cobb, Gwinnett, Clayton, and Fayette County became the destinations of young White people seeking safe communities where they could raise families; as you will see in the pages that follow, Black people, though they politically controlled Atlanta—and eventually Fulton County—weren't capable of creating the same economic prosperity found wherever White refugees (or White transplants from across the nation) decided to reside, so they followed.

Interestingly, the same moral and economic conditions that White people escaped—and which are almost exclusively found in Black communities (high rates of unemployment, little economic development, outrageous rates of crime, rampant out-of-wedlock birthrates and incredibly low property value)—follow Black people wherever they have decided to move in the metro Atlanta region.

Tamar Jacoby, writing in her book *Someone Else's House, America's Unfinished Struggle for Integration: The Effects of the New Racism* noted that the situation in Atlanta, what she called an "uneasy coexistence" might be "as good as it gets" when it comes to race relations in America.

But she is wrong. And it's not just the words of a former Black mayor who vowed to "fight to the death" to maintain affirmative actions in the city that prove this reality.[1]

Though a world class city grew out of the same soil where once an invading army trampled upon the dreams of a people to create a new nation, a long dormant flower is beginning to bloom in Atlanta.

The flower of secession:

---

[1] NYT, "Atlanta's Mayor Defies Threat."

With a belly full of grouper and anger, a Buckhead resident stood before his neighbors at 103 West in the affluent north Atlanta community and unleashed his frustration.

"When is someone going to have them indicted and taken to trial?!?" he barked, eliciting head nods from fellow disgruntled taxpayers picking at their three-course lunches.

The "them" he refers to is the Atlanta municipal government—namely, the public school system, mayor, city council and bean counters who helped dig the $140 million hole in which the city finds itself. The angry man's audience consists of more than 200 Buckhead residents, a well-to-do group of citizens in the city's most well-to-do community.

The occasion? The Fulton County Taxpayers Foundation's luncheon to discuss the controversial—and extremely complex—notion of Buckhead severing ties with Atlanta, a city full of confusion that Glenn Delk, an attorney and 20-year resident of the community, said is subsidized by he and his neighbors' largesse.

Delk, whose study about Buckhead's possible cityhood has kickstarted a serious look into the matter, informed the audience right away that he neither intended to run for political office nor owned commercial property in Buckhead. He appears to simply be a person who doesn't like paying high taxes for what he considers to be subpar services. Plus, he doesn't trust the money management skills of City Hall. To him, and to many in this room, the time has come to break free.

"You will hear some people say this is about race and money," he said. "There's only one color that matters in this debate—and that's the color green."

The crowd ate this up. The city was broken, Delk said, and the same woes it faces today it faced in the past. And as Delk rattled through a laundry list of statistics—the community comprises 15 percent of Atlanta's population yet generates 45 percent of its revenue; a city of Buckhead could be run on $150 million, half the taxes residents pay today to the city—the crowd of predominantly white men and women nodded their heads in agreement.[2]

The question is simply this: why would the residents of Buckhead want to secede from Atlanta, an almost entirely Black-run city? The most obvious reason is property value, followed closely by the supplying of the majority of the tax revenue that goes to support Atlanta and the city services (which primarily are used by Black residents of the city).

In the pages that follow, you'll be treated to the real history of Atlanta and metro Atlanta; you'll be treated to the history of one of America's top cities *after* Jim Crow was toppled; you'll be treated to the history of Atlanta under Black political control. And it is that firm vise on control that Black people refuse to give up, as evidenced by the 2009 Mayoral election in the city:

> The campaign for mayor of this city, which has long promoted its racial tolerance, veered into controversy Thursday with the release of a memo urging black voters to unite around an African-American candidate and block the election of a white mayor.
>
> A local group known as the Black Leadership Forum called for African-Americans to consolidate their support around Lisa Borders, president of the Atlanta City Council and one of several African-American candidates, according to a memo circulated on the Web and to local media.
>
> The group said Ms. Borders had the best chance of winning support from white business leaders and defeating Mary Norwood, a white city councilwoman and a leading candidate for the Nov. 3 election, according to polls.
>
> "For the last 25 years Atlanta has represented the breakthrough for black political empowerment in the South," read the memo. "In order to defeat a Norwood (white) mayoral candidacy we have to get out now and work in a manner to

---

[2] Wheatley, "Buckhead secession movement gains."

defeat her without a runoff, and the key is a significant
Black turnout."

The memo was the sharpest signal yet of overt racial politics creeping into the competition to replace Shirley Franklin, elected as the city's first female mayor in 2001. Atlanta
was the first major Southern city to elect an African-American mayor, Maynard H. Jackson, in 1973. No white candidate has mounted a serious campaign for the office since
then.[3]

Though Mary Norwood would win a plurality of the votes in the
initial election, she would lose in a runoff to Kasim Reed,
thanks largely to the votes of Black men and women, whose
cousins, brothers, sisters, and other family members living in
South Fulton County would take part in a nightmarish scene
in 2010, when more than 30,000 Black people battled over the
right to sign up for subsidized housing vouchers[4].

By less than 1,000 votes did Norwood lose to Reed, in a race
that accentuated the racial divide in Atlanta.

The highest turnout was in Buckhead—the city's whitest,
most affluent area and Norwood's home turf—where more
than 53 percent of registered voters cast ballots. On the
city's heavily black southside, Reed's base of support, better
than 41 percent of registered voters showed up there.

Reed, who ran both of the current mayor's campaigns,
was seen in some corners as the heir to Maynard Jackson.
Jackson was elected the city's first black mayor in 1973,
when blacks wrested control of City Hall from whites after
years of being shut out of city politics. Since then, blacks
have fiercely defended Jackson's legacy, which has been as
much about access as appearances.

During the election, Reed was embraced by Jackson's
family, as well as former mayor and civil rights icon Andrew

---

[3] Bauerlein, "Race Enters Atlanta Mayoral Vote."
[4] MyFoxAtlanta Staff, "Chaos As Crowd Waits."

Young and Franklin—affirmations that may have struck a nostalgic chord with some black voters.

"There are folks who are here who struggled to see the election of black mayors and a majority black city council and school board and a municipal work force," Emory University political science professor Michael Owens said. "That still has a lot of meaning for people, the image of people like them being in control of political resources."[5]

It is in the pages of "Black Mecca Down" that you'll learn if Jacoby's belief that Atlanta is as "good as it gets" when it comes to race relations in America, it might be time to pull the plug on the whole idea of integration once and for all.

---

[5] Haines, "Slim win for mayor."

1

MARTA: Moving Africans Rapidly Through Atlanta (and Employing Them to Tune of 83 Percent of 4,000+ Employees)

October 18th, 2012

Did you ever want to get a taste of the type of waste that comes with the Black-Run America (BRA) racial cronyism that exists in major cities? Atlanta offers a picturesque microcosm for the type of transfer of wealth schemes common around the nation, where White taxpayers pay for the artificial creation of a Black middle class through a public agency completely run for the betterment of Blacks.

Or completely run as an employment agency for Blacks.

The way MARTA (the light rail system) in Atlanta is run crystallizes the problem of how government—be it local, state, or federal—is run for the betterment of a particular racial group.

Back in 1998, the Christian Science-Monitor reported that Mayor Bill Campbell appointed Laura Lawson, a resident of Atlanta's 99 percent Black public housing, as MARTA board chairwoman:

> The new leader of Atlanta's mass transit board will never need to interview riders to find out how well the subway and bus system serves them. She is one of them, depending daily on rail and wheel to take her to her job, church, and children's schools. It's a first for Atlanta—having a transit chief

who doesn't even own a car—and unusual even in cities where public transportation is more a part of life than it is here.

But while the move makes sense, the promotion of Laura Lawson

from Metro Atlanta Rapid Transit Authority board member to MARTA board chairwoman has stirred quite a storm. At its eye are questions of whether common man or powerbroker should lead this organization, and where the organization should be led: to serve affluent suburban commuters or the car-less?

Critics have focused on her years in public housing and wondered if she will be beholden to players such as Mr. Beasley and Mayor Campbell who have helped her achieve what she has. "We know that she describes herself as a paid community organizer of Herndon Homes," writes Atlanta commentator Dick Williams. "Paid by whom? Is she a political operative? A conduit for street money?"

As MARTA chairwoman, she'll be paid $75 per meeting, the same rate as other board members. The board meets once a month.

Lawson stresses that her role as chairwoman of the MARTA board is to solicit input from the 16 other members and work with them to reach a decision agreeable to all— not to push her own agenda. She talks often of teamwork.

"First and foremost I want each and every board member to know that I respect their opinion on every issue," she says. "I wouldn't want any member to feel like their input is not important."

Except for the fact that she lives in public housing, Lawson's path to public service mirrors that of many women leaders today. She first became active in her four children's parent-teacher associations and went on to lead the equivalent of a neighborhood association. She parlayed that into her multiple roles on appointed city boards and now says a run for city council may be in her future.[6]

A perfect representative for the city of Atlanta and a wonderful figurehead for MARTA indeed. This of racial cronyism, putting residents of public housing in charge of a board controlling a quarter of a billion dollars a year, can only be highlighted through employment numbers of the 4,000+ person organiza-tion:

Now, currently MARTA serves only DeKalb and Fulton County. (DeKalb is roughly 55 percent black and 35 percent white; Fulton is roughly 49 percent white and 47 percent black.) But a look at the 2011–2012 employment data show that Sen. Fort and Mr. Evans' fears of discrimination are entirely unfounded: MARTA is currently plagued by a gross lack of diversity, with 83 percent of the 4,527 employees be-ing black.

Of 50 employed dispatchers, only one is not black; 96 per-cent of the 1,227 operators are black; 100 percent of the re-cruiters are black; 85 percent of the 42 MARTA representa-tives are black; 94 percent of 295 people employed in ser-vices are black; 95 percent of the station agents are black; 84 percent of the superintendents are black; 88 percent of the 171 supervisors are black; and 82 percent of the transit police are black.[7]

Why is all the racial data of the employees of MARTA im-portant? Eighty-three percent of the employees of MARTA be-ing Black represents a racial stranglehold on good paying jobs within a system that is hemorrhaging money. Worse, it's a sys-tem that has always been a Black jobs program and a system designed for, ahem, Moving Africans Rapidly Through Atlanta.

Public transportation can work: however, when it's run as a jobs program for otherwise unemployable-in-the-private-sector

---

[6] Nifong, "Atlanta's New Transit Chief."
[7] WND Staff, "Atlanta's tax hike bankrolls."

Black people, and as a dumping ground for social engineering by appointing a Black woman living in public housing as the board chairwoman . . . public transportation will be ineffective and costly.

Just how costly is MARTA (whose ridership is 78 percent Black) being a dumping ground for otherwise unemployable Black people?

MARTA is spending $50 million above the national average for employee benefits, but if it revamped its health care, retirement and worker compensation plans, it could erase a projected $33 million operating deficit, an audit released Monday reveals.

The transit authority will have to cut services even more in a few years if it doesn't control runaway costs, according to the KPMG audit, commissioned by the authority's board of directors to give it a blueprint for stabilizing the troubled finances and to expand its services.

The audit said that, in addition to the labor and retirement savings, the authority could save between $60 million and $142 million over five years by outsourcing many functions. According to the audit, the five-years savings if cleaning services were privatized would be $29 million to $49.5 million.

Moreover, the report said, the high rate of employee absenteeism cost MARTA about $11 million a year, while worker compensation claims were costing $5.5 million more than the national average.

The report will undoubtedly provide ammunition to MARTA's critics in the legislature, who have long contended that the authority's finances were out of control. State Rep. Mike Jacobs, R-Atlanta, who chairs the legislative committee that monitors the quasi independent MARTA, has advocated privatization of some areas, such as payroll, human resources and cleaning.

"The amount of the savings is pretty staggering," he said Monday. "I think it is pretty clear that there are things to be done."[8]

The audit of Black-run (but largely funded through White tax dollars) MARTA also showed this:

> Whoever is chosen for the Atlanta job will be heading an agency with projected financial shortfalls of $114 million by fiscal 2016 and of $248 million by 2021, according to the audit. That could mean potentially large service cuts. The audit also found that the authority needs another $6 billion to $7 billion for capital improvements by 2021.
>
> "For long-term fiscal sustainability, MARTA must alter its revenue or funding sources or decrease its cost structure by a minimum of approximately $25 million annually," the audit said.[9]

Black-Run America is unsustainable.

But don't think this won't stop those Black people in charge of protecting primarily Black MARTA employees:

> MARTA union leaders don't see the recent management audit of the financially troubled transit agency as a blueprint for survival. They see is as an assault on labor.
>
> "It is a clear attack on labor, and ultimately it is an attack on the community," said Curtis Howard, president of the Amalgamated Transit Union chapter at MARTA. "We've been giving concessions (for years) to keep our jobs. We don't have any more to give. . . . We're down to the bone."
>
> Howard said the audit—which says the transit agency is spending $50 million above the national average for employee benefits—glosses over realities and management shortcomings and makes it appear that employee benefits and loafing workers are pushing the transit agency toward

---

[8] Visser, "Audit: MARTA spends $50M."
[9] Ibid.

insolvency. Bad management is the root of the problem, he said.

"This issue is critically important to the future of MARTA, our customers and our employees," MARTA spokesman Lyle V. Harris said. "But any attempt to draw conclusions about how we intend to proceed, or to predict outcomes, is extremely premature at this point."

KPMG auditors delivered a draft of their in-depth analysis of the transit agency—which has a $33 million operating deficit—last month to MARTA officials. The auditors zeroed in on key areas to focus on to reshape MARTA finances and made the following recommendations:

- Revamping the health care, retirement, and workers' compensation plans the audit said were pushing benefits so high above the national average.
- Outsourcing agency functions such as payroll and cleaning—privatization—to save between $60 million and $120 million a year.
- Attacking high rates of employee absenteeism, which cost MARTA as much as $11 million a year (MARTA officials say further analysis puts the number at $8 million), and use of workers' comp, which costs about $5 million more than the national average.[10]

Chronic absenteeism? MARTA's personnel is 83 percent Black. Who's to blame here? The evil auditors who dared point out the inefficiencies in the almost entirely Black workforce of MARTA?[11]

But here's the key quote:

Moreover, he said, assaults on bus drivers prompt absenteeism—and the union has been pushing to make buses more secure. Last November, *The Atlanta Journal-Constitution* documented a rise in physical assaults on drivers over the

---

[10] Visser, "Union leaders say MARTA."
[11] WND Staff, "Atlanta's tax hike bankrolls."

first quarter of the fiscal year—15 assaults and seven robberies.

"If I get assaulted, I'm not coming to work tomorrow,"
Howard said, adding that assaults lead to stress. "That is
absenteeism."

MARTA is currently spending $17 million to install video
cameras on buses and trains—partly funded with a $9 mil-
lion federal grant—that transit officials say will help police
investigate crime and the agency resolve customer complaints.[12]

MARTA ridership is . . . what again? Oh, 78 percent Black. And
assaults are up on MARTA employees (83 percent Black). Correlation?

Perhaps you now know why White people stay away from
MARTA, and the organization with huge financial shortfalls is
trying to remake its image:

MARTA's No. 1 image problem is a perception that the system is unsafe, but that could be fixed, in part, with a few
well-placed Coca-Cola vending machines. So says a marketing proposal to renovate MARTA's image as the transit
agency embarks on a $700,000 program this month to win
more riders and expand its reach. People feel safe and com-
forted when they're near the familiar red-and-white Coke
logo, says the Atlanta marketing firm Turner Fernandez
Turner.

Acknowledging "this is going to sound crazy," the firm
suggests that putting Coke vending machines on MARTA
trains would conjure up "all sorts of positive images of child-
hood, security, stability and Americana."

In many ways, MARTA's image problems are typical of
systems throughout the country.

---

[12] Visser, "Union leaders say MARTA."

"People in the suburbs think MARTA is a black, transit-dependent system," said the agency's chairman, Bill Moseley. "Some people are saying they don't like the MARTA name."

For three decades the MARTA acronym has been the subject of a racially charged joke: "You know what MARTA really stands for, don't you? Moving Africans Rapidly Through Atlanta."[13]

Some things never change.

MARTA's No. 1 image problem—like public transportation across the nation—is because it's a Black-run system, whose primarily Black ridership makes it unsafe for sorely needed higher White ridership levels.

Just how unsafe is MARTA. Back in 2011, two employees of Delta Airlines were attacked by 30+ Black people aboard a Marta train:

MARTA police said they were investigating the incident. A witness said he watched the violent attack unfold Sunday.

"We were intimidated. Everyone was terrified. People were trying to run, but there was nowhere to run," the man, who requested anonymity, told Channel 2's Erica Byfield. Around midnight, a MARTA train pulled up to the Garnett Station in Downtown Atlanta, authorities said. The witness said up to 30 people boarded the southbound train." Once the doors opened, it was like a bum rush of people," he told Byfield. "The next thing you know, they started just beating him. There was blood everywhere. People were hollering and screaming," he said. A MARTA police report identified two victims as Delta Airlines employees.

The report said one victim had a soda can smashed in his face and his wallet stolen, while the other was punched repeatedly in his face. The witness said the attackers were teens chanting "B. F. P. L." "I don't know if that's a gang," the witness said. By the time the train made it to West End

---

[13] McCosh, "MARTA calls on marketers."

stop, some riders were desperate to get off, but the car doors would not open, the witness said. "So basically we were just trapped," he said. The witness told Byfield he saw the teens exit the train at the Oakland City stop. "For people to have to witness that it is ridiculous," he said.[14]

The *Atlanta Journal-Constitution* called the group of thirty-plus attackers "teens," though a correct description would be "Black teens," but that is not allowed in BRA:

"There was blood everywhere, people were hollering and screaming," a witness told Channel 2 Action News. "We were intimidated. People were terrified. People were trying to run. But there was nowhere to run."

Flight attendant Parker Stanea, 28, told officers a diminutive black male, no taller than 5'4", emerged from the pack of teens to hit him over the left eye with a soda can. Stanea was pushed to the ground by the other youths and his wallet, stolen.

His friend, Jose Souza, said he was assaulted by the same suspect, according to the MARTA police incident report. The pink-clad teen punched him in the lip, the 24-year-old Delta employee said, but before they could take anything two unidentified male passengers intervened.

Meanwhile, witnesses said they heard the youths chanting "B.P.F.L," an Atlanta gang that appears to have established a presence within Zone 3 on the south side. They departed the train at the Oakland City station.[15]

There, in a nutshell, is the reason America is failing. Just one public transportation system serves as a powerful reminder of the impediment to growth and stability that the endless promotion of 13 percent of the United States population represents.

---

14 WSB-TV, "Delta Employees Attacked."
15 Boone, "Horde of teens attack."

2

"You Keep Using That Word. I Do Not Think It Means What You Think It Means"

October 17th, 2012

Something incredibly strange is happening in Buckhead (one of the wealthiest areas of the country) that should cause the thinking person to pause, however briefly, and realize we are about to enter a new phase of intellectual life in America.

And, of course, it deals with that word "racism." Or, more precisely, the charge of being a "racist."

Located in North Fulton County (uh-oh, the affluent White part of Atlanta), North Atlanta High School is experiencing extreme turmoil, which is once again bringing unwanted scrutiny to the Atlanta Public Schools (APS) system. You remember APS, right? Home to the almost entirely Black academic scandal?

Buckhead is roughly 76 percent White, but the sons and daughters of the majority in this Disingenuous White Liberal (DWL) enclave would never be sent to be educated with Black kids. Never.

So North Atlanta High School, though located in the wealthy (White) part of Fulton County, is a majority Black school at 55 percent African-American, 22 percent White, 16 percent Hispanic, 7 percent other. The average SAT score is 1439, one of the higher scores in all of the county.[16]

---

[16] Badertscher, "State: No plans to take."

It seems six key administrators at the school, including interim principal Mark MyGrant, were removed by the APS Superintendent Erroll Davis:

> At a community meeting Tuesday night attended by hundreds, Atlanta Public Schools Superintendent Erroll Davis told North Atlanta High parents that under the state's old accountability system the Buckhead school could have been "seized" by officials because of failure to meet academic goals. That system was ditched this year in favor of a new system of evaluating schools, which shows North Atlanta High is in good standing.
>
> Davis discussed the school's low performance in connection to recent leadership changes at the school, but said they did not play a role in the timing of the abrupt dismissal of interim principal Mark MyGrant and five of the school's top administrators. MyGrant was retired and scheduled to leave at the end of this month; an assistant principal and three academy leaders were reassigned, while another academy leader retired.
>
> Davis said the school, which is located in one of Atlanta's most affluent communities, is underperforming. He cited a sluggish graduation rate and new student growth data, which shows the school is slightly above average in terms of how much students are learning in a year.
>
> MyGrant said the removal dealt with charges of racism against two staff members he hired last year. Davis said he could not address personnel issues.
>
> In a statement to *The Atlanta Journal-Constitution* late Wednesday, MyGrant said "it is time for us to move on."[17]

Underperforming? Shouldn't some of the Black students at North Atlanta High School be the Black sons and daughters of Black multimillionaires living in Buckhead?

---

[17] Ibid.

Before we get the "charges of racism" MyGrant spoke of, just how poorly are students at this majority Black high school located in posh 75 percent White Buckhead performing?

A sampling of data reviewed by *The Atlanta Journal-Constitution* shows the school located in Buckhead, one of Atlanta's most affluent communities, has a mixed academic performance.

About 62 percent of its students graduated in 2011, 10 percentage points above the district's average of about 52 percent. The highest graduation rate was at Carver Early College, where 97 percent of students earned a diploma.

Davis highlighted North Atlanta's rate in his comments Tuesday night, when he noted that four out of 10 students won't graduate from the school.

Under the state's old accountability system, which was ditched this year, North Atlanta High for years failed to meet annual academic goals. Only three other schools in the district had a worse track record of meeting benchmarks than North Atlanta, according to state data.

But the school is among the district's best in other subjects. State data from 2011 shows North Atlanta's SAT score of 1,439 was the second-highest in the district, just behind Grady High's of 1,455.

Passing rates on the End of Course exam in math 2 were the fourth-highest in the district.[18]

Low standards, even for a county where the almost entirely Black high schools in the South Fulton consistently perform at standards that are the worst in the state of Georgia, if not the entire country.

So what's this charge of hiring a racist all about?

---

[18] Sarrio, "N. Atlanta High's poor performance."

A North Atlanta High teacher has left her position at the school following accusations of racial discrimination, according to a letter obtained by *The Atlanta Journal-Constitution.*

Amy Durham worked as a language arts teacher at the school, where a little more than a week ago six key administrators were replaced, including interim principal Mark MyGrant.

In a letter to school officials, Durham said her position was never officially approved by the school board because she was told there were "outstanding questions" about how she was selected for the position.

Durham said in September she was told about a charge of racial discrimination made against her related to her part-time work at the school's college and career counseling center in 2011-12. She said she has tried to get clarity from Atlanta Public Schools about the allegations, but has gotten no response.

As a result, Durham sent the letter, dated Oct. 10, saying she was leaving her position at the high school.

"As you can understand, the initial enthusiasm that I had to be an Atlanta Public Schools teacher has been considerably diminished," she wrote.

On Oct. 5, APS officials reassigned four North Atlanta High administrators—an assistant principal and three academy leaders. Two other administrators—interim principal MyGrant and academy leader Reginald Colbert—both retired. A new principal takes over Oct. 29.

MyGrant said he would present evidence that the replacements grew out of what he considers politically motivated and baseless allegations that two of his recommended hires—a graduation coach and an English teacher—were racists. He delivered 25 pages of documents to the central office Tuesday that he said would exonerate him and the other administrators. Late Wednesday, he released a statement saying, "It is time for us to move on."[19]

---

[19] Sarrio, "N. Atlanta High teacher quits."

Again, so what are these "racist" charges that went to the APS? They seem to be the underlying rationale for removing the leadership of a school that was merely producing the SAT scores and graduation rates that have become expected of Black students.

Would you believe Durham was accused—by an anonymous individual—of racism, because she didn't have a reception for a Black student that was accepted into Harvard (no questions or insinuations if this student got in because of affirmative action . . . promise! Whoops. . . .):

Weeks before Atlanta Public Schools Superintendent Erroll Davis replaced six key administrators at North Atlanta High, two school board members exchanged emails over parents' complaints of "institutional racism" at the school and how to deal with it.

In the emails obtained by *The Atlanta Journal-Constitution* through an open records request, school board chairman Reuben McDaniel and District 4 board member Nancy Meister disagreed over how to investigate the allegations.

Davis said Tuesday the district gets allegations of racism frequently. In this latest case, the district reviewed the allegation and decided not to investigate. It was passed along to the principal, he said.

APS officials swept into North Atlanta High on Oct. 5 and replaced the interim principal, Mark MyGrant, and five administrators. The upheaval sparked protests from parents and teachers—and triggered rumors that the shakeup was tied to alleged racism at the school.

Davis defended the staff moves by saying the school for years has been underperforming academically.

"It's clear nothing much has been done about (performance issues), or if something has been done, it's been done ineffectively by the leadership team," Davis said this week.

On Aug. 18, MyGrant emailed Davis that he had investigated anonymous allegations that a teacher about to be hired, Amy Durham, was accused of racism for not having a reception for a black student who will be attending Harvard University.

"I am not sure how to respond to the racist comment other than to say that I have worked with her [Durham] for 10 years and have never had any concerns or complaints," MyGrant wrote.

Three days later McDaniel sent an email to Associate Superintendent Steve Smith, asking him to collect data from North Atlanta that breaks down the school's graduation rates, and other performance metrics, by race. He asked for an ethnic breakdown of teachers and staff who were recommended for positions by interim principal MyGrant.

"I think it is critical that we understand these issues as we go through the principal selection process so that we can factor in some of the skills required to address the racial issues at North Atlanta in our new leadership," McDaniel wrote.

Meister responded in an email 35 minutes later that the analytical search for evidence of racism shouldn't be focused just on North McDaniel wrote back that he agreed gathering data across the district "would be interesting," but not practical. He wrote: "My purpose for requesting the data is to begin to understand statistically the evidence I have received from parents at North Atlanta indicating that we have a problem there that is based in an institutional racism mentality."[20]

What? No party for a Black student getting into Harvard—obviously, they were accepted into Harvard because they are Black—can only, only be due to extreme racism on the part of the North Atlanta High School teacher.

Again, you are probably asking yourself "What the f—?" but the city of Atlanta is run with the same type of mentality that A. Reginald Eaves had

---

[20] Scott and Sarrio, "In emails Atlanta Public Schools."

when he was appointed director of public safety—serving as the super chief for all police, fire, and public safety services in Atlanta—by the city's first black mayor, Maynard Jackson, in 1974. An extreme example of racial cronyism—having no police experience—Eaves promoted African Americans to every level of administration in the Atlanta Bureau of Police Services so that they were a substantial number and percentage of the sergeants, lieutenants, captains, majors, and deputy directors. Eaves successfully carried out Jackson's mandates in the Bureau of Police and he made it reflect and represent the people that it was supposed to serve. He stated that he wanted as many "black police administrators as possible making decisions about black lives" in Atlanta. African Americans in Atlanta began to believe that the Bureau of Police Services was their friend and on their side.[21]

No, Atlanta isn't the fight against black-on-black, or black-on-anyone crime. It's a dangerous place, with every public department still run by the same type of racial cronyism Mr. Eaves bragged about implementing in the 1970s.

Not throwing a party for a Black kid going to Harvard can even get you fired, and the principal removed.

Back in 2010, the AJC reported that White parents were considering saving some money and instead of splurging on private school tuition, they might actually use the public schools their tax dollars fund:

Parents living in Atlanta's tony Buckhead have for years enrolled their children in the city's elementary schools, later opting for higher performing private middle and high schools. That left the North Atlanta area's one middle and one high school underpopulated.

Talk to old-timers, and they throw out a number of reasons: Marketing. Racial bias. Academics.

---

[21] Poinsett, "Atlanta's Winning Fight Against."

Nancy Dillon, a real estate agent with Coldwell Banker Buckhead, said families without children in public schools often move out of the city because of its higher taxes. "But if they think their money is going toward something good, you've got something that's a draw," Dillon said of the new high school. "It's all about quality."

The Buckhead cluster contains six elementary schools, Sutton Middle and North Atlanta High School, which offers an International Baccalaureate program begun in 1982—the Southeast's oldest.

Still, "parents had a perception," said Sidney Baker, principal of Buckhead's Sarah Smith Elementary School since 2000. "What some people saw [was] the racial makeup." Many consider Buckhead the center of Atlanta's white business and civic community. The city school system overall is predominantly black, reflecting the city's demographics. Yet both are diversifying.

North Atlanta had magnet programs that drew students from all over the city, including for international studies and for the performing arts. Ten years ago, 69 percent of the student body was black and 20 percent was white. In October, after the system remade the magnet programs into "small learning communities," the percentage of black students stood at 59. White students made up 17 of the student body and Latino students made up another 17 percent.

But there were other factors that fed into parents' perceptions. North Atlanta was no athletics powerhouse, in large part because students went there for reasons other than its sports teams. And despite the prestige and awards earned by both the school's magnet programs, parents felt the school's academic prowess did not seem as strong as that of nearby private schools, some of which are nationally recognized.[22]

---

[22] Torres, "More kids stick with Buckhead schools."

Wait a second. North Atlanta High School has consistently been the dumping ground for the best performing Black students in the region, but even they can only muster a graduation of 62 percent. But they still know how to complain about "racism" when a party isn't thrown in their honor.

One day, not far from now, someone is going to start a revolution by simply laughing at an accusation of "racism" by saying—channeling Inigo Montoya from *The Princess Bride*—and say, "You keep using that word. I do not think it means what you think it means."

With a smile, they'll add, "let me show you what it means."

Does that sound "inconceivable" to you?

No?

Good.

It shouldn't.

3

I Bless the Rain Down in Africa: Atlanta Symphony Orchestra Declares Cobb County High Schools "Too White" to Play with Them

August 16th, 2012

It seems the Atlanta Symphony Orchestra—though boasting virtually an all- White lineup of musicians—is mad about the racial makeup of high school chorus groups that perform with them. 11 Alive, the NBC affiliate in Atlanta, reports:

COBB COUNTY, Ga.—After a four-year partnership, two suburban Cobb County high school choruses will not be performing with the Atlanta Symphony Orchestra this coming fall.

That's because they've been told they are not racially diverse enough.

The Walton High School Chorus has received many honors and performed all over the world.

So, too, has the Lassiter High School Chorus.

But they won't be back with the ASO for a joint holiday concert this coming December.

11Alive was first alerted to the change by e-mails from some angry parents, none of whom would go on camera.

But a spokesperson for the Cobb County School District confirmed the breakup.

In a response to an 11Alive e-mail, school system communications director Jay Dillon wrote that "the schools were informed by Symphony officials that their choruses are not diverse enough, and that the Symphony would be inviting a third, more diverse chorus."

Dillon said Walton and Lassiter were still welcome to participate but, "because of limited space, only a portion of the Lassiter and Walton choruses would therefore be able to attend."

He added that the schools chose not to leave any chorus members behind and "would not be able to perform with the Symphony."

Dillon also wrote, "Cobb County School District choral programs are open to all students, and participation is determined on the basis of merit alone."

The Atlanta Symphony Orchestra sent us a written reply from marketing VP Charlie Wade.

"We've been thrilled with the quality and performance of Lassiter and Walton choruses for four straight years; they are terrific," Wade wrote. "But we felt it was simply time to let another set of kids participate."

He said Atlanta's Grady High School chorus had been added.

Meanwhile, we also asked about the racial diversity of the ASO itself.

A 2008 study by the League of American Orchestras found that 87% of musicians in U.S. symphonies are White.

But Melissa A.E. Sanders, the Atlanta Symphony Orchestra's senior director of communications, wrote, "It is against our policy to share the race and/or ethnicity of our musicians, so I am unable to share that information."[23]

Those hideously White schools in Cobb County, Walton and Lassister, aren't exactly hives of homogeneity: out of 2500 students, Walton is 75 percent White and 5 percent Black;[24] out of just under 2000 students, Lassiter is 80 percent White and 10 percent Black.[25]

---

[23] 11 Alive Staff, "Atlanta Symphony thinks two."
[24] "Walton High School," School Digger
[25] "Lassiter High School," Find Good School

Grady High School, which has replaced these horrifyingly White schools from Cobb County, is thankfully 67 percent Black and 27 percent White. Whereas 50 percent of the students at Grady are eligible for free or reduced lunches, less than 10 percent are eligible at both Lassiter and Walton.[26]

Perhaps there's a correlation to hunger and vocal ability?

The Atlanta Symphony Orchestra (ASO) has always been on the lookout for the great Black hope, with Robert Shaw—the music director of the ASO from 1967–1988—being radically devoted to enriching the all-White ASO with much-needed diversity:

> When he arrived in Atlanta in August 1967, he found the ASO already in the midst of an effort to upgrade itself. Atlanta's cultural leaders had long been working toward raising the Orchestra's budget, extending the length of its season and building a permanent hall for its performances. They turned to Shaw because he was both a musician of international stature in both orchestral and choral realms and a rising conductor who could bring the ASO to prominence as his own reputation grew.
>
> He came in like a whirlwind, presenting ambitious concerts of difficult music, speaking about Atlanta's need for a conservatory of music, looking for black musicians to play in the all-white orchestra, successfully lobbying to have black members added to the ASO's Board, and introducing the city to more contemporary music than it had ever heard before. Hard though he may have driven his players and singers, he pushed himself harder. His attention to detail and his capacity for endless hours of score study and preparation were phenomenal. Unlike most high-profile conductors, he had no other orchestra half a globe away, and he accepted few dates to conduct elsewhere. Shaw had come to Atlanta to be Music Director, and he considered it a full-time commitment.

---

[26] Atlanta Public Schools, "What Does Grady Have to Offer?"

Throughout his career, Shaw was known for his commit-ment to racial equality and to broadening opportunities for minority musicians in the classical field. Under his leader-ship, the ASO actively sought black and other minority in-strumentalists for vacancies in the Orchestra. During the 1980s the Atlanta Symphony participated in the Music As-sistance Fund's "Orchestra Fellows Program," designed to help rising black string players gain the experience for suc-cessful symphonic careers. At the front of the stage, many black soloists, both instrumental and vocal, performed with the ASO. His commitment was further reflected in his full staging in 1972 of the world premiere of Scott Joplin's opera Treemonisha, in his frequent work with glee clubs from Morehouse and Spelman Colleges, in his leading the ASO at the inaugural ceremony for Maynard Jackson, Atlanta's first black mayor, and in his commissioning of new music by composers such as Frederick Tillis, Billy Taylor, John Lewis, T.J. Anderson and Alvin Singleton. Anderson and Singleton were also chosen by Shaw to be Composers in Res-idence with the ASO.[27]

So, how'd all that diversity and inclusion work out for Mr. Shaw in trying to "Blacken" up the ASO? Lonely Stephen Wil-son, who plays in the brass section of the ASO, is the lone Black member of the Atlanta Symphony Orchestra in 2012.[28] In the city that we know and love called "The Black Mecca," the fine Black citizens of the metro Atlanta area can only muster one lone musician worthy of inclusion in the ASO.

White people, no matter how much talent, are to be replaced in Black-Run America (BRA) with a continued energetic—and rapacious—drive for "diversity." Someone cue up the Toto and hit replay on "Africa."

---

[27] Atlanta Symphony website Robert Shaw "About" page
[28] Atlanta Symphony website Conductors and Musicians "About" page

4

The Gordian Knot Appears: Untie Atlanta, Untie America

July 6th, 2012

The Gordian Knot. The ultimate problem that vexed the ancients was one Alexander of Macedonia solved:

> While at Gordion, the Macedonian king learned about a special wagon that was situated in the Temple of Zeus. The pole of the wagon was tied to the wagon body with an intricate knot of cornel bark, and a prophecy had foretold that whoever could unfasten the knot would go on to rule over Asia (or even the whole settled world, in one version). Seized by a longing to test the prophecy, Alexander tried to unfasten the knot by unraveling it, but when he was unable to do so, he drew his sword and cut right through it. From this comes the proverbial expression "to cut the Gordian Knot," meaning to cut right to the heart of a matter without wasting time on external details.[29]

At the end of this month, metro Atlanta will go to the polls to decide if there will be an increase of taxation[30] so that the burden of commuting around the city can be lessened:

> On July 31, 2012, residents across the 10-county Atlanta region including Cherokee, Clayton, Cobb, DeKalb, Douglas, Fayette, Fulton, Gwinnett, Henry and Rockdale counties, as

---

[29] Penn Museum, "Gordian Knot."
[30] Galloway, "Trust and the transportation sales tax."

well as the City of Atlanta have the opportunity to vote on a referendum that would fund $8.5 billion in transportation improvements through a regional one percent sales tax.[31]

It has already been established that Atlanta has the worst traffic in America. The longest commutes. A public transportation system that does little more than serve as a jobs program for Black people and Move Africans Rapidly Through Atlanta (MARTA ridership is 78 percent Black).[32]

For those who support the transportation referendum, a website has been set up with the historically interesting title of Untie Atlanta. The site (UntieAtlanta.com) states:

The Crisis

Traffic is choking metro Atlanta. Billions of dollars are wasted in traffic congestion each year, costing the average metro commuter $924 annually in wasted fuel and lost time. Businesses are discouraged from moving to our region and creating jobs because of the added costs and hassles of traffic congestion. And home values suffer as homebuyers avoid clogged communities.

The Solution

A yes vote on July 31 will help to untie our traffic knot and make our region more competitive again. Investments in regional transportation will help create and support 200,000 mid-to high-paying jobs—and will free up our clogged roadways so we can be more productive at work and spend more time at home. Investing in our region will bring jobs, prosperity and an improved quality of life for decades to come.

Who can be against the creation of jobs, right? Well, *The Atlanta Journal-Constitution* published an article which illustrates the project has virtually no accountability nor transparency:

---

[31] From the Atlanta Regional Commission website.
[32] Schmitt, "In Tight Times for Transit Budgets."

The battle over how the region would spend $6.14 billion to fix metro Atlanta's transportation quagmire is in full roar.

Little noticed in the din: $1.08 billion in tax revenue that would go directly to local government, part of the $7.2 billion expected from the proposed 1 percent sales tax.

Each of the region's counties, cities and towns would get a share of the $1 billion to spend on transportation. But unlike the regional $6 billion fund, there is no requirement to list a single project for the $1 billion local fund. In many cases, voters at the polls July 31 will have no way of knowing where the projects are that the local money would build. [33]

Look, no project in the Black Mecca has ever had accountability (save former Mayor Bill Campbell's mad dash to keep Affirmative Action in The City too Busy to Hate, lest Black people no longer have access to public jobs). The entire reason Atlanta has crushing traffic problems is completely, 100 percent due to White people's attempts to create cities and communities free of the Black influence that makes Atlanta one of the most violent in all of America.

That we live in Black-Run America (BRA) where no White person can speak honestly about race without fear of social ostracism and career suicide shows the totalitarian nature of the current political system.

Traffic isn't suffocating Atlanta; our inability to openly talk about race and the harmful effects of the Black Undertow Phenomenon (consult the history of Clayton and DeKalb County, as well as Stone Mountain) are suffocating Atlanta.

The city of Atlanta is where other municipalities mirrored their affirmative action policies from; because of government contracting rules that mandated work with the city, county (Fulton), and the Hartsfield International Airport, the city attracted Black people from around the nation to work in an artificially created middle class.

---

[33] Hart, "Public 'in the Dark.'"

And because Black people are responsible for virtually all the crime in the metro Atlanta area, White people must continually seek safe cities (read: free of the Black Undertow) to raise children in.

Though Whites are moving back into a city they long ago abandoned,[34] the entire metro Atlanta is plagued by high foreclosure rates and property devaluations directly correlated to the influx of Black people.[35]

The Metro Atlanta area has some of the greatest disparities of wealth in America. This is primarily because Black wealth is created via a monopoly on public jobs in predominately Black counties and the City of Atlanta, but also because of the law of the Visible Black Hand of Economics, which states that any area that is majority Black will not be capable of sustaining any semblance of a vibrant, diversified economy.

In the *Travel Patterns of People of Color* (prepared by the U.S. Department of Transportation Federal Highway Administration, June 30, 2000) we learn of the spatial mismatch hypothesis, which "suggests that employment rates and poverty rates are higher for inner city Blacks in large part because they are isolated from employment opportunities located in the mainly suburban and exurban metropolitan regions areas that ring central cities."

Forever blame Whitey for the plight of Black people, who lack the ability to sustain a business or create new industries (just look at the sorrowful nature of Sweet Auburn, historically the pride of the Black community in Atlanta).

Funny, the counties that go majority Black (Clayton, DeKalb) quickly prove the spatial mismatch hypothesis wrong, because once-thriving business districts dry up as the tax base evaporates. In *The Spatial Mismatch Between Jobs and Residential Locations Within Urban Areas* by Keith Ihlanfeldt of Georgia State University, we learn this:

---

[34] Dewan, "Gentrification Changing Face."
[35] Bluestein, "Firm: Georgia Foreclosure Rate."

Within central cities, white flight from neighborhoods undergoing racial transition has been an important historical
phenomenon. These results may not carry over into a suburban setting, however, since the cost of moving—in terms
of additional travel time—from the city to the suburbs may
be quite different from the cost of moving from one suburban
location to a more distant suburban location. At some point,
the desire for access to the central city may work to impede
the mobility of white households.

Some evidence on suburban black infiltration/white
flight in Atlanta during the 1980s is provided in Table 4
DeKalb, Clayton, and South Fulton Counties are inner-sub-
urban areas that experienced considerable black in-migra-
tion during the 1980s. Each county has been divided into
the superdistricts defined by ARC for planning purposes.
The black population increased in all but one of the 14 superdistricts, and in 11 of these 13 cases the decline in the
white population was substantial.

As has previously been stated here, Black people—and White
people escaping from living near Black people—represent the
greatest ecological threat to the United States. Some call it suburban sprawl; we simply call it escape from Black people
(though you might hear neighbors, family members, or pundits
call it "searching for good schools"). The Sierra Club published
a report in 1998 where they labeled Atlanta as the worst city
for "sprawl" (read: White people escaping from Black crime and
property devaluations):

1998 Sierra Club Sprawl Report: 30 Most Sprawl-Threatened Cities
    Ten Most Sprawl-Threatened Large Cities
    Number One: Atlanta
    *Every week, five hundred acres of green space, forest,
and farmland in the Atlanta metro area are plowed under.*
    Atlanta is one of the fastest growing regions in the coun-
try, and the environmental impacts of unplanned sprawl in

the Atlanta area are among the most significant and wide-spread in the nation.

Atlanta's urban land area expanded 47 percent between 1990 to 1996, following a 25 percent expansion between 1980 and 1990. Pressure to expand will continue as the population grows disproportionately in the outer suburbs. From 1990 to 1996, the population outside Atlanta's urban core increased almost 40 percent, but only 2 percent inside the city limits. Some experts believe that the region's population could double in the next 50 years. With no natural barriers, few cities are growing as fast as Atlanta.

Green space is being gobbled up by sprawl faster than in any metro region in history (according to a real estate research firm and reported by the *Atlanta Journal Constitution*). Every week, five hundred acres of green space, forest or farmland are plowed under to build parking lots, shopping malls and housing subdivisions. Between 1982 and 1992, the amount of open space lost to development in the Atlanta metropolitan area increased by 38 percent. The rate of land developed nearly doubled in outer suburban counties such as Gwinnett, Henry and Paulding.

The Chattahoochee River was named one of the nation's most endangered rivers in 1998 by the environmental group, American Rivers, which identified rampant growth in the suburbs as the most significant threat to the river. The Chattahoochee is seriously degraded from overflowing sewage systems, city street runoff and other pollutants.

Air quality is also alarmingly poor. The 13-county region is in violation of clean air standards and has lost the right to spend federal money on new road projects. Children with asthma go to the hospital every summer because of high levels of ozone pollution. Cars and trucks are the largest source of air pollution in the nonattainment area. Yet, state, regional and local agencies cannot agree on a plan to clean up the region's air.[36]

---

[36] Sierra Club, "Ten Most Sprawl-Threatened Large Cities."

But there is no escape. The entire metro Atlanta represents a giant Black Hole, and the vote on July 31 will only perpetuate this into the future with funding to the tune of billions of dollars.

All of this will allow Whites to continue to flee the problems that so few people dare confront publicly, namely that Black political stranglehold over both MARTA, Fulton County, and the City of Atlanta (increasingly DeKalb, Rockdale, and Clayton County) has created an ecological nightmare around the city too busy to hate.

All of the could end, if someone would just dare cut the Gordian Knot in Atlanta. With this act, BRA ends.

"Untie Atlanta" . . . it's a catchy marketing term used by those who favor perpetuating an insane transportation system that does nothing but enslave metro Atlanta citizens to the cycle of forever vacating a thriving city once too many Black people move there, overwhelming the judicial system and breaking the back of the local economy due to business closures.

Back in 1996, *The New York Times* wrote "Atlanta is Burning," meaning its future is uncertain because of the instability of "the Atlanta Way."[37]

America's Gordian Knot is Atlanta, home to corporations that have slavishly prostrated themselves before BRA (looking at you, Coca-Cola) and the origins of sinister "equality" programs and affirmative action mandates[38] in contracting and public employment that have polluted cities across the nation, creating barriers to employment for more qualified White males.[39]

Traffic isn't suffocating Atlanta; our inability to be honest about race is suffocating not just Atlanta, but America.

The Gordian Knot is ready to be cut.

---

[37] Goldberger, "Atlanta Is Burning."
[38] Smothers, "Atlanta Affirmative Action Plan."
[39] Sack, "Atlanta Leaders See Racial."

5

An Honest Look at DeKalb County: America's Second-Best County for Black People . . .

June 1st, 2012

Equipped with his five senses, man explores the universe around him and calls the adventure Science.
    – Edwin Powell Hubble, *The Nature of Science*

Watching the steady implosion of the Black Mecca offers a glimpse of what will soon transpire across the entire nation. Property value is plummeting in metro Atlanta after years of Black migration from other parts of the nation to the promised land of public jobs and preferential contract work with the city of Atlanta, Fulton County, and Fortune 100 companies with offices (and aggressive affirmative action hiring programs) there.

As the metro Atlanta counties become "Blacker" (i.e., greater percentage of Blacks than other racial groups), the tax base shrinks. Clayton County offers the best glimpse of what happens to a once thriving county when the Blacks take over.

DeKalb County is the Prince Georges County of metro Atlanta for Blacks (54 percent Black and 33 percent White), considered by many to be the best place in the Black Mecca to call home (if you are Black—just ask former CEO of DeKalb County Vernon Jones, who tried to remake the city government in a Black image).[40] Look at this quote from *USA Today* in 2001,

---

[40] Dewan, "Georgia."

where the Blacks talk about the glory of segregated communities:

"Segregation doesn't necessarily speak to bias and discrimination in all cases," says William Boone, political science professor at Clark

Atlanta University. "Sometimes, people make a rational choice."

Choice is what created many black suburban enclaves around Atlanta. Some of them are among the most affluent black neighborhoods in the country. In DeKalb County, subdivisions of million-dollar homes are being developed by blacks for blacks.

"People say in code when they come, 'I want to go where people look like me,'" says Pamela Holmes, a real estate agent and chief of staff for DeKalb County's chief executive. "In Atlanta, they can get a $200,000 or $300,000 home or million-dollar home and still be with people who look like them. And that's an asset."

Holmes and her husband, Benjamin, live in the suburbs. Their subdivision in Stone Mountain, which has 175 homes, was built in 1994. They were the third black family to move in. "We had no idea which way it would go," she says. The subdivision is now 85% black, 10% Hispanic and 5% Asian. The Holmes' neighbors are athletes, doctors, teachers and executives.

Boone, who is black, also lives in a predominantly black suburb. He says that as blacks gain financial and political clout, the need to integrate decreases. In the past, blacks had to move to white neighborhoods to find good homes, good schools, low crime and better public services, he says.

Now, blacks are more influential and can get the same types of services in black neighborhoods. "We have to rethink this whole question of who wants integration and why we want integration," Boone says.[41]

---

[41] Nasser, "Minorities Make Choice."

If it's such a great place to live (and a wonderful, affluent place for Black people),[42] why is there such a huge budget deficit for the DeKalb school system. In particular, one that is 71 percent Black—K–12—and where nearly 64 percent of the students are eligible for free or reduced lunches.[43]

DeKalb County saw eighteen thousand of its residents fore- closed upon in 2010, the third-highest number in Georgia, which contributed to the county seeing a drop in tax digest in early May of this year.

Now, reports CBS Atlanta, the situation is getting dire for what is touted as one of the best counties in all of America for Black people:

> The DeKalb County School system faces a $73 million short- fall for the upcoming school year, and they said much that deficit can be blamed on falling property values in the county. About 40 percent of the school district's revenue comes from property tax revenues, according to school dis- trict spokesman Walter Woods.
>
> Those property values fell 6 percent last year, he said, when the district was only expecting them to fall 4 percent.
>
> "You've seen this around the metro area," Woods said. "You've seen other metro counties face this—Gwinnett, Cobb, Fulton, Atlanta Public Schools all face declining prop- erty values. That's our chief source of income."[44]

No one wants to mention the correlation between race and property value (in many cases—such as Fayette and Forsyth County—property value is tied to K–12 school system perfor- mance, which is directly tied to the race of the students en- rolled), so it falls on SBPDL to point out that the halcyon days of unlimited growth in the Black Mecca are done.

---

42 Stewart, "In a Pocket of Prince William."
43 As of the writing of this article, from the district website.
44 Frampton, "DeKalb County schools."

DeKalb County test scores (on the CRCT Test) indicate that those affluent Black parents didn't exactly earn their jobs on merit:

> The DeKalb County School System is one of the lowest performing systems in metro Atlanta in several subjects and other school systems are improving faster than DeKalb's according to 2011 CRCT results.
> When compared with other systems such as Atlanta Public Schools, Clayton County Public Schools and Fulton County Schools, DeKalb, although making slight improvements, is still improving more slowly than the systems surrounding it. [45]

It's time to call metro Atlanta for what it is: the black hole of America.

Already, graduation rates are abysmal[46] in a school system that is nearly 75 percent Black. Black scores on the NAEP tests were . . . bad, when compared to the standard set by White students (a dwindling percentage of all school systems in America) Who's going to be able to do anything—and pay taxes—in this future America?[47]

The USA Today in May 2012 reported that American test scores on the science portion of the NAEP are slumping (does no one dare point out the correlation to race and the fact that more and more of American K–12 students are non-White?),[48] which could easily have been foretold from a simple data set available in DeKalb County: the decline of Fernbank Science Center.

The Atlanta Journal-Constitution reports:

> In 1967, the Fernbank Science Center opened with the goal of building science literacy through exhibits, instruction and

---

45 Beauregard, "DeKalb Schools improvement slower."
46 Johnson, "Graduation Rates Amongst African."
47 Downey, "NAEP science: Scores rise."
48 Toppo, "Schools try to pull."

other experiences. Visitors can view a range of taxidermy including birds and animals native to Georgia. Pythons and boa constrictors slither in display cases. Honeybees buzz around a hive. Part of the Apollo 6 space shuttle sits just across from a pictorial display of the Tuskegee Airmen. The forest serves as a living laboratory for visitors to examine flora and fauna, while the observatory is reported to have the largest telescope in the southeast. Experts in

fields ranging from biology to astronomy teach DeKalb school children everything from sex education to space missions.

As one of 13 centers built in a national pilot program, the Fernbank Science Center is the only one that still exists, said a Science Center spokesperson. Other than a nominal fee for the planetarium, entry to Fernbank Science Center is free. At its height, the center reportedly hosted more than 800,000 visitors per year. Recent estimates are closer to 160,000. Staffing has been dramatically reduced and the $4.7 million in funding is the same as it was in 2004.[49]

Why does this matter? Science is obviously of the Stuff that Black People Don't Like, so why not cut this museum out of DeKalb's budget?

Each year, about 160,000 people, many of them schoolchildren, learn about frogs, snakes, bugs and other animals and plants during visits to Fernbank Science Center.

The decades-old institution, owned and operated by the DeKalb County public school district, has offered a hands-on education to students and other visitors from across metro Atlanta and elsewhere. However, it might close, under a recommendation Thursday by the school board's budget committee. Fernbank Science Center, which includes a planetarium, is near the Fernbank Museum of Natural History, which is operated by a separate nonprofit.

---

[49] AJC, "Dekalb Under the Gun."

At an annual cost of $4.7 million, the building and its 56 full-time employees now are looking like a luxury to school officials. They are struggling with a $73 million deficit, and may have to cut teachers and school days to balance the budget.[50]

No, Mr. Hubble, it's only the White man that dares explore the universe. Within forty years of assuming political power in the city of Atlanta, and creating this most radical affirmative action programs and minority contracting regulations in America (thereby inviting all Black professionals to flock to the metro area as part of the Black Gold Rush), Black people are on the verge of crippling an entire region.

DeKalb County, on paper one of the top counties for Black people in America. But when you actually try and read that paper, it crumbles like sand in your hand.

Just like Prince Georges County.

---

[50] Tagami, "DeKalb schools cuts could."

6

"The Atlanta Youth Murders and the Politics of Race"

June 30th, 2012

Over at *VDARE*, Nicholas Stix has an interesting piece on the city too busy to hate. He brings up much that can be found in the archives of SBPDL, but two important facts must be quickly addressed. Reginald Eaves, the first Black public safety commissioner for Atlanta, was praised to the high heavens by *Time* in an article from 1976. As Stix notes:

Newly elected Mayor Jackson appointed the Atlanta PD's first black public safety commissioner, A. Reginald Eaves, back in 1974. Eaves discriminated mercilessly against white cops, driving them off to the suburbs and replacing them with incompetent blacks. The Department has never recovered. In 1978, Eaves was caught giving black patrolmen the answers to the sergeant's exam, and fired.

In a characteristic example of the new dispensation, a 1980 murder case had to be thrown out because the police had lost the case file and evidence. A prosecutor explained, with a shrug "Keystone Kops."[51]

Time magazine had no problem propping up Eaves as a Black Wyatt Earp, despite a complete lack of empirical evidence to support these accolades.

---

[51] Stix, "Never Too Busy to Hate."

But it is a book that Stix mentioned had me laughing. I just finished *The List* by Chet Dettlinger and Jeff Prugh, and plan to write about the Atlanta Child Murders. Hint: there was no serial killer in Atlanta; Wayne Williams did kill a few people, but the "Atlanta Child Murders" were just your run-of-the-mill Black murders that were aggregated together as some Professor Moriarty or KKK scheme.

Here's what Stix wrote:

Under black rule, life became very cheap in Atlanta.

In the now-forgotten (because the perp turned out to be black) so-called Atlanta as of 1979-1981 (few of the victims were children and several were adult, although all were African American), leading black lawmen such as Louis Graham promoted, without any supporting evidence, a conspiracy theory that the culprit was the KKK, which was allegedly driving around in black neighborhoods, grabbing black kids off the street and killing them at will.

Federal investigators saw how ludicrous this notion was when they drove around some of the neighborhoods that had been hit. When residents saw white men, they immediately stopped what they were doing and stared.

White lawman and policing theorist Chet Dettlinger came in to solve the crimes. Dettlinger was a racial liberal, but in his 1983 book *The List* (ghosted by Jeff Prugh), he wrote unsparingly of the racial chaos and corruption he observed. He reported that the Atlanta PD's negligent crime scene investigators would typically leave half of the evidence on the ground, and its officers suffered from fundamental "ignorance about valid cause-and-effect relationships."[52]

Sorry, Mr. Stix: life is cheap wherever Black people are found.

The best part of *The List* that Stix doesn't bring up is that the Black Atlanta Police hierarchy enlisted the help of psychics

---

[52] Ibid.

from around the nation, in a ludicrous attempt to stop the "serial killer" from claiming more Black victims. Yes, Atlanta's first Black mayor, Maynard Jackson, despite precious little evidence that these "psychics" were aiding in stopping the murder of Black Atlanta children—almost all in slum areas of Atlanta that were 99 percent Black—still stood by contracting out these soothsayers in bringing the non-existent "serial killer" to justice.

It is in *The Atlanta Youth Murders and the Politics of Race* (Elmer H Johnson & Carol Holmes Johnson Series in Criminology) by Dr. Bernard Headley that an unpleasant truth about Black crime in Atlanta—during the period of the "Atlanta Youth Murders"—slips out: each year, roughly ten Black children fell victim to Black-on-Black violence in Atlanta.

Over a span of three years, roughly twenty Black children were found. (The numbers are inflated, because teenagers and young adults were added to "the list.") Nothing out of the ordinary, save the hysteria created by Organized Blackness in trying to blame White people for the deaths of these young Black kids.

Blacks in Atlanta were whipped into a frenzy during this time period, attacking White firemen when they traveled into the areas where the "serial killer" was preying upon Black children, all because Organized Blackness had pointed an incriminating at a shadowy White person being behind these killings.

In actuality, it was just Black people killing Black people. It shouldn't have taken a psychic to help Atlanta's political class and police to figure this out, but then why would the federal government (Ronald Reagan authorized millions of dollars in aid to help combat the "serial killer") and the nation's media care about Black people randomly killing Black children? That's not a juicy story!

It's a fast read. And hilarious. You can learn about the "psychics" that the Atlanta Black political class enlisted to stop the "serial killer" that targeted Atlanta's Black children in the slums of Black Atlanta.

7

The Death of "The Atlanta Way":
New York Times Profiles Sandy Springs

June 26th, 2012

You might recall that we quoted from *A Man in Full* in a story detailing President Obama's gratuitous use of street slang in campaign material directed at Black people (African-Americans for Obama: "Got Ya Back!"), all of which was hilariously parodied in Tom Wolfe's book on Atlanta racial politics that was written in 1998.

The below scene from Wolfe's book (found on p. 97) brings us a conversation on the Atlanta Way, between the light-skinned Black Mayor Wes Jordan (naturally, a Morehouse man) and Roger Too White:

> "Atlanta's a small world," said the Mayor. If you look closely, there's a handful of people who do everything."
>
> It's not very complicated," said Wes. "He thinks he's going to win. In these all-black elections, I don't see white businessman wasting time on ideology and issues. It's more like 'Can I do business with him or not?' and I'm sure Armholster (Inman Armholster, fictional white businessman in Wolfe's *A Man in Full*) is all ready to do business with Andre Fleet. That's what is known as 'the Atlanta Way.'"
>
> "The Atlanta Way?"
>
> "Exactly," said [Atlanta Mayor] Wes Jordan, "the Atlanta Way. Did you ever unravel a baseball?"
>
> "No."

"It's not a particularly illuminating exercise, but I used to enjoy doing it when I was ten or eleven years old. After you take the white horsehide cover off, you come across a ball of white string, or it's like string. There's about a mile of the stuff, once you start unraveling it, all this white string. Finally you get down to the core, which is black, a small hard black rubber ball. Well, that's Atlanta. The hard core, if we're talking politics, are the 280,000 black folks in South Atlanta. They, or their votes, control the city itself. Wrapped all around them, like all that white string, are three million white people in North Atlanta, and all those counties, Cobb, DeKalb, Gwinnett, Forsyth, Cherokee, Paulding. . . . So how do those white millions deals with that small black core? That's what leads to the Atlanta Way. Remember that billion-dollar expansion of the airport back when Maynard (Young, Atlanta's first Black mayor) was Mayor? Well, Maynard got the "business interests" together and, "Boys, here's a billion-dollar project." So they're salivating, of course, and then he says, 'And 30 percent of its going to minority contractors.' They gulped—but only for a moment. Seven hundred million was nothing to look down your nose at, either, and in no time they were salivating all over again, and they figured they'd just make do with the minority contractors some way or other. Later on Maynard said, "That airport created twenty-five black millionaires.' He was proud of it, and he had every right to be. That's the Atlanta Way."[53]

The Atlanta Way. For more than sixty years, one of the world's greatest cities (well, the Coca-Cola company would have you believe it) has survived on a steady racial truce: the progressive White business leaders, who provide the economic life-blood of the city (tax revenue redistributed to Black people in the forms of city and county jobs) ceded power to an entrenched Black

---

[53] Wolfe, *Man in Full*, 97–99.

political class that has strived to enrich only itself and connected parties, all the while ignoring rising rates of Black underclass reliance on the government for . . . everything.

It shouldn't take a genius to understand that this situation
wasn't going to be sustainable forever. With the anointed Black
political class laying a welcome mat for any Black person with
an IQ over 95 (or below) to ditch the city they live in and head
to the "Dirty South" to seek their fortune, that hard Black rubber ball that served as the center of Wolfe's metaphor on Atlanta has now slowly seeped into those once prosperous White
counties.

The consequences of the migration to Atlanta by hundreds
of thousands (if not millions) of Black people since the "Welcome to the Black Mecca" sign was turned has been catastrophic.

On March 28, 2011, Katie Leslie wrote an article for *The
Atlanta Journal-Constitution* that hinted at the Atlanta Way
ending (Lawsuit seeks dissolution of Dunwoody, Sandy
Springs, Johns Creek, Milton, Chattahoochee Hills: Suit says
"super-majority White neighborhoods" were created). In this
piece, the Georgia Legislative Black Caucus filed a lawsuit "to
dissolve the city charters of Dunwoody, Sandy Springs, Johns
Creek, Milton and Chattahoochee Hills. Further, the lawmakers, joined by civil rights leader the Rev. Joseph Lowery, aim
to dash any hopes of a Milton County."

Here's what Leslie wrote:

> The lawsuit, filed in a North Georgia U.S. District Court
> Monday, claims that the state circumvented the normal leg-
> islative process and set aside its own criteria when creating
> the "super-majority white" cities within Fulton and DeKalb
> counties. The result, it argues, is to dilute minority votes in
> those areas, violating the Voting Rights Act of 1965 and the
> Fourteenth and Fifteenth Amendments to the Constitution.
>
> "This suit is based on the idea that African Americans
> and other minorities can elect the people of their choice,"
> said Democratic State Sen. Vincent Fort.

According to the 2010 census, Fulton County is 44.5 percent white and 44.1 percent black. About 54 percent of DeK-
alb County residents are black, and 33.3 percent are white.

Sandy Springs, created in 2005, is 65 percent white and
20 percent black. Milton, formed a year later, is 76.6 percent
white and 9 percent black. Johns Creek, also formed that
year, is 63.5 percent white and 9.2 percent black. Chattahoochee Hills, formed in 2007, is 68.6 percent white and 28
percent black, while Dunwoody, created in 2008, is 69.8 percent white and 12.6 percent black.[54]

Translation: Black people realize the gravy train of the Atlanta
Way will end if White people dare flex any political power and
decide they no longer want to pay for the proliferation of the
Black Underclass (what we have dubbed the Black Undertow,
which has overwhelmed much of Metro Atlanta).

White people have one purpose in Atlanta and the rest of
Black-Run America: pay taxes so that Black people can live in
a cradle-to-grave society, while simultaneously keeping their
mouth shut about this one-sided proposition.

Well, David Segal of *The New York Times* on June 23, 2012
profiled one of those dissenting "White" cities that dares dis-
rupt the flow of capital from White taxpayers to the Black political class. Sandy Springs, a renegade majority-White city in
North Fulton County, might be engaging in the first example
of open warfare with the system known as BRA that "could"
become the model for separation that rich, majority-White cities employ to escape the crushing taxation needed to keep alive
counties under Black political domination.

Segal writes:

If your image of a city hall involves a venerable building,
some Roman pillars and lots of public employees, the version offered by this Atlanta suburb of 94,000 residents is a
bit of a shocker.

---

[54] Leslie, "Lawsuit Seeks Dissolution of Dunwoody."

The entire operation is housed in a generic, one-story industrial park, along with a restaurant and a gym. And though the place has a large staff, none are on the public payroll. O.K., seven are, including the city manager. But unless you chance into one of them, the people you meet here work for private companies through a variety of contracts.

With public employee unions under attack in states like Wisconsin, and with cities across the country looking to trim budgets, behold a town built almost entirely on a series of public-private partnerships—a system that leaders around here refer to, simply, as "the model."

Cities have dabbled for years with privatization, but few have taken the idea as far as Sandy Springs. Since the day it incorporated, Dec. 1, 2005, it has handed off to private enterprise just about every service that can be evaluated through metrics and inked into a contract.

To grasp how unusual this is, consider what Sandy Springs does not have. It does not have a fleet of vehicles for road repair, or a yard where the fleet is parked. It does not have long-term debt. It has no pension obligations. It does not have a city hall, for that matter, if your idea of a city hall is a building owned by the city. Sandy Springs rents.

Does the Sandy Springs approach work? It does for Sandy Springs, says the city manager, John F. McDonough, who points not only to the town's healthy balance sheet but also to high marks from residents on surveys about quality of life and quality of government services.

But that doesn't mean "the model" can be easily exported—Sandy Springs has the built-in advantage that comes from wealth—or that its widespread adoption would enhance the commonweal. Critics contend that the town is a white-flight suburb that has essentially seceded from Fulton County, a 70-mile-long stretch that includes many poor and largely African-American areas, most of them in Atlanta and points south.

The prospect of more Sandy Springs-style incorporations concerns people like Evan McKenzie, author of "Privatopia:

Homeowner Associations and the Rise of Residential Private Government." He worries that rich enclaves may decide to become gated communities writ large, walling themselves off from areas that are economically distressed.

"You could get into a 'two Americas' scenario here," he says. "If we allow the more affluent to institutionally isolate themselves, then the poor are supposed to do—what? They're supposed to have all the poverty and all the social problems and deal with them?"

The champions of Sandy Springs counter that they still send plenty of tax dollars to the county and that race had nothing to do with the decision to incorporate. (The town's minority population is now 30 percent and growing, they note.) Leaders here say they had simply grown tired of the municipal service offered by Fulton County.

"We make no apologies for being more affluent than other parts of the metro area," says Eva Galambos, the mayor of Sandy Springs. And what does she make of the attitude of the town's detractors? "Pure envy," she says.

Sandy Springs residents still send roughly $190 million a year to Fulton County through property taxes, about half of which goes to schools, including those in Sandy Springs. But by incorporating, the town gets to keep $90 million in taxes a year to spend as it pleases.

Has this financially hurt the rest of Fulton County? It has, says the county manager, Zachary Williams, who calculates that the incorporation of Sandy Springs, and neighboring towns that incorporated after it, cost the county about $38 million a year. Mr. Williams described the figure as "significant," especially given the strains imposed by the economic downturn.

"I would bet that Atlanta is top five in the country in terms of foreclosures," he says. "I think our vacancy rate is 14 to 18 percent."

Some Georgia politicians outside Sandy Springs regard it and other breakaway towns as "the first shot in the battle to destroy Fulton County," as State Senator Vincent Fort, a Democrat whose district includes part of Atlanta, put it.

"What you have is the northern section of the county," he went on, "which is mostly white, seeking to leave the rest of Fulton County, and doing so with what I think are racially tinged arguments about the corruption and inefficiency of local government."

Town leaders say race had nothing to do with it. Mayor Galambos said, "A 94 percent vote in favor of incorporation speaks to the broad community support for self-government and a desire to have local dollars remain local."[55]

That the Department of Justice has not stepped in and declared war yet on Sandy Springs for depriving the rest of Fulton County (outside of Buckhead, and pockets of Urban Pioneers in South Fulton, the county is the Black Undertow personified) of much needed White tax dollars to redistribute to "the Black hard core of Atlanta" is a mystery that will one day need an answer.

Because if Sandy Springs successfully leaves Fulton County and creates a new county (with those other majority-White cities), then you have the blueprint for a secession movement that would instantly spring up in other major cities that are heavily segregated but under Black political control.

Birmingham, Charlotte, Memphis, Chicago, Philadelphia, Baltimore, Indianapolis, Kansas City, Milwaukee, St. Louis, Montgomery . . . you will be looking at wave of secession movements that are basically about denying an entrenched Black political class (Blacks control city hall, but have yet to turn this into economic power—the Visible Black Hand of Economics in action) the ability to redistribute White tax dollars.

But here's the problem, which was delineated in Connected Capitalism: this model is basically the grounds for creating mini-South Africas in America—hundreds of them. As Black Undertow continues to get worse, cities will begin to privatize

---

[55] Segal, "Georgia Town Takes."

their own security forces (can you say XE/Blackwater?) and implement the same draconian measures we see the dwindling
White minority in the Rainbow Republic of South Africa take.

This is the great quandary of BRA's coming collapse: if the
Sandy Springs model is successfully implemented in other cit-
ies and counties, the inevitable will only be delayed, and the
South Africanization of America will be crystallized.

Opposition to this system can longer be supplied via ab-
stractions: if America is a nation of laws, what does it matter
what people live here and abide by them? What does it matter
what language they speak?

If the move to incorporate Sandy Springs is about abstrac-
tions, so be it. But if Vincent Fort is right, and the move is to
deprive the Black political class in Atlanta of the precious flow
of White tax dollars, then a moment that could paralyze the
world is near.

The City Too Busy to Hate . . . devastated by White people
daring to understand that self-determination means no longer
being forced to pay for the proliferation of a Black Underclass
that commits virtually all the crime in Atlanta, nor pay the
bloated public salaries for Black city/county employees that
create an artificial Black middle class.

The Atlanta Way has been the blueprint for too many other
municipalities and how racial dynamics have been governed in
them, and America, for far too long.

8

Gone with the Wind:
Atlanta, Affirmative Action,
and White Managerial Elites

May 20th, 2012

Ronald H. Bayor's *Race & The Shaping of Twentieth-Century Atlanta* is one of Disingenuous White Liberal (DWL) scholarly books that blames the current state of the Black Mecca on the lingering vestiges of White racism.

Despite Atlanta—since 1973—being a city firmly under the iron Black heel when it comes to who controls City Hall and the hiring/firing of public employees (not to mention the creation of the Minority Business Enterprise, which mandates a significant portion of city projects go to minority firms), Bayor's book places all the blame for the city too busy to hate's shortcomings on White people.[56]

Just as in Detroit, it was White flight from Black criminality to virtually crime-free White suburbs surrounding the city that allowed Black people to become the majority of Atlanta by 1970 and elect Maynard Jackson in 1973. This event was the culmination of years of cohesive actions by the Black community in Atlanta:

---

[56] Adenekan, "Maynard Jackson."

The black response to a city being shaped by segregation was to form their own self-help organizations, develop businesses and colleges to serve the African-American community, negotiate for land and housing, fight for political inclusion, and, most important, to continually point out to white Atlantans what should have been obvious: measures that diminished black life in the city also had negative effects on whites. Black Atlanta's community development, resistance to or bypassing of white policies, and implementation of their own policies after 1973 were some of the shaping aspects of race that one could see in Atlanta.[57]

Black Atlanta did implement their own policies starting in 1973 (minority contracting mandates, which transferred tax revenue to the Black community) as outlined here:

The election of Maynard Jackson, who has died of a heart attack aged 65, as the first black mayor of Atlanta, Georgia, in 1973 was a major landmark in the southern US city's history.

It signposted a change of guard in the local political class from white to black; no white person has since been elected mayor.

Jackson, who served three terms in office, was a prominent exponent of affirmative action.

In his first two terms, he rattled Atlanta's old cosy business relationships, alienating some, but wooing them back in his third term with deft deal-making skills. In 1978, he signed a law requiring 25% of the city's projects to be set aside for minority firms. The policy, which still operates today, made Atlanta the most hospitable place in America for black entrepreneurs.

He also pushed through an affirmative action program that made it mandatory for contractors to take on minority-owned businesses as partners, and forced the city's major law firms to hire African-American lawyers. He threatened

[57] Bayor, *Race and the Shaping*, 247–9.

that "tumbleweeds would run across the runways of Atlanta airport" if blacks were not included in city contracts.[58]

This is the reason Atlanta is known as the "Black Mecca"; an aggressive affirmative action program implemented to enrich Black citizens of Atlanta, that resulted in enticing Black people from around the country to return to the city (and surrounding metro Atlanta area) to get a piece of the pie. An article from *Ebony* in 2002 notes:

> Though Census figures show that Atlanta's Black population has dipped slightly (it peaked at 282,911 in 1980 and stands at 255,689 today), more than 150,000 African-Americans still moved into the city during the 1990s. The real boom was in the surrounding bedroom communities in DeKalb, Fulton and Cobb counties. More than half a million Blacks swelled the population of those communities in the 1990s. In fact, more Blacks moved to metropolitan Atlanta than to any other metro area in the country during the last decade.
>
> Even in once-segregated strongholds like DeKalb County, which cuts a small swath through the city of Atlanta, Blacks have changed the face of the social and political landscape. In November 2000, DeKalb residents elected 41-year-old Vernon Jones as the county's first Black chief executive. "The times are definitely changing in and around this metropolitan area," Jones maintains. "The whole area is just much more diverse, and that's changing things. There are some glass ceilings, too. We still don't have a Black senator or a Black governor. But the population is growing. More and more Black people are moving here, affluent Black people. That is making a difference."
>
> Today, Atlanta boasts more Black-owned companies per capita than any other city in the nation except Washington, D.C., according to the U.S. Department of Commerce. It is

---

[58] Adenekan, "Maynard Jackson."

home to the nation's second-largest Black insurance company, Atlanta Life. Citizens Trust Bank, the fourth-largest Black bank, also is based there.

"There are business role models here like Jesse Hill and Herman Russell who allow young people to see what the possibilities are," says Thomas Dortch, national chairman of 100 Black Men of America.

But the new economic landscape produced by the labor, lobbying and civil rights leadership of Atlantans such as Dr. Martin Luther King Jr., Andrew Young and Congressman John Lewis also has created scintillating opportunities in areas where Blacks previously were shut out. As Atlanta has grown, so too have the fortunes of scores of Black businessmen who have participated in its amazing development. With the backing of Maynard Jackson, who is credited with initiating the building boom that put Atlanta on the map (some call Hartsfield airport "the airport that Maynard built"), business owners like construction magnate Herman J. Russell, whose H.J. Russell & Co. is the 14th-largest Black business in the country, literally paved the way for the unprecedented success of the Black businesses that followed.

Using aggressive affirmative action initiatives, Jackson ushered in an era in which the percentage of the contracts Black businesses received from the city grew from less than one-tenth of 1 percent in 1970 to more than $250 million today. It is said that 90 percent of the contracts that go to minority-owned firms that do business with American airports are at Hartsfield. Herman Russell, along with his partner, pioneering restaurateur James Paschal, operate several of those concessions, but many young Black business owners also have broken into this lucrative territory.[59]

More and more Black people—who are vacating cities they helped ruin during the Great Migration of 20th century—are

---

59 Whitaker, "Is Atlanta the New Black Mecca?"

moving back to Atlanta. Fittingly, there is a correlation to property value drops, lower tax revenue collected—resulting in
teacher and public employee layoffs and a lack of funds for improvements in infrastructure (and increased crime)—and further White flight from these counties Black people are settling
in.

Attracted by affirmative action policies that helped enrich
one segment of the population, one wonders if metro Atlanta's
White population would ever dare unite to defend their interests? The looming showdown over North Fulton vs. South Fulton would lead one to say "yes, they will."

But it's not just affirmative action policies that have helped
enrich Black people in the private sector.

In describing Freaknic—a raucous Black spring break event
that was eventually evicted from Atlanta—in the opening
chapter of *A Man in Full*, Tom Wolfe writes:

> Atlanta was their city, the Black Beacon, as the Mayor
> called it, 70 percent black. The Mayor was black . . . and
> twelve of the nineteen city council members were black, and
> the chief of police was black, and the fire chief was black,
> and practically the whole civil service was black, and the
> Power was black.[60]

But going back to that quote from Boyer, one glaring incon-
sistency with logic sticks out:

> to continually point out to white Atlantans what should
> have been obvious: measures that diminished black life in
> the city also had negative effects on whites.

Actually, it's measures that improved Black life in the city that
have had negative effects on Whites. More importantly, it's had
negative effects on Black people. Despite these affirmative action programs, poverty (and crime, which has no relation to

---

[60] Wolfe, *Man in Full*, 17.

poverty) in the Black community in metro Atlanta is at levels that rival any in all of America:

Atlanta's status as a haven for African-Americans was greatly reinforced by the election of the city's first Black mayor, Maynard Jackson, in 1973. This accomplishment was due not to the progressive sentiments of the majority of Atlanta's White population, but rather their departure from the city in big numbers. In the book *Imagineering Atlanta: The Politics of Place in the City of Dreams*, Charles Rutheiser reports:

> He (Jackson) assumed a confrontationalist posture vis-a-vis the white business community, arguing passionately for a greater distribution of the benefit of growth among African-Americans. In a showdown over the new airport, Jackson succeeded in establishing a minority business enterprise program that became widely regarded as a model for minority set-asides for municipal contracts. Together, with extensive affirmative action hiring by Atlanta-based corporations like Coca-Cola and Delta Airlines, and an already-established black business community, the set-aside program made Atlanta a nationally known center for African-American economic opportunity in the latter part of the 1970s and 1980s.

> Despite economic opportunities for the middle class and a continuous black presence at city hall for two decades, Atlanta was far from being a decent place, much less a paradise, for the majority of its African American residents. By any and every statistical measure, from poverty and unemployment to graduation rates and crime, the quality of life "enjoyed" by the city's African-American majority plummeted during this period. The percentage of black households living in poverty nearly doubled between 1980 and 1990, to more than a third of all households. Over half of the city's children lived in poverty.

> Nowhere was the divide between the two black Atlantas more manifest than in the area of crime. Atlanta was nationally renowned for its high crime rate in the late 1960s

and early 1970s. Its homicide rate more than doubled between 1965 and 1970, making the city the country's "murder
capital." Atlanta has retained the dubious honor of being
one of the nation's most violent cities to the present day. The
vast majority of these crimes occurred, then as now, in the
cities poorest census tracts to the south, east, and west of
downtown, areas that are more than 95 percent African
American.[61]

Violent crime hasn't stopped in Atlanta (where Black people
have a virtual monopoly on crime), it's just no longer reported
by the police or *The Atlanta Journal-Constitution*.[62]

A simple question has to be asked at this point: who were
those White people in power in Atlanta that caused Black people to unite and create cohesive organizations that would, in
turn, consolidate political power in their own hands (both in
the public and private sector)? Who were these White people
that allowed Atlanta to become the Black Mecca?

An incredibly close-knit group of friends, neighbors, and
business partners from the city's posh Northside, the power
structure shared a common history. "Almost all of us had
been born and raised within a mile or two each other," remembered Ivan Allen Jr., a member of the group who would
succeed (William) Hartsfield as Atlanta's mayor from 1962
to 1970. "We had gone to the same schools, to the same
churches, to the same golf courses, to the same summer
camps. We had dated the same girls. We had played and
worked within our group." Member of the power structure
not only shared a common past and present; they shared a
common vision of the future. In Allen's telling, they were
"dedicated to the betterment of Atlanta as much as a Boy
Scout troop is dedicated to fresh milk and clean air."[63]

---

[61] Rutheiser, *Imagineering Atlanta*, 44–45.
[62] Stix, "Could Atlanta Property Crime?"
[63] Kruse, *White Flight*, 29.

The actions by the White elite (what can only be described as the White "Managerial Elite" of Black-Run America) from 1940–1970 resulted in the vacating of the city by middle class Whites (who couldn't insulate their families from Black crime and integrated schools as the Northside elite could with private schools) and, in turn, resulted in the nightmarish of 2012 metro Atlanta: an entire metro area witnessing property deprecia-tion, increased crime, and staggering costs for commutes.

Interesting that despite government mandated policies of affirmative action, minority contracts, and hiring practices that have turned all public jobs (tax supported) in the metro Atlanta area into a Black vocational program, Black communi-ties there are in complete disarray.

Those areas that stayed White (despite a hostile govern-ment, private sector hiring practices that favor non-Whites, and an onus on entrepreneurship): thriving. Atlanta has been rebuilt up Georgia 400 to Roswell, Sandy Springs, Alpharetta, and Forsyth County.

The tallest buildings in all of suburban America, the 30+ story King and Queen Towers—The Concourse at Landmark Center in Sandy Springs—recently went on the market, and analysts predict the sale[64] will rival what the tallest building in the southeast (which was foreclosed),[65] the Bank of America Plaza, went for. The former complex is located outside the pe-rimeter, in a city that is majority White; the latter located in downtown Atlanta.

Sandy Springs is one of these primarily White cities in North Fulton that could secede from the county tomorrow and instantly see property values rise dramatically.

Since 1973, untold financial investing in the Black Mecca (through primarily White tax dollars and the appropriation of collected revenue toward minority contracts and the establish-ment of an entrenched Black monopoly on public jobs) has re-sulted in the creation of a Black elite in Atlanta, which should

---

[64] Suggs, "Atlanta's Royal Couple Apparently."
[65] Small, "Foreclosed for $235M."

now represent a sunk cost. No matter how many private companies enact affirmative action policies in hiring, this, too, will represent a sunk cost over time.

Atlanta, *The City Too Busy to Hate*, represents a microcosm of how one can look at the entire nation after Black-Run America (BRA) rose to power: The White managerial elite rushing to cede power to Blacks, who have and always will maintain a close racial cohesion. It has been the zeitgeist in America for some time to be seen as "progressive" when it comes to Black America.

The state of 2012 Atlanta and the metro Atlanta area is directly correlated to two things: 1) Blacks moving from around the nation to city to take advantage of affirmative action policies enacted in 1973 that have created the facade of a "Black Mecca," only because of the misappropriation of tax dollars by a racially cohesive drive to augment Blacks, and, 2) White people trying to avoid living anywhere near Black people. No matter the distance of the commute, having limited interaction with Black people is preferred.

One will never be able to quantify (nor qualify) what might have been for Atlanta—and metro Atlanta—were a race-based policy not enacted in 1973 and instead, a merit-based policy enshrined into law.

The White managerial elite of Atlanta sold the city to Organized Blackness; as a result, everyone has suffered.

Such is the case for all of America.

To look back at what Mr. Buyer stated in his book, it should become clear: the day that White people decide to do any of things he listed as the Black response to "segregation" in Atlanta, is the day BRA ends.

Hilariously, it looks like it will be in the very Northside of Atlanta (North Fulton) that sees secession attempted and a new county created.

The seeds of BRAs destruction are in the soil of Atlanta.

9

"We Need More Dead Thugs": Atlanta Is on the Brink (Plus, Buy a House for $61,000 in Nearly All-Black Riverdale)

June 17th, 2011

The story of Deshon Marman is illustrative of the problem plaguing college football. Because of "special admission" status, those 50 percent of Black males who graduate high school are admitted to colleges where they are incredible ill-prepared to perform anything classified as academic work.

Marman's story is hilarious and indicative of why states that wish to ban "baggy pants" are wrong; "baggy pants" are a positive demarcation that Black males, who commit a disproportionate share of the murder and crime in America (hence why so many are locked away in prison), voluntarily display that allows law-abiding citizens to know trouble might be near.

All he had to do was cooperate with the authorities, pull up his pants, and this would never have happened:

> The Transportation Security Administration identifies many, many official threats to our skies, from contact lens solution to gel shoe inserts to throwing stars. Even in the wake of the "Underwear Bomber," though, boxer shorts have been considered generally safe—unless, that is, as New Mexico safety Deshon Marman discovered Wednesday at San Francisco International Airport, airline personnel can see a little bit too much of them:

On Wednesday, San Francisco police got a call about 9 a.m. that someone was exposing himself outside a US Airways gate, Sgt. Michael Rodriguez said.

An airline employee spotted Marman before he boarded Flight 488, bound for Albuquerque, and complained that Marman's pants "were below his buttocks but above the knees, and that much of his boxer shorts were exposed," Rodriguez said.

The employee asked Marman to pull up his pants before he boarded the plane, but he refused, Rodriguez said. Marman allegedly repeated his refusal after taking his seat on the plane.

"At that point he was asked to leave the plane," Rodriguez said. "It took 15 to 20 minutes of talking to get him to leave the plane, and he was arrested for trespassing." Marman allegedly resisted officers as he was being led away.[66]

These are the type of athletes that Predominately White Institutions (PWI) spend vast sums of money to recruit and court so that they will represent an overwhelmingly White student body on the football field and basketball courts.

Once on campus these Black athletes, who come from cities long since abandoned by White flight, fail to acclimate to the mores and morals and still dress in a manner befitting ghetto styles. All Marman had to do was pull his pants up, and the stereotype of the Black thug who rebels against societies norms would have instantly vaporized.

Perhaps it is this image that prompted Neal Boortz (thanks OD) to make this comment regarding the city that is erecting a police state to stave off "urban" (read: Black people) violence:

> Ed Schultz said he is worried about right-wing rhetoric after playing a clip of a talk show host calling for the streets of Atlanta to be "littered" with "dead thugs."

---

[66] Hinton, "Grieving New Mexico safety."

Speaking on his Wednesday show, Schultz challenged conservative talk show host Neal Boortz to appear on his MSNBC show and defend controversial comments he made about Atlanta on Monday:

BOORTZ: We got too damn many urban thugs, yo, ruining the quality of life for everybody. And I'll tell you what it's gonna take. You people, you are—you need to have a gun. You need to have training. You need to know how to use that gun. You need to get a permit to carry that gun. And you do in fact need to carry that gun and we need to see some dead thugs littering the landscape in Atlanta.

"There's something very ugly and dangerous going on in this country," Schultz said. "Right wing talk show hosts seem to be amping up racist and reckless rhetoric like never before. . . . The level of racist and violent rhetoric on hard-right wing radio today is off the charts."

He said that, in his opinion, Boortz "just advocated murder in the streets of Atlanta," and guessed that "Neal wasn't thinking of white thugs." Schultz also called Boortz "reckless, stupid and a racist."[67]

Boortz is right. Chicago, Baltimore, Washington D.C., Newark, Memphis, Birmingham, Charlotte, Milwaukee, St. Louis, Cincinnati, Cleveland, Knoxville, Columbia, Richmond, and many others—not just Atlanta—have way too many urban (Black people) thugs that threaten the safety and well-being of the law-abiding.

Schultz is wrong. It is Black people—who wear baggy pants—that are amping up the levels of racism and violence in this country, attacking White people in Chicago, New York, and Washington D.C. It is the Mainstream Media, led by Disingenuous White Liberals (DWLs), who refuse to report on the race of these attackers.

Slowly, those on the right are becoming aware of the problem.

---

[67] HuffPost Media, "Ed Schultz: Neal Boortz."

Recall that *The Atlantic* magazine pointed out—much to White liberals' bafflement and chagrin—that Black crime followed the patterns of where Section 8 housing vouchers were passed out in the lovely city of Memphis. Here is more on that story:

> Richard Janikowski and Phyllis Betts don't look as if they're inclined to stir up trouble.
>
> He is tall, a sharp dresser who laughs easily. She is short and motherly. They live in suburban Countrywood with two dogs and three cats.
>
> Yet stir up trouble the couple did when a long article in the July/August issue of The Atlantic—"American Murder Mystery" by Hanna Rosin—brought to national attention their theory that shifting patterns of crime in Memphis can be linked to or at least run parallel with the demolition of old public housing in inner-city neighborhoods—Lamar Terrace and Dixie Homes, Hurt Village and LeMoyne Gardens, Lauderdale Courts and Fowler Homes ·and the transfer of former inhabitants to new neighborhoods on Section 8 vouchers.
>
> In other words, crime follows poverty wherever it goes.
>
> "Well, that's a bit of a simplification," said Janikowski, associate professor in the Department of Criminology and Criminal Justice at the University of Memphis and director of the Center for Community Criminology and Research, "though that's the way our studies have been interpreted. Crime and poverty are inextricably linked, there's no question, but it's not that poverty causes crime. Poverty creates a contact point that exacerbates all sorts of stresses on people. It's not that there's any one cause. It's a confluence of stresses."[68]

No. Crime doesn't follow poverty. Crime follows Black people. Take a look at this recent story from Atlanta:

---

[68] Koeppel, "Couple's findings link crime."

The 2010 census makes it clear that there is a modern-day migration underway, as black families leave Atlanta and relocate to the suburbs.

But contrary to what a lot of people thought, it's not the displaced poor who are behind those numbers.

During the last decade, the city's urban landscape underwent a profound metamorphosis, as the public housing projects were demolished one-by-one. In many cases, new upscale developments replaced what were basically dangerous crime factories.

But in order to do that, thousands of residents had to be uprooted and displaced.

The conventional wisdom was that they left the city and went to suburban communities like Clayton, Cobb, and Gwinnett counties, all of which saw large population spikes among African-American residents.

But researchers say that's a myth, quite literally an urban legend. Because most of the former public housing tenants stayed in Atlanta.

"80 to 85 percent of the people in our study moved within the city limits," said Georgia State University sociology professor Deirdre Oakley. "And typically they moved within three miles. That's the average moving distance from their public housing homes. So we didn't find very many at all that moved outside the city of Atlanta Professor Oakley says the reason people stayed put is simple: Public transportation.

Most relocated near MARTA lines.

While some of the displaced residents returned to the new and improved developments, many more simply took their vouchers

from the Atlanta Housing Authority and relocated to other places. Typically these were still poor communities, but respondents to the survey felt the neighborhoods also had less crime and fostered less fear. [69]

---

[69] Reporting from 11 Alive.

Just as crime followed Black people in Memphis, crime follows Black people in Atlanta, in New Orleans and Birmingham. And we can't forget Washington D.C., where the artificially created Black middle class wages war on each daily in Prince Georges County.

We have talked about Clayton County before, but Riverdale is a town I know very well. Just look at this article from *Atlanta Magazine* (starting on page 88) that describes a county whose school population—67 percent of which receive free lunches—is 70 percent Black and 7 percent White:

> After a rash of violent episodes, including the beating of a Forest Park High School teacher by three students, school officials implemented precautions, such as random use of metal detectors in the system's high schools, searches by drug-and-gun-sniffing dogs and new dress codes that ban baggy, oversized pants. Police presence had to be increased at football games after several shooting incidents last fall. A teenager was charged when two men were shot after a Riverdale-Lithonia football game in September. A month earlier, two people were shots after a game in the Morrow High School parking lot. Finally, the system as a whole did not meet "adequate yearly progress" as required by No Child Left Behind.

Riverdale and Clayton County sound like a great place to live and raise a family, right? Well, look what *The Atlanta Journal-Constitution* just published:

> Riverdale is Georgia's most affordable housing market, according to a new Coldwell Banker Real Estate's 2011 Home Listing Report.
>
> The report, released Wednesday, looks at the average listing price of a four-bedroom, two-bath home in 2,300 North American
>
> markets between September 2010 and March. The survey examined 97 real estate markets in Georgia and found

Riverdale, with an average listing of $61,618, was the most affordable.

Dunwoody is the state's most expensive market, with an average listing of $379,866. Nationally, a four-bed, two-bath home averaged $293,251, well above the Georgia average of $180,373.

Nationally, Riverdale's housing market was second only to tourist magnet Niagara Falls, N.Y. where the average list price was $60,820. Two other Georgia cities made Coldwell's top 10 list of most affordable U.S. markets: College Park was fourth ($72,477) and Lithonia was eighth ($77,385). The report noted that all three cities are within a 20-mile commute of Atlanta, which had an average list price of $255,000.[70]

Dunwoody, the state's most expensive market, is one of the White enclaves that Black lawmakers are talking about suing. No one is threatening to sue Clayton County, except banks who continue to foreclose on Black homeowners there.

Clayton County schools—and by extension Riverdale—are veritable police states, jails that house Black students until the bell sounds. No wonder property values are so low.

Like the Comedian from *Watchmen*, I find all of this hilarious. Riverdale and College Park were once thriving White communities (30 years ago), but the Black Undertow moved in and Whites fled. Atlanta and its suburbs are a microcosm of every major city.

It's all a joke.

We could have been on Mars, but we had to fund our own dispossession. Our major cities rot, to point where crackhead infestations in Detroit and Black citizen's attempts to ward them off are major news stories.

The Los Angeles Times asks if we should be preparing for European-style riots this summer. Chicago already offers a

---

[70] Joyner, "Riverdale named Georgia's most."

glimpse of what is coming; as does Newark, Baltimore, and Atlanta preparations.

Knowing that a disproportionate number of criminals are Black, and knowing that a disproportionate of people who eschew wearing belts are Black, the chances that a Black person wearing baggy pants being a criminal are large.

Or as Boortz was careful to identify them: "urban thugs."

And so we march to the inevitable moment when Atlanta becomes a full-on Section 8 riot, and Disingenuous White Liberals blame libertarians like Neal Boortz for antagonizing a population that has already antagonized White people to build suburbs 40–50 miles away from the epicenter of Black-Run America (BRA) looming demise.

But hey, you can buy a lovely abode in Riverdale for $61,000 if you want your kids to go through metal detectors at school.

As the Comedian said in *Watchmen* when asked what happened to the American Dream, "What happened to the American Dream? It came true. You're looking at it."

10

The Black Mecca Underwater:
Atlanta Inches Closer to Implosion

April 27th, 2012

This book has predicted that the concept of Black-Run America (BRA) will be dealt a terminal blow in Atlanta, the city too busy to hate. The metro Atlanta area represents the perfect storm for BRA, for the very history of the region over the past 60 years has been that of White people fleeing Black people.

It has nothing to do with a search for "better school systems" or "safer communities"; it has everything to do with finding a city with few Black residents, the best way to ensure high property value in the metro area. Finding these cities means locating an area of metro Atlanta where the Black population is negligible and the White population represents more than 90 percent of that city's inhabitants.

But the cost of this is increasing. Already metro Atlanta has the worst traffic in America, with your average suburban White commuter spending 60 hours a year stuck in traffic. Because White people must travel great distances to live in peaceful suburbs free from the pernicious influence of the Black Undertow, only 29 percent of metro Atlanta residents get to and from work in less than 20 minutes.[71]

---

[71] ABC, "Forbes: Atlanta traffic the worst."

Wasted productivity and time spent away from family and friends, all because you're stuck in a car as it's not safe to raise a family in a city with too many Black people. Plus, your property value will be embarrassingly low if you do.

As OD points out, the time is coming where a real conversation about race is near. It can start in Atlanta, where the greatest ecological threat to America (Black people) has forced White people—merely trying to raise a family in a decent suburb—to spend an average of $5,280 annually on gas:

> Metro Atlanta commuters might have a new reason to consider carpooling or alternative forms of transportation.
>
> A new survey from AAA finds that the average cost of driving climbed 1.9 percent in the past year, to nearly 60 cents a mile.
>
> In metro Atlanta, where the Clean Air Campaign estimates an average daily commute of 35 miles, that's $21 a day and $5,250 annually if you work 250 days in the year.
>
> "The average driving cost for 2012 is up due to relatively large increases in fuel and tire costs, and more moderate increases in other areas," said John Nielsen, AAA director of automotive engineering and repair. "Those increases were offset by a decrease in depreciation resulting in an overall increase of 1.9 percent."
>
> The cost of fuel rose 14.8 percent for the year, to 14.2 cents a mile for sedan drivers, AAA found. Tire costs, meanwhile, rose 4.2 percent to 1 cent per mile. Maintenance costs rose 0.7 percent while insurance costs rose 3.4 percent. The cost of depreciation fell 4.9 percent.
>
> The news is worse for minivan and SUV drivers, who pay 63 cents and 75.7 cents a mile, respectively. Small sedan drivers pay only 45 cents a mile, AAA found.

When these White people return to their homes well Outside the Perimeter (OTP)—after battling horrific traffic from similar White drones who are merely punching a timecard to pay for greater benefits and entitlements for America's growing non-White population—they should be warned the value is dropping to levels not seen since the Olympics were held in the city:

> Home prices fell much more sharply in metro Atlanta than in other U.S. cities in February, dragging the region's average to 1996 levels, according to a widely watched survey.
>
> Metro Atlanta prices dropped for the seventh straight month in the Case-Shiller Home Price Indices report, which tracks 20 metro areas. The average annual decline for all cities in February was 3.5 percent. For metro Atlanta it was 17.3 percent—double the decline in Las Vegas, the next worst city.
>
> "Atlanta continued its downward spiral, posting its (steepest) annual rate of decline in the 20-year history of the index . . . " said David M. Blitzer, Chairman of the Index Committee at S&P Indices.
>
> The survey gives a big picture view, while real estate experts note that price trends depend heavily on specific location. They also say dropping inventory and the state's falling unemployment rate are positive signs.
>
> "I know in the first quarter we established a new bottom, but the numbers toward the end were more stable," said Steve Palm of SmartNumbers, a Marietta real estate data firm. "New construction is up 20 percent. I think April is going to be the truth-telling month in our market."
>
> The Case-Shiller report uses repeat sales to arrive at an index figure based on a value of 100 for January 2000. Metro Atlanta's index peaked at just over 136 in mid-2007, dropped when the housing bubble burst and then stabilized just above 100. But Atlanta's index dropped below 100 last September and has slid further each month since.
>
> In February it reached the lowest level since October 1996.
>
> Only one city in the Case-Shiller report—Detroit—had a lower index than Atlanta in February, although nine of the 20 posted new post-housing bubble lows, Blitzer said.

Experts say the biggest culprit in Atlanta's recent slide is the effect of foreclosures and other low-priced distress sales. Georgia has been a top-five state for foreclosures and about half of all home sales in 2011 were foreclosed proper- ties.

Georgia's higher than average state unemployment rate left consumers feeling less confident about buying, and lend- ing has been tightened. Some homeowners who want to move are not putting homes on the market to avoid taking a low price. [72]

Welcome to America, where your government is no longer con- cerned with maintaining high property values for its produc- tive citizens, but is more concerned with putting in Section 8 Housing in cities where crime only happens on television. It's more concerned with transferring wealth from the very people who spend much of their most productive years in cars on 400, I-85, I-75, or 285 because it's not safe to take MARTA or live near Black people . . . to those same Black people.

One needs to only look at Clayton County to understand America in 2012. When plans were being made for MARTA (At- lanta's incredibly inept and poorly run light rail system, which is basically a jobs program for otherwise unemployable Black people) to expand into Clayton County nearly two scores ago, the county was almost 95 percent White. The city leaders didn't want MARTA coming into their county, for the understandable fear that it would allow low-income Black residents to move into the city:

Fifty-six-year-old Carolyn McMillan considers herself lucky. To get to work, she can drive to the Home Depot parking lot on Jonesboro road in Clayton County Georgia, then take a bus to her clerical job in downtown Atlanta.

"I'm just barely making it," McMillan says. "Because I have to put gas in the car. I'm just barely making it." Not

---

[72] Quinn, "Atlanta home price index."

too long ago, McMillan could take a local bus before switch-
ing to the Atlanta system, or MARTA. But Clayton County
isn't part of MARTA, and last year, Clayton eliminated all
bus service. Today it stretches south of Atlanta in an endless
string of fried chicken joints, tattoo parlors, check-cashing
stores and used car lots.

In the 1970s, when Clayton County voted not to become
a part of MARTA, it was then a mostly white, rural place.
Now, as more affluent whites flock to downtown Atlanta,
Clayton County is mostly black.

"Transportation in Atlanta has always been mired in
race and racism," says Robert Bullard, director of the Environmental Justice Center at Clark Atlanta University.
When Atlanta began building its commuter rail system in
the 1970s, white communities like Clayton County wanted
no part of it.

"Public Transit was equated with black people and poor
people and crime and poverty. And when the Metropolitan
Atlanta Transportation Authority was created MARTA, it
was a running joke that MARTA"—he spells it out—M-A-R-
T-A—"stood for moving Africans rapidly through Atlanta."

"It's transportation apartheid," he says.[73]

MARTA never came to Clayton County, though a steady trickle
of Black people into the county eventually forced White people
to make an important decision: stay put and watch your property value plummet, or leave for another suburb?

Now? Clayton County is the foreclosure capital of the nation.[74] Racially, it is has completely flipped:

The last quarter-century has seen significant change in the
racial composition of the county's population. In 1980, Clayton county's population was 150,357—91% white and 9%
minority, while in 2006 the population was approximately

73 Bernstein, "Back of the Bus."
74 Shaw, "Atlanta property taxes."

271,240—20% white and 80% minority. Many of these minority groups lived in Clayton County's housing projects
that were built around the time these minority groups
moved to Clayton County; since then many of the housing
projects have been redeveloped due to high crime.[75]

Whereas the almost exclusively White residents of Clayton
County rejected MARTA in 1971, the almost exclusively Black
residents of Clayton County in 2011 approved of a non-binding
referendum to join MARTA.[76] The problem? The primarily
Black residents have property values that reflect the environment of Clayton County,[77] one that Black people have a tendency to create regardless of the state. There's no tax base left
in Clayton County, for Black people have no purchasing power
that the federal government doesn't give them (25 percent of
Black people were on food stamps in 2009 there).[78] Because
home prices are so low (a reflection of the horrendous quality
of life Black people create in terms of schools, livability, and
through the local economy via the business community), tax
revenue collected for local government is dropping, which
means cutting services:

> Last year, they saw little relief in their tax bills and valua-
> tions even though property values were plunging. But this
> year, the numbers are dramatically different, leaving some
> wondering whether their valuations are too low, while oth-
> ers are sure theirs are still too high.
>
> The county's typical appraised value for 2010 was
> $90,589, according to the AJC's analysis, a decline of 25 per-
> cent from last year. The typical sale price, meanwhile, was
> $80,656.

---

[75] "Clayton County, Georgia," Wikipedia.
[76] Cardinale, "Clayton County Votes in Favor"
[77] Joyner, "Riverdale named Georgia's most."
[78] Bloch, et al., "Food Stamp Usage Across the Country."

The reductions in 2010 tax bills cut one way for county taxpayers and the other way for county officials: Lower tax bills mean more money for property owners and less money for local government.[79]

There's a reason that Riverdale (located in Clayton County) has the "most affordable" housing prices in all of Georgia. $61,000 is the average listing: Black people have absolutely devastated the city.[80] The New York Times has an amazing interactive map that showcases government benefits and illustrates, "The share of Americans' income that comes from government benefit programs, like Medicare, Medicaid and Social Security, more than doubled over the last four decades, rising from 8 percent in 1969 to 18 percent in 2009."

Remember that Clayton County was almost 100 percent White in 1970; 90 percent White in 1980; 65 percent White in 1990; 40 percent White in 2000; less than 20 percent now. Let's see how the change from White to Black impacted the county when it came to reliance on the government as the overall share of the Clayton County residents' income:

1969: 3.1%
1979: 6.41%
1989: 7.2%
1999: 10.83%
2000: 23.2%[81]

America will no longer be a global power if we continue to see this type of change take place. Atlanta is not an aberration, either; the same type of Climate Change is happening in the suburbs of Kansas City, Memphis, Birmingham, Chicago, Cleveland, Philadelphia, Washington D.C., Houston, Dallas, Detroit . . . well, you get the picture.

---

[79] Shaw, "Atlanta property taxes."
[80] Joyner, "Riverdale named Georgia's most."
[81] White, et al., "Geography of Government Benefits."

Clayton County was almost 100 percent White in 1969; the reliance on government benefits as a percentage of the share of income for the counties citizens was incredibly low. Now, with Clayton County an overwhelmingly Black county, the share of income derived from *your* tax dollars is almost one fourth of the citizens' income.

Atlanta will be the city where White Americans finally stopped being so busy—probably because they were stuck in traffic on 400—and remembered what type of country they had when "hate" simply meant the freedom to speak openly and honestly about Black people.

11

"The Day the EBT Cards Run Out":
A Glimpse of the Chaos from Clayton County

August 11th, 2011

The Reality of Clayton County, again.

We write about that wonderful county located in Metro-Atlanta a lot here. Whether it is a Black sheriff firing all the White police officers and putting Black snipers on the roof as they are marched out, humiliated in the process; whether it is the first county in America in 40 years to lose its academic accreditation; whether it is the county in all of Georgia with the lowest property value (and some of the worst academic test scores by the children who live there), highest foreclosure rates, and highest rates of crime; or whether it is the city that now gives us a glimpse of the impending "day the EBT cards run out," Clayton County is just the gift that keeps on giving.[82]

The overwhelming majority of Clayton County is Black, with nearly every elementary, middle, and high school in the county providing free lunches to Black students whose parents (okay, parent) lack the financial acumen to provide monetary assistance to their children and feed them, themselves, on their own dime.

White people have fled Clayton County. In 1980, they represented 91 percent of the population.[83] They built an economic

---

[82] Gray, "Clayton County Food Stamp."
[83] "Clayton County, Georgia," Wikipedia.

infrastructure out of nothing, only to see it erode once they fled from the Black Undertow pouring in from Atlanta:

> Between 2000 and 2009, Clayton County had a significant change in its racial and ethnic composition, a much greater change than experienced by the state. The county's African-American population rose 9.9 percent, and its Hispanic population rose 4.8 percent to make-up 62.1 and 12.2 percent of Clayton County's entire population, respectively. The county's White population declined 11.0 percent, and in 2009 comprised 30.4 percent of the county's total population.[84]

Clayton County offers the most stunning visual proof of what happens when White flight meets the Black Undertow; once thriving schools become academically inept, because the students who made those schools academically thrive are gone, their parents moving them to safer cities; the business infrastructure collapses—sustained by the purchasing power of White people who made the county economically viable and attractive to big box stores and business investments—and ultimately replaced with empty strip malls replete with dollar stores, nail and hair salons, and payday loan stores. That is the economy of the Black Undertow.

Here is the story that signifies all that Clayton County became, courtesy of *The New York Times*:

> On his first day at work, the new sheriff of Clayton County called 27 employees into his office on Monday, fired them and had snipers stand guard on the roof as they were escorted out the door.
>
> A judge on Tuesday ordered him to rehire the employees.
>
> The sheriff, Victor Hill, 39, defended the firings and said he had the right to shake up the department in whatever way he felt necessary.

---

[84] Georgia Tech, "Clayton County Community Needs."

Sheriff Hill also said it was necessary to fire the workers the way he did, including taking some deputies home in vans normally used to transport prisoners because the deputies were barred from using county cars.

Sheriff Hill was among a spate of black candidates elected last year in the county, which was once dominated by rural whites. The fired employees included four of the highest-ranking officers, all of them white. Sheriff Hill told *The Atlanta Journal-Constitution* that their replacements would be black.[85]

That was in 2006. Clayton County is a reflection of what Black people are capable of . . . destroying. The Black Undertow obliterated a once thriving county in a matter of two decades. As of 2009, 25 percent of Black people in Clayton County were on EBT/food stamps, not to mention that almost every school in the county provides free lunches to the predominately Black student body. Indeed, all of Metro Atlanta has counties where more than 20 percent of the Black population (in some cases, 40 percent) are sustained via EBT cards.[86]

And then, something happened in Clayton County earlier this week that offers us that tiny glimpse of the pandemonium that will soon ensue across the entire nation when EBT/Food Stamps no longer work:

> Anger and frustration from dozens of Clayton County parents who say their children are going hungry after their food stamps were suddenly cut off.
>
> State officials admit that something went wrong down in Clayton County at the office that administers food stamps and Medicaid but they're still not sure what.
>
> Parents say they can't buy food without those food stamps.

---

[85] Associated Press, "Georgia Sheriff Fires Workers."
[86] Bloch, et al., "Food Stamp Usage Across the Country."

Terry Clark says she stood in line for more than six hours at Clayton County's Human Services Office because food stamp help for her six children unexpectedly ended.

"There's no telling my kids we can't eat. I'm not taking no. We don't deserve that. Nobody should go hungry here in Georgia," said Terry Clark.

State officials say the office was overwhelmed Tuesday with dozens of families facing a similar problem. The food stamps are just not there.

"Me and my kids they haven't ate since this morning. I was supposed to get my food stamps yesterday and I got nothing," said a mother.

A state spokesperson says what happened was out of the ordinary and unexpected but she said they don't know yet what went wrong—what was the glitch that lead to this mess?

"Our budgets have not been increased, they've been decreased," said one official.

The office director admitted there were problems as he tried to calm fears.

In a statement, a state spokesperson says, "We have both state and county staff working to understand the cause of the problem today. We are working to ensure people receive their food stamps as soon as possible."

"I'm a cancer patient. I need these pills to survive," said Candace Bennett.

Candace Bennett says her cancer medications have nearly run out

and after spending all day at the office. Her Medicaid and her food stamps are both still on hold.

State officials say that the Clayton County office was closed Monday because of furloughs and that could have contributed to the lines. They are investigating whether some sort of paperwork or computer problem might have lead to some families getting their benefits cut off by mistake.[87]

---

[87] Gray, "Clayton County Food Stamp."

In 2010, Atlanta had a Section 8 voucher riot. 30,000 Black people rioted for the chance to sign up for Section 8 vouchers that won't be available for five to seven years. We learned in the tragic Brittney Watts story that all of the violent crime in Atlanta is monopolized by Black people; the same can be said of virtually all of the surrounding counties:

A crowd of people hoping to get federal housing assistance became unruly Wednesday morning with reports of fights breaking out in the crowd.

Thousands of people were lined up at the Tri-Cities Plaza shopping center, hoping to apply for a voucher from the East Point Housing Authority that will give them a discount on their rent.

People began lining up at the shopping center two days ago, and by Wednesday morning the crowd had grown to over several thousand people. East Point police, some wearing riot helmets, were patrolling the area. Firefighters and EMTs were attending to people who were overheating in the sun. Police from College Park, Hapeville, Fulton County and MARTA assisted in crowd control.

Felecia McGhee told the AJC she arrived around 6:30 a.m. Wednesday. She said the major problem began when people started breaking into the line and officials started moving the areas where they were handing out applications. She said she saw at least two small children trampled when the crowd rushed the building where the applications were to be handed out.

"It's a real mess out here," she said.

East Point Police Sgt. Cliff Chandler said most of those treated were suffering from heat-related illnesses. He did not have a total number of people treated but knew of at least a half-dozen cases. He said a toddler was treated earlier in the morning for "some type of seizure." He estimated the crowd at 8,000 to 10,000.[88]

---

[88] Markallwood, "Crowd in East Point."

Atlanta Public Schools (APS) has just had a hilarious Black cheating scandal exposed that the Atlanta Chamber of Commerce tried to help cover up, because they know new businesses will not want to move into the city if accreditation is lost. Where will these new investors in the city too busy to hate send their children? A school run by cheating Black teachers, trying to help academically inept Black students meet the standards set by their White counterparts in the lily-White (peaceful) suburbs?

Atlanta will be the city where Black-Run America (BRA) dies. The day the EBT cards no longer work . . . Clayton County has given us a glimpse, just a glimpse of the anger that will appear. All across this country exist counties where a majority or near majority of Black people subsist on EBT Cards/food stamps. The Day the EBT Card no longer provides free food to a certain segment of the population that believes it is their right, their duty to continue receiving welfare and other amenities from the government, is the moment the experiment of BRA officially ends.

Again, a once thriving county in Georgia (when it was White) offers a glimpse of the future for those cities, towns, and counties that allow the Black Undertow to take over. White Flight happens first; commerce and business investments next; and you are left with Black people in control of every level of government, courts, police, the schools, and the Chamber of Commerce.

The Reality of Clayton County is the reality of the power of the Black Undertow. White people can continue building new cities out of the wilderness, but they will inevitably be abandoned when it is no longer feasible to raise children in a healthy, crime-free environment.

12

Water Bills in Atlanta: Not for Black People to Pay
(or the Black-Run City Government)

April 16th, 2012

Last March, CNN published a story that showcased the high prices for water that Atlanta residents were forced to pay for this public utility.[89]

"Skyrocketing water bills mystify, anger residents" was the headline of this story out of the city known as the Black Mecca of America.

Shouldn't that have been enough to give away the answer? In a city that has been completely run—politically—by Black people since Maynard Jackson took power in 1974, wouldn't you wager that one group of people aren't paying their water bills, deferring to those who actually pay their bills higher rates?

Though Atlanta is the city in America with the fastest grow-ing White population, Black residents still comprise 54 percent of the city's inhabitants.

The city too busy to hate has the highest water bills in America, and the reason is because a significant portion of the Black population (and businesses owned by Black people) simply don't pay their water bills.[90]

---

[89] Zamost and Phillips, "Skyrocketing Water Bills Mystify."
[90] Stirgus, "Is Atlanta Drowning."

Back in 2008, WSBTV did a report showing that the city of Atlanta owed $8 million and that $28 million of uncollected water bills were past due:

The City of Atlanta wants raise water rates by 15 percent. Customers who'll be paying more may be interested to know that thousands of water customers don't bother to pay at all, and many of them are government agencies, starting with the City of Atlanta itself.

Channel 2's Richard Belcher sorted through the list of delinquent accounts.

The City of Atlanta is looking for ways to close a 9-figure budget shortfall.

Of course, the budget might be in even worse shape if city agencies actually had to pay their water bills.

The list is 158 pages long—more than 8,000 customers—a total of $28 million in unpaid bills.

Most are companies and individuals, but it is surprising how many of the big bills are for government agencies.

There are at least 36 accounts listed as City of Atlanta with total unpaid bills of nearly $7.9 million.

But that doesn't include the separate account at the city court. The unpaid water bill there is nearly $173,000.

Other unpaid bills include Chastain Amphitheater at $98,000, Piedmont Park at nearly $88,000, or Fire Station #4 on Edgewood with $67,000 worth of water yet to be paid.

In fact, the list includes 29 separate agencies with the word fire in somewhere their names.

Total unpaid water bills for these firefighters more than $328,000.

The Fulton County Jail is deadbeat number two overall with a total unpaid water bill of more than $1.3 million.

There are at least four other Fulton County bills in the top 100. The unpaid total of those is $268,000.

If you think that's bad, Grady Hospital has 31 separate water accounts showing unpaid bills of more than $4.5 million.

If this distresses you as you're paying your soon-to-be-higher Atlanta water bill, keep this in mind—you're in the majority.

There really are more people who pay than don't pay. It's just that some who don't have been collecting your tax dollars and not paying their bills.[91]

No problem. The city of Atlanta (full of accounting wizards whom Ernst & Young stated in a 2004 audit of the department had financial employees clearly unqualified for the job: any guess as to the race of the economic titans?)[92] will just write these uncollected water bills off the balance sheet and find new ways to offset these uncollected bills.[93]

Funny: Baltimore (a city with a greater percentage of Black people than Atlanta) is having a similar crisis right now. *The Baltimore Business Journal* reports:

> City Council President Bernard C. "Jack" Young on Monday called for a two-year moratorium on placing liens on properties because of unpaid water or sewer bills.
>
> Young plans to introduce a formal resolution at Monday's council meeting, he said, followed by an ordinance to enforce the moratorium by March 26.
>
> The move comes in response to a recent city audit that revealed a dysfunctional system of charging businesses and residents for water and sewer usage. Baltimore, according to the audit, has overcharged 38,000 water and sewer customers by more than $4 million. The city so far has failed to correct the inaccurate bills, leaving many customers to either pay more than they could afford or choose not to pay their bills at all, Young said.
>
> "I've encountered too many constituents on fixed incomes who routinely have to choose between feeding their families

91 WSB-TV, "City of Atlanta Accountable."
92 Henry, "Chinks in Shirley's armor."
93 Stirgus, "Outstanding Water Bills Reach $811,011."

and buying needed medication or paying improperly estimated water bills, which, if left unpaid, have the danger of
forcing them into homelessness," Young said in a statement.[94]

No one wants to ask the question, so we will: could these Baltimore residents (and the odds that we are talking about almost exclusively Black residents are at 100 percent) afford the
water rates even if the correct bills were being supplied by the
city?

You can't have a community if residents—and the city—decides it doesn't need to pay water bills, deferring higher costs
for H_2O onto those who actually pay their bills and are productive members of society.[95]

But isn't it wrong to assume—without credible evidence—
that it is the Black residents of both Atlanta and Baltimore
that aren't paying their water bills? No.

It's not.

Because the one city that keeps on giving provides the answer. Yes, we are talking about Detroit, where an estimated
40,000 Black people had their water turned off in the mid-
2000s for failing to pay their bills. Extrapolating this out, it
seems we can conclude that Stuff Black People Don't Like includes paying utility bills.

The citizens of Detroit—89 percent Black—have no White
residents to transfer the burden of paying a utility to in the
form of higher rates for a service they can't provide themselves.
Those Black people without water in Detroit suffer—even
though the city has relatively low rates—because White people
live in the prosperous suburbs they created in escaping the
plague of the undertow.

Without a White scapegoat to fit the higher bill, the Detroit
Water and Sewage Department (DWSD) has no alternative.

Atlanta and Baltimore do.

---

[94] Briggs, "Young Calls for Suspending."
[95] Bennett, "Atlanta water, sewer rates."

Such is life in Black-Run America (BRA). We could have been on Mars, but instead you have to pay for the never-ending sins of a past you had nothing to do with.

Even in something as trivial as utility bills, you can have the burden of those who held to no financial accountability by the state fall on your shoulders. If you are a White Atlanta resident, the next time you get your water bill (or you decide to add up what you have already paid), imagine where that money could be going, were we not living in BRA.

The Black Mecca of America . . . without a substantial (and growing) White population maintaining the business sector and keeping the city competitive, Atlanta would be nothing more than the Detroit below the Mason Dixon Line.

With Black people spreading out across Metro Atlanta to once exclusively White suburbs (counties), the greatest ecological crisis in America is becoming clear.[96]

---

[96] Stafford and Davis, "Minority populations make strides."

13

I've Seen the Future and It Will Be:
Atlanta's Minority Mandates Governing
City Contracts (and Bids) for Blacks Only?

May 11th, 2012

It's called the Black Mecca. But why? Because Atlanta has one of the most powerful affirmative action programs in place (plus rules that mandate 35 percent of city contracts go to minority contractors) in the entire nation:

> It was the place to be, we were told throughout the Eighties and Nineties. The housing was cheap, the weather benign, the social and business networks poppin', the elected officials black and enlightened, and the opportunities limitless. Twenty years before it had been "the city too busy to hate." Now it was the "Black Mecca," and pilgrims streamed in by the tens of thousands each year.
>
> Maynard Jackson was elected Atlanta's first black mayor in 1973, only 5 years after the death of Dr. Martin Luther King. According to a June 29, 2003 *Atlanta Journal-Constitution* article by Ernie Suggs:
>
> "In 1973, fewer than 1 percent of the city's contracts went to minorities. Five years later, it was 38.6 percent. At one point, more than 80 percent of all minority contracts at U.S. airports were in Atlanta, prompting Jackson once to boast that he had helped create 25 new black millionaires . . ."
>
> Those first 25 millionaires, with the assistance of the next three black Atlanta mayors, have helped to create

scores of additional black millionaires along with the thriving, empowered, well-connected and ambitious business and professional class which identifies with the people who run Atlanta to this day.[97]

Those Black people who benefit from Atlanta's intense affirmative action programs, help to uplift Black workers without any oversight from the EEOC or the Department of Justice. In fact, 82 percent of jobs created by Black-owned business will go to Black people.[98]

Were that number implemented by White-owned business (82 percent of jobs going to other Whites), you'd have the federal government suing on behalf of a huge number of aggrieved Black workers denied jobs because of their race.

The heart of America's Black middle class might be in Atlanta, but the blood is pumped directly from mandated minority contracts (Minority Business Enterprise) and government jobs. Without these, there is no Black middle class in Atlanta.[99]

Black Atlanta's power is fracturing, as the city moves to being a majority-minority municipality. And now, other racial groups—not Whites, who know they have no voice in Black-Run America (BRA)—are hoping to fight to the front of the line for minority-mandated contracts:

ATLANTA—Critics charge that when it comes to awarding lucrative city contracts, Atlanta's anti-discrimination policy discriminates against certain minorities.

FOX 5's I-Team found that the city's minority goals in multimillion dollar construction contracts are set aside for African American and female business owners only. Latino and Asian business owners aren't eligible.[100]

---

[97] Dixon, "Atlanta Leads Nation."
[98] Boston, Affirmative Action and Black Entrepreneurship, Ch. 3.
[99] Darnell, interview.
[100] Russell, "City minority contracts investigated."

We could have been on Mars. Never forget that. Now, the fu-ture of America is a Jerry Springer racial free-for-all over who gets what exclusive-to-non-White contracts that come courtesy of primarily White taxpayers.

This should put the 2009 "Black Mayor Memo" into a new perspective, knowing that the Black establishment in Atlanta knows that if they ever lose their vice on power, the gravy train for creating Maynard Jackson's "Black millionaires" could come to a crashing end.

14

Black People Responsible for Virtually All
Crime in Atlanta, Judge Marvin Arrington Confirms

May 6th, 2012

OD has done the tremendous task of compiling the color of crime for the city of Atlanta (looking at statistics from April 2011 to April 2012). The results:

In Atlanta, African-Americans are 54 percent of the population, but are responsible for 100 percent of homicide, 95 percent of rape, 94 percent of robbery, 84 percent of aggravated assault, and 93 percent of burglary.[101]

But statistics and data are misleading, right? In the Black Mecca, that City Too Busy to Hate—which is completely run by an entrenched Black political establishment—there has to be some lasting vestige of institutional racism *making it seem as if* Black people are responsible for all the crime in Atlanta.

Perhaps we should just ask a former judge in Atlanta—the very Black Marvin Arrington—his thoughts on the Black monopoly of all crime in the city. It was Judge Arrington in 2008 who made national headlines by asking all the White people in his courtroom to leave so that he could admonish the criminals (i.e., Black people) in the room:

---

[101] Wallace, "Atlanta: The Color of Crime."

Judge Marvin Arrington insists he's not a racist; despite ordering white lawyers out of his courtroom on Thursday.

The Fulton County Superior Court judge said he was just fed up seeing a parade of young black defendants in his courtroom.

"I came out and saw the defendants, about 99.9 percent Afro-Americans, and some point time I excused some of the lawyers, most of them white, and said to the young people in here 'What in the world are you doing with your lives,'" he told WSB-TV Channel 2 reporter JaQuitta Williams.

Arrington said he thought his message might have more power if it was delivered to a blacks-only audience.

"I didn't think about racism or reverse racism, I practiced law for 30 years and 75 percent of my partners were white," he explained.

The judge said the majority of people who appear before him accused of crimes such as murder, rape and robbery are black and he wanted to do something about it, one on one.

"I didn't want them to think I was talking down to them; trying to embarrass them or insult them; be derogatory towards them and I was just saying 'Please get yourself together,'" he said.

Arrington added that he may make a similar speech next week, but this time he'll allow everyone to hear it.[102]

Interviewed by NRP, Judge Arrington would go even further with his declaration of Black monopolization of crime in Atlanta:

Judge ARRINGTON: And I just said, my God. Will we ever stop? We are executing each other. They appeal before me. They can't read. They cannot write, have no character, no morals, or what have you. And I just exploded.

Judge ARRINGTON: Oh, you just said it for me. I said, would the white defendants and all whites excuse themselves? I want to talk to my brothers one-on-one. And they

---

[102] WSB-TV, "Judge Orders Whites Out."

excused themselves, and I really asked myself a thousand times. I don't see what I'm doing—did wrong. If asking some people not to kill, shoot, you know, to have sex with your daughter, to rape, if that is wrong, I don't want to do right, because I see that as my role, and I said it to my children.[103]

In his autobiography, *Making My Mark*, Arrington would write this about the people he encountered throughout his legal career:

I just wish that more of the cases that come before the court today held the same sense of pride for me. As I've settled into this position and gained more perspective on what it means to sit where I sit, I'm distressed by so much of what I see. So many young people, black and white—but particularly African Americans—come through the system on drugs, especially crack cocaine. There is so much violence, senseless violence. That's largely what I meant

earlier when I said the job of helping young people succeed is such a serious challenge. So many of our black youngsters today seem lost. Their education and training are lacking, as is any motivation or sense of purpose. I see it every day. Young men come with little or no regard for human life, with little or no ambition. More of them come through the courtroom than I care to count. Young women come also, who can hardly read or write, and who don't fully understand what's going on in their lives, or in the courtroom.[104]

Back in 2011, the federal appeals court in Atlanta upheld the armed-career criminal conviction of one Ronregus Jordan, though he tried to claim "racism" in his defense. The court rejected his claim he was targeted for an enhanced penalty because he was a Black man:

---

[103] NPR, "Judge: Whites, Step Aside."
[104] Arrington, interview.

In a decision Wednesday, the court found that Ronregus Jordan failed to produce enough evidence to establish a selective prosecution claim. Jordan was convicted at trial in 2009 and then sentenced to 20 years in prison for being found in possession of a .38-caliber revolver in August 2007 and having more than three prior felony convictions.

In pre-trial motions, Jordan's attorney presented documentation that showed African-Americans accounted for about 93 percent of the armed-career criminal prosecutions by the U.S. Attorney's Office in Atlanta, while blacks accounted for significantly less than that percentage of the population. [105]

More of the type of Black career criminals, okay, Black people Judge Arrington tried to scold in a segregated moment of clarity. *The Atlanta Journal-Constitution* reported this about Judge Arrington, who admitted to once being an inner-city thug himself:

Judge Marvin Arrington had seen and heard enough.

The parade of black men and women—criminals and mothers of criminals—he saw every day frustrated him.

What he did to address it, some observers say, was classic Arrington. Others say it was arrogance.

"You guys are destroying your lives," he admonished—after asking the few whites present to leave his Atlanta courtroom. "Black people, please, turn your life around."

The scolding quickly became national news earlier this month. Arrington's "fireside chat," as he later called it, was being compared to the more public criticism first voiced four years ago by actor Bill Cosby, who criticized some African-American families for not raising their kids right, slammed black youth for wearing their clothes backward and berated them for failing to master the queen's English. [106]

---

[105] Rankin, "Court Denies Selective Prosecution."
[106] Staples, "Honorable 'Was A Thug.'"

Asking White people to leave the courtroom so that he could address the source of Atlanta's criminal problem (Black people) was a nice gesture by Judge Arrington, considering that in 2005 new Clayton County Sheriff Victor Hill (once an all-White, prosperous county to the southwest of Atlanta, it has subsequently been Detroit-ed by the influx of Black people and outward migration of Whites) fired all the White police officers and had snipers put on the roof of the police station as they left:

> On his first day at work, the new sheriff of Clayton County called 27 employees into his office on Monday, fired them and had snipers stand guard on the roof as they were escorted out the door.
>
> Sheriff Hill was among a spate of black candidates elected last year in the county, which was once dominated by rural whites. The fired employees included four of the highest-ranking officers, all of them white. Sheriff Hill told *The Atlanta Journal-Constitution* that their replacements would be black. [107]

Just don't ask Judge Arrington about his plan on how to deal with Black crime:

> Fulton County is giving young law breakers with limited criminal histories a chance to turn their lives around.
>
> As many as 40 low-level offenders ages 17 to 30 are slated to participate in Operation Turn Around. Fulton County District Attorney Paul L. Howard Jr. and Fulton County Superior Court Judge Marvin Arrington unveiled the program on Thursday.
>
> Arrington sees it as an extension of the tough-love talk he delivers from the bench that, like that of comedian Bill Cosby, has attracted media attention and sparked debate.
>
> The judge considers "mind bogging" the number of African-Americans incarcerated in the nation's prisons and

---

[107] Associated Press, "Georgia Sheriff Fires Workers."

jails. He also remembers once being young, crazy and unwilling to listen to anybody until black school teachers pushed him to do better.[108]

Operation Turn Around isn't a bad name, but the manners in which it is being conducted are wrong: mandatory sterilization for all repeat offenders will ensure that crime drops dramatically in Atlanta (indeed, in all of America) in as little as one generation. That's the real Operation Turn Around America needs today.

Though it can't be turned around, the actions of Brian Nichols in 2005, a Black criminal who killed a judge, court reporter, Federal agent and a Sheriff's Deputy in Atlanta, represent exactly the type of individual Judge Arrington was trying to reach. He decided to wage a racial war in the name of perpetually oppressed Black people:

> The Atlanta courthouse gunman said in letters that he escaped from guards and then killed four people in a shooting rampage to fight back against what he believed was a racist justice system, according to documents obtained by The Associated Press.

In the letters, which were among thousands of Georgia Bureau of Investigation documents reviewed exclusively by the AP, Brian Nichols lays out his motive for the March 2005 slayings in stark racial terms.

"Certain dogs you can kick and they tuck their tail between their legs and run," he wrote in a July 2005 letter to a man who criticized him. "Others if kicked will turn and bite the individual responsible. I hate to say it, but it's the truth that Black men have done way too much tail tuckin'."

While awaiting trial on rape charges, Nichols overpowered a guard at the Fulton County Courthouse and fatally shot a

---

[108] Reid, "Judge Arrington wants to turn."

judge, court reporter, deputy, and federal agent. He was sentenced to life in prison without parole in December 2008.

Trudy Brandau, the sister of slain court reporter Julie Ann Brandau, said the letters show Nichols is delusional.

"If you want changes made, make smart, intelligent choices that would actually wind up causing improvement," she said. "What he wound up doing was extremely selfish and hasn't changed a thing for anybody."

Nichols said he was infuriated that the judge, Rowland Barnes, was holding him without bond on rape charges while other inmates awaiting trial were set free.

He compared himself to Dany Heatley, a former Atlanta Thrashers star, whom Barnes allowed to remain free on bail after he was charged with vehicular homicide in a 2003 crash that killed a teammate. "White boy, driving crazy killed somebody. Was he not a threat to the community having killed a person as a result of his reckless behavior?" he wrote.

He said "no Black man has ever made a stand such as mine" and insisted the shootings sent a message.

Perhaps my children of another generation won't find their back against the wall, subjected to unequal treatment under the law. Unfortunately, my sacrifice is not enough to prevent that from happening, but perhaps it's a start. . . .

And believe me, in Fulton County, where there are a large number of people pissed off at the way the criminal justice system treats people, it can happen. . . . All I need is the right people on the jury, and I go home. I've got to put in the grass-roots effort it takes to pull something like that off.[109]

It might be too late for Operation Turn Around America, if we're to believe Nichols. Or, if we are to believe the story surrounding the death of Dr. Eugenia "Jeanne" Calle, who was killed in 2009.

---

[109] Quoted in Bluestein, "Letters: Courthouse gunman angry."

"The start of our day here at the American Cancer Society was quickly punctuated by the rumor—and then the confirmation ·that one of our friends, a valued colleague and mentor, lost her life in a horrific crime sometime Tuesday in Atlanta.

Jeanne Calle was a member our society family since 1989. She was vice president of epidemiology here at our national home office in Atlanta.

She was an epidemiologist who worked incessantly to unlock the secrets of what population·based information can tell us about the causes and risk factors that lead to cancer. There are few researchers in this country who have labored so hard and been so successful at bridging the gap between what we learn from epidemiology research and how we apply that information to our everyday lives.

We have lost someone very special. Her death was tragic and needless, and defies explanation."[110]

Calle was striving to better society through groundbreaking research in fighting cancer that would have lasting implications on the health and well·being of countless individuals, regardless of race or creed.

Sadly, a condo·less, Black Atlanta resident decided to take her life in a cold·blooded manner that seems to defy explanation. Lawrence Auster of View from the Right reported:

"Their fateful meeting at the high·rise Midtown condo complex—the prominent cancer researcher and the young man described by police as a two·bit criminal—was nothing but chance.

Eugenia "Jeanne" Calle, who had a condo on the Aqua building's 20th floor, was walking her gray poodle.

Shamal Thompson, 22, fresh off a meal at a nearby Checkers fast·food restaurant, wandered in under the pretense of shopping for condos in the luxury building that

---

[110] ABC News, "Remembering Dr. Eugenia 'Jeanne' Calle."

boasts private elevators, around-the-clock security and sky-line-view homes that cost as much as $2.5 million.

Calle undoubtedly thought she was seizing on an oppor-tunity to sell her condo. But it was Thompson, police say, who was looking for opportunity.

Early Thursday morning, authorities arrested Thomp-son and charged him with beating Calle to death as she showed him around her penthouse condo. After the killing, and after he went on a spending spree with Calle's credit cards, Thompson got bolder, returning to the scene of the crime late Wednesday night and trying to con his way back inside her condo, police said.

"He was extremely brazen," said Atlanta police Lt. Keith Meadows, commander of the department's homicide unit. "It's a little unsettling when people are that bold. I can't even put it into words."

Just two weeks into retirement, Calle wanted to sell her condo so she could move in with her fiance."

Would you like for me to escort him up?" the guard asked Calle, according to Meadows.

"No, it'll be fine," Calle responded. "I don't want him to think that we don't trust him."

It's not clear whether Thompson seriously intended to buy a home in Aqua or had the money to do so. Meadows said he suspects Thompson wanted to case the condos for valuables and didn't realize beforehand that the first two were vacant.

Surveillance footage captured Thompson on camera, but he had given a fake name to the real estate agent, Meadows said. He had used his own cell phone to set up the condo viewings, however, and police subpoenaed his phone rec-ords.[111]

A White female doctor striving to rid the world of cancer: dead. A Black career criminal: alive.

Crime in the metro Atlanta is a Black phenomenon. Hence,

---

[111] Morris and Eberly, "Police: 'Brazen' Suspect Returned."

why White people have for sixty years been fleeing for suburbs surrounding the city that quickly turn into flourishing Whitopias, only to be eventually overwhelmed by the Black Undertow. Thus, the need to move even further outside the city to find peace, tranquility, and temporary solace from Black crime. This *Atlanta Journal-Constitution* from 2010 tragically illustrates that importing poverty to metro Atlanta counties only means seeing White people leave and Black people replace them:

> According to the data, Atlanta is on the verge of no longer being a majority black city—a major shift in its cultural identity.
>
> Averaging the samples from 2005 to 2009, Atlanta's population was 50.1 percent black and 43.1 percent white. The rest were either Asian, Native American or a combination of two or more races.
>
> (Hispanic is an ethnic rather than a racial category; Hispanic people may be of any race.)
>
> At the same time, northern communities saw substantial increases in the number of black residents as well as Hispanics.
>
> Both Cobb and Gwinnett counties remained predominantly white, but the trend was strongly toward greater diversity. In Cobb County, the number of black residents rose by 20 percent and the number of Hispanics by 47 percent. In Gwinnett County, those figures were 52 percent and 54 percent, respectively.[112]

Judge Arrington's dismissal of White people from the courtroom almost four years confirms the findings by OD of Atlanta's crime problem. But those findings could be for any big city in America with a significant Black population. They are not an anomaly. Guns don't kill people; dangerous minorities do.

---

[112] Schneider, et al., "Census data show gap."

15

In the Air Tonight: White North Fulton vs. Black South Fulton County

May 8th, 2012

Reading the book *White Flight: Atlanta and the Making of Modern Conservatism (Politics and Society in Twentieth-Century America)* gives you the impression there was some grand opposition to Black-Run America (BRA) being implemented in Atlanta.

There wasn't.

White people just fled the city and created what is now metro Atlanta, home to the worst traffic in America and the steepest property value drops in all the nation.

As Tamar Jacoby notes in 1990s book *Someone Else's House: America's Unfinished Business Struggle for Integration*, the outcome of the 1970s in Atlanta—when Black people became the dominant population group in the city and took political control—was not integration, but an "uneasy coexistence":

> Even so, many whites used crime as an excuse to avoid downtown, and blacks and whites divided up the landscape like a battleground. Sometime in the '70s, localized shopping nodes eclipsed the old central hub, and by the end of the [Maynard] Jackson era, Atlanta had two downtowns: the deteriorating black downtown in the center city and the new white downtown, Buckhead, six miles to the north.

With the city's upscale restaurants, its choicest hotels and newest office towers, Buckhead paid taxes to Atlanta and in an important way helped keep it alive, but its residents had less and less to do with the black on the south side of town.[113]

Those White people who remained in the city—ensconced in Disingenuous White Liberal (DWL) enclaves—made a deal with the emerging Black establishment in the 1960s that the dwindling White majority in Detroit failed to make before the riots of 1967 forced their hands; it was a Faustian Pact that won't end pretty.

No deal with the devil ever does.

This is why the following story published at *The Atlanta Journal-Constitution* on May 7 is so interesting; battle lines between the White Northside and the very Black Southside are being drawn:

> The latest eruption of Fulton County's north-south tensions has one elected official calling out another for publicly taking swipes at the Northside.
>
> Liz Hausmann, who represents most of north Fulton, has asked Vice Chair Emma Darnell to stop insulting her and her district, and while she's at it, stop haranguing county staffers called before the commission dais.
>
> "All this does is continue the drumbeat to separate the county," Hausmann said.
>
> The spat is another setback in Chairman John Eaves' efforts to improve the county government's image. The commission directly governs less than 10 percent of the population but provides libraries, criminal justice, health services, senior centers, property tax assessments and other services to nearly 1 million people.

---

[113] Jacoby, *Someone Else's House*, 371.

Last week, while talking about unincorporated south Fulton's share if voters in the region approve a new transportation sales tax in July, Darnell told Hausmann to pipe down because she doesn't represent that area. Hausmann had stated that $2.9 million per year, the south's projected share for local projects, is a significant sum.

The commission is unincorporated south Fulton's governing body, making decisions on zoning matters and its property tax rate, among other things. Hausmann pointed out that she would be voting on which transportation projects south Fulton gets.

Darnell said later, while talking about buying new cell door locks for the county jail, that she never agrees with Hausmann on anything because of the area she speaks for.

Hausmann told Darnell in a letter Friday, copied to the whole board, that it's time for her anti-north rhetoric to stop.

North Fulton, mostly white, affluent and conservative-leaning, makes up a third of the county population.

Dissatisfaction with the county led four Fulton communities—three of them in north Fulton—to vote to form cities during the past decade, changes made possible by Republican gains in the Legislature. There's also a movement to split the six Northside cities into their own county.

Darnell, who represents northwest Atlanta and part of south Fulton, has railed against such efforts. She did not return phone messages or emails seeking comment Monday and Tuesday.[114]

South Fulton is full of Black people whose mere existence is predicated upon the redistribution of tax dollars collected from the North Fulton residents.[115] Jim Goad profiled some of those residents in *Blight of the Living Dead*.[116] As the AJC article points out, those residents of North Fulton are largely White.

114 Edwards, "County Official Asked to Stop."
115 Edwards, "Battle Brews over Proposal."
116 Goad, "Blight of the Living Dead."

Tired of playing Atlas for Fulton County's Black residents, the largely White residents of Sandy Springs, Johns Creek, and Dunwoody have decided to finally shrug. The catastrophic effects to Black Atlanta would be instantaneously felt were this to happen, as the city becomes Detroit-ed overnight:

> In the cradle of the civil rights movement, a new secession effort is under way that would break off Atlanta's predominantly white, wealthy suburbs to the north from poorer, black neighborhoods in the south. There's a renewed push to take some suburbs out of Fulton County, Georgia's most populous and home to most of the city of Atlanta, and put them under the now-extinct Milton County. Its supporters hope resurrecting the county would give residents there more responsive government.
>
> But opponents say the measure is racially motivated and will open up a deep rift between black and white, rich and poor in a state with a complicated racial history. The area that would be split off is more than 75 percent white, while a large block of the remaining portion of Fulton County is 90 percent minority. "It sends a message when you say the hometown of Dr. Martin Luther King is going to be split apart in a kind of latter-day secessionist movement," said state Sen. Vincent Fort, an Atlanta Democrat.
>
> It was frustration with Fulton County that led to the creation of the new cities of Sandy Springs in 2005, Milton in 2006, and Johns Creek in 2006. Those suburban enclaves—along with Alpharetta, Roswell and Mountain Park—would constitute the newly formed Milton County. What used to be Milton County is now largely white and Republican and affluent. Atlanta and its southern suburbs are mostly black, are controlled by Democrats and have neighborhoods with some of the highest poverty rates in America. Buckhead, a trendy Atlanta neighborhood known for its clubs, restaurants and mansions, would remain in Fulton County.

"There's no doubt in my mind that race is part of the equation here and it has been since Day One," said Brooks.[117]

This is why in March of 2011, the Georgia Legislative Black Caucus declared war on White flight:

The Georgia Legislative Black Caucus filed a lawsuit Monday against the state of Georgia seeking to dissolve the city charters of Dunwoody, Sandy Springs, Johns Creek, Milton and Chattahoochee Hills. Further, the lawmakers, joined by civil rights leader the Rev. Joseph Lowery, aim to dash any hopes of a Milton County.

The lawsuit, filed in a North Georgia U.S. District Court Monday, claims that the state circumvented the normal legislative process and set aside its own criteria when creating the "super-majority white" cities within Fulton and DeKalb counties. The result, it argues, is to dilute minority votes in those areas, violating the Voting Rights Act of 1965 and the Fourteenth and Fifteenth Amendments to the Constitution.

"This suit is based on the idea that African Americans and other minorities can elect the people of their choice," said Democratic State Sen. Vincent Fort.

According to the 2010 census, Fulton County is 44.5 percent white and 44.1 percent black. About 54 percent of DeKalb County residents are black, and 33.3 percent are white.

Sandy Springs, created in 2005, is 65 percent white and 20 percent black. Milton, formed a year later, is 76.6 percent white and 9 percent black. Johns Creek, also formed that year, is 63.5 percent white and 9.2 percent black. Chattahoochee Hills, formed in 2007, is 68.6 percent white and 28 percent black, while Dunwoody, created in 2008, is 69.8 percent white and 12.6 percent black.[118]

---

[117] Associated Press, "Atlanta secession effort raises race issues."
[118] Leslie, "Lawsuit Seeks Dissolution of Dunwoody."

Metro Atlanta in 2012 offers the most important domino in the ultimate collapse of Black-Run America (BRA) legitimacy. Though the White people who form the aristocracy and establishment of Atlanta are some of the vilest humans to have ever existed (as evidenced by the attempts of the White business community, the executives of the Metro Atlanta Chamber of Commerce, to cover-up the Atlanta Public Schools cheating scandal), they will, like rats, eventually scurry from the sinking ship that is Atlanta.[119]

Recall that in 2009, the "Black Memo" was circulated among the Black political elite of Atlanta as to why Black people must unite around mayoral candidate to ensure that Black political gains remained intact:

> A memo arguing that African-Americans should unite behind a single black candidate in the race for mayor of Atlanta is about to become a prime topic of debate.
>
> The material, which we include below, is said to be distributed by Aaron Turpeau, a long-time City Hall figure, on behalf of something called the Black Leadership Forum.
>
> Introduction
>
> The debate over the best strategic option for black leadership and the African American community as we approach the Mayoral election in Atlanta has become critical based on the fact that for the last 25 years Atlanta has represented the breakthrough for black
>
> political empowerment in the South.
>
> It is debatable to what extent the objective socio-economic and political position of the African American community has improved. At the same time, most would agree that the Jackson [Maynard Jackson, Atlanta's first Black mayor, who was elected in 1973] breakthrough represented an unprecedented opportunity for black political representation nationwide.

---

[119] Saporta, "How Biz Community Dealt."

A passionate argument has been made for us to develop a unity of purpose and position, and for that to be defined immediately, given the short amount of time remaining between now and November 2009 election day (two and ½ months from now).

There are unstated assumptions that need to be examined. Perhaps the most critical factor is the lack of an agenda against which to evaluate candidates. An agenda, beyond just electing a Black Mayor, would allow us to move from the margins of the debate to controlling the expectations associated with gaining our support.[120]

Back in 1988, *The Atlanta Journal-Constitution* published a number of investigative articles by Bill Dedman, which became known as *The Color of Money*.[121] This report detailed how Atlanta's White banks weren't lending money to Black people to pursue the American Dream of home ownership.

The value of homes in Metro Atlanta has been devastated by the availability of cheap credit, which resulted in some of the highest foreclosures rates in the nation. All of this in the mindless pursuit of putting Black people in the position to own homes, a goal that Bill Dedman once won a Pulitzer Prize for reporting that they were rightfully denied for a lack of collateral or credit (a punishing takedown of Dedman is coming, for this report was instrumental in passing legislation that ultimately birthed Steve Sailer's Minority Mortgage Meltdown).

Atlanta is the domino that must be pushed first; that must fall first. No one cares about 90 percent Detroit anymore, but the Black Mecca in the Dirty South is the vibrant home of America's favorite Black celebrities.[122]

There was no opposition to BRA becoming the law in Atlanta. But BRA's legitimacy is on the line in Atlanta (the Black political elite know this, hence the memo from 2009).

---

[120] Galloway, "Memo that's about to shake."
[121] Kovach and McCutchen, eds, *Color of Money*.
[122] Severson, "Stars Flock to Atlanta."

The push of that domino—the first domino—will come when DWL residents of the Northside attempted to form their own county. The Department of Justice will attempt to intervene, thereby showing that White people have only one role and one duty in BRA: to continue working and paying taxes to support Black people's proliferation (and, increasingly, other non-White minorities).

The Black Mecca is underwater. Once the push comes, the legitimacy of BRA will end. The salvation of Real America ironically begins in the same city where the dream of the Confederacy was burned to the ground.

From all ashes rise a new hope.

16

The Reality of Race in the Divide Between
North and South Fulton County

October 1st, 2012

If you've been paying attention to SBPDL, you know that we believe 2013 will be the year all eyes turn to Atlanta. The battle between primarily White, affluent North Fulton County vs. overwhelmingly Black, poor South Fulton County will come to a head. We have noted at *VDARE* that the smell of 1861 is in the air, and the time is ripe for a nation-shattering moment.

The Atlanta Journal-Constitution inadvertently added more fuel to the fire with writer Jeffry Scott sticking strictly to "Journalism 101" in a story on the great divide between SAT scores produced by the students in North Fulton versus those of South Fulton:

> Fulton County could serve as a core sample of all the ethnic, cultural and economic diversity of metro Atlanta, stretching about 80 miles from the north to the south, from the suburbs through the heart of the city. When SAT scores were announced last week it was like taking the latest reading on the impact of those influences on public schools.
>
> By many measures, Fulton excelled. Six of the top 10 performing public schools in the state were in the county, and the district's overall increase of 20 points bested that of its rival core counties of DeKalb, Gwinnett and Cobb (which showed a 2 point drop).

But there was an undertow to the numbers: The average score for the 11 north Fulton high schools was 1613 out of a possible 2400. That was 362 points higher than the average of 1251 scored by the five high schools in the less-affluent south end of the county—Banneker, Creekside, Langston Hughes, TriCities and Westlake.[123]

Noticing any important information missing? The racial data would be incredibly important to determine if, once again, that pesky racial gap in achievement is present in Fulton County, too. That 362-point difference is important, if not a bit skewed. Only those students hoping to go to college take the SAT, and because South Fulton is overwhelmingly Black, you have to wonder what percentage of these students opted out of taking the SAT.

Had they taken the test, what would the point differences have been?

But doesn't the SAT score difference between the sons and daughters of North/South Fulton County bespeak something much, much more important? Namely, why North Fulton is full of thriving communities, high

property value, and the center of job growth/private industry employment in the Atlanta area; conversely, why South Fulton is the area of the city most reliant on welfare and public employment, and where job stagnation and blight is most commonly found.

In the important Brookings Institute study *Moving Beyond Sprawl: The Challenge for Metropolitan Atlanta* let slip some hugely important stats in understanding the racial divide between North and South Fulton:

- The Atlanta region's poverty challenge has a strong racial dimension. A 1999 study found that 91 percent of the welfare recipients in the City of Atlanta are African-American, and only 4 percent are white. In the Atlanta

---

[123] Scott, "Great divide lurks beneath."

region as a whole, 70 percent of welfare recipients are African-American and 19 percent are white. Welfare recipients who are black are concentrated in predominantly black, high-poverty neighborhoods; fewer than 10 percent of welfare recipients in the City of Atlanta live in neighborhoods that are less than 50 percent African-American. By contrast, white, and to some extent Hispanic, welfare recipients are dispersed. In the region as a whole, less than 5 percent of white welfare recipients and about 10 percent of Hispanic welfare recipients live in high-poverty neighborhoods.

- There is little or no job growth in majority non-white neighborhoods. South Atlanta had a net loss of nearly 1,000 jobs in the 1990s. South DeKalb County, about 83 percent non-white in 1998, had a net gain of 324 jobs between 1990 and 1997. This is minuscule growth compared to the rest of the region.
- In Fulton County, the northern suburbs account for 62 percent of the county's job growth. The area around Alpharetta in northern Fulton saw a 175 percent increase in jobs[124]

The onus on the residents of North Fulton to keep alive the economic engine powering the entire region is dramatic. The study used words like "distressed neighbors" to describe those areas of Atlanta where Black people are found in large numbers. Actually, blaming the residents for the "blight" and "distressed" quality of the neighbor would instantly require those studying why "sprawl" (i.e., White flight) exists to factor in racial differences in ability.

That ain't gonna happen. Instead, the good people of North Fulton (remember, disproportionately White and educated) have set their sights on doing what they do best: building thriving communities that become the envy of their neighbors (remember, those in South Fulton are overwhelmingly Black).

---

[124] Daley and Katz, "Atlanta Can Flourish in Global Economy."

Sharon Adams bemoaned this racial imbalance when she wrote:

- A study conducted by the Institute of Race and Poverty at the University of Minnesota Law School, indicates that a disproportionate share of the region's poor and moderate-income residents live near the southern region of Metro Atlanta where job growth is the slowest. "Thirty percent of African Americans are more likely to work in areas where job clusters are declining compared to 20 percent of whites," informs Myron Orfield, executive director of the University of Minnesota Institute of Race and Property. The study also shows that job centers in the Atlanta business district grew modestly during the 1990s by 4,400 reflecting a 3.9 percent increase, compared to the second largest and fastest growing job center located in Sandy Springs/Dunwoody, which grew by 62 percent in the same time span. Other areas of increased growth include Cobb and Gwinnett counties and Alpharetta. According to the 2000 United States Census, African Americans represent 7.2 percent of north Fulton County's population, which includes the cities of Roswell and Alprahretta and whites represent 82.6 percent; where as the demographics of south Fulton County is 73.97 percent African American and 21.85 percent white.
- As job clusters are seemingly racing toward the north, it poses an increased burden for those who have to fight the traffic each day to keep up. "One of the biggest impacts in this type of imbalance for the region as whole [is that] it creates, among other things, an extreme burden on transportation," says Tom Weyandt, director of the Comprehensive Planning Department of the Atlanta Regional Commission.[125]

Those Disingenuous White Liberals (DWLs) are sneaky: "job clusters" are the offspring of White people (as evidenced by the

---

[125] Adams, "No Jobs Near?"

population data this article by Adams provides), while the greatest detriment to job creation seems to correlate unfortunately with a high-clustering of Black residents.

"Blight," "Distressed neighborhoods," and empty business districts are the hallmark of an all-Black area. Know what else is hallmark of an all-Black area? Ethnocentric politicians who were elected specifically to defend Black interests:[126]

> The latest eruption of Fulton County's north-south tensions has one elected official calling out another for publicly taking swipes at the Northside.
>
> Liz Hausmann, who represents most of north Fulton, has asked Vice Chair Emma Darnell to stop insulting her and her district, and while she's at it, stop haranguing county staffers called before the commission dais.
>
> "All this does is continue the drumbeat to separate the county," Hausmann said.
>
> North Fulton is 68 percent white and makes up more than a third of the county population. Its median household income is $93,555, according to north Fulton chamber data.
>
> Dissatisfaction with the county led four Fulton communities—including Sandy Springs, Johns Creek and Milton in north Fulton—to vote to form cities during the past decade, changes made possible by Republican gains in the Legislature.
>
> Northside residents have long complained that the county government siphons their tax money to the south while ignoring their needs, while Southside leaders contend that their money helped build up north Fulton, so it ought to reciprocate. The dispute has sparked a movement to split off the six northern cities and re-form old Milton County.
>
> Were that to happen, what remained of Fulton would have a $36,930 median household income, according to a 2009 study by researchers at the University of Georgia and Georgia State. South Fulton is 81 percent black and Atlanta

---

[126] Edwards, "County Official Asked to Stop."

is 54 percent black, according to census statistics.[127]

So there's your 2012 racial breakdown: North Fulton is 68 per-cent White; median household income is $93,555. South Fulton is: 81 percent Black; median household income is $36,930.

Now, why couldn't Jeffry Scott's article on the differences in the SAT scores between the two factions of Fulton County have included this information?

We already know that Sandy Springs (located in North Ful-ton) has successfully incorporated, but this article published in Scott's AJC just prior to the vote provides some stark data on just how reliant the Black population of Atlanta—and, by ex-tension, all of Black America—is on the White population for job creation:[128]

Sandy Springs stands on the verge of becoming the second-largest city in metro Atlanta. But whether or not its voters approve cityhood in a June 21 referendum, the community will not be the shoreline for waves of white flight its found-ers inhabited when they first tried to incorporate in the 1960s.

That first population boom escalated into a barrage: Families came from Atlanta and northern cities through the '70s, apartmentseeking baby boomers and yuppies into the '80s and '90s, and now immigrants willing to occupy older, smaller dwellings.

Urban gateway

Today, Sandy Springs is more of an urban gateway than it is a "Golden Ghetto," the community's nickname when it was Atlanta's wealthiest suburb a generation ago.

At least one-third of the community's residents are His-panic, Asian or African-American. Few disagree with de-mographers' predictions that whites will someday become another minority in this community tucked between Buck-head to the south and Roswell to the north.

---

[127] Ibid.
[128] Farber, "Race colors Sandy Springs' future"

The browning of Sandy Springs could color future deci-sion-making as prospective city pioneers prepare to wrest control of government from Fulton County.

Racism charge disputed.

Diversity is a sensitive issue for city proponents. Their loudest critics come from south Fulton and Atlanta—the center of Georgia's black political power.

Unincorporated south Fulton alone would lose $25 mil-lion annually if Sandy Springs starts collecting and allocat-ing its own taxes. The most severe critics call city advocates racists bent on victimizing blacks.

Sandy Springs advocates, noting the community's grow-ing diversity, call the charge ironic.

"Whether they're black, white or Hispanic, they need more representation for themselves, too, and they'll have it when they're in a new city," said Gabe Sterling, a co-chair-man of the city campaign.

SANDY SPRINGS POPULATION
1960 total: 16,456
White (16,286): 99%
Black (167): 1%
Other (3): 0%
1970 total: 39,050
White (38,883): 99.6%
Black (109): 0.3%
Other (58): 0.1%
1980 total: 46,877
White (45,804) 97.7%
Black (626): 1.3%
Asian (257): 0.6%
Other (190): 0.4%
1990 total: 67,842
White (60,797): 89.6%
Black (5,152): 7.6%
Asian (1,106): 1.6%
Other (787) 1.2%
2000 total: 85,781
White (66,522): 77.6%

Black (10,332): 12.0%
Asian (2,820): 3.3%
Other (6,107): 7.1%
2004 total (estimate): 86,567
White (64,742): 74.8%
Black (11,126): 12.9%
Asian (3,212): 3.7%
Other (7,487): 8.6%
2009 total (projected): 90,998
White (65,617): 72.1%
Black (12,224): 13.4%
Asian (3,833): 4.2%
Other (9,324): 10.3%

Sandy Springs is roughly 75 percent White today, debt-free, and poised to lead the incorporating areas of North Fulton County (and those cities incorporating in DeKalb County) to the promised land of secession: the creation of Milton County.

In closing, it should be noted that in the hotly contested 2009 mayoral race for Atlanta, the battle went to a runoff between Kasim Reed, the Black candidate, and Mary Norwood.

Norwood was the respectable White candidate, who thanks to changing demographics in Atlanta, forced a runoff with Reed (though she got the majority of the votes in the initial voting). The vote went strictly down racial lines, as 11Alive (an NBC affiliate in Atlanta) noted.

If austerity ever comes to America, the reality of race is going to come smashing directly in the face of the egalitarian course the nation has been headed for the past 70 years.

Nowhere is this more evident than Atlanta, where the divide between North Fulton and South Fulton is purely a racial one.

And with the move to secession (the creation of a new county), the amount of money flowing from North Fulton County, now a torrent, to keep afloat the primarily Black residents of South Fulton becomes less than a trickle.

17

The Great Tree Lighting: What Christmas in Atlanta says about the Black and White Community

December 17th, 2012

What if the origins of the "War on Christmas" date back far, far longer than we previously care to admit? What if in the roots of one of the South's great traditions resides the formula for the "War on Christmas" that is so subtle that few even gave it a passing thought?

I'm referring to the tradition of the lighting of the Rich's Great Tree in Atlanta, now known as the lighting of the Macy's Great Tree since Rich's has long ceased being a functioning department store.

Started in 1948, the grand tradition of lighting the Rich's "Great Tree" was a brilliant marketing ploy by the Rich family, who owned what was then one of the biggest department stores in the nation.

Known as a "Southern Tradition Since 1867" (wait . . . where was Rich's before, oh never mind), Rich's fortunes ebbed and flowed with the demographics in Atlanta. It's flagship store, located in the heart of downtown, would close in 1991. No longer was it necessary for the suburban residents of the city to travel into Atlanta to go shopping, when safe malls with the same merchandise was available closer to them.

But it was the lighting of Rich's "Great Tree" on Thanksgiving night that would attract hundreds of thousands of suburban Atlanta residents and people from all across the southeast to the city, to watch, what Celestine Sibley would write in her 1967 book *Dear Store: An Affectionate Portrait of Rich's*, the powerful lighting of the "Great Tree":

> From the big tree a radiance reflects on the faces of children standing below in the darkness and sometimes it makes prisms of tears on the faces of grownups.[129]

That her 1967 book was published in the centennial year of Rich's existence should prove that it served as nothing more than hagiography for the company history is one thing; that the book shows the Rich's "Great Tree" was, from its inception as a "tradition" in 1948, never referred to as officially as a "Christmas Tree" is another.

Why wouldn't Rich's dub the event the lighting of the "Great Christmas Tree"? The popularity of this event was (and still is) immense; *Time* magazine put an image of the lighting of the tree on the cover of its December 15, 1961 issue (with the corresponding story "Customs: But Once a Year" being little more than a rundown of the commercialization of Christmas and how department stores across the nation had successfully monetized the holiday).

And there can be no denying that during the first initial decades of the Rich's "Great Tree" lighting in Atlanta, there was a distinct Christian sentiment. In Jeff Clemmons's recently published *Rich's: A Southern Institution*, he notes that Rich's would the tree in "spectacular" fashion, with the over 70-foot tree sitting atop the famed Crystal Bridge connected to Rich's, with all the nearby businesses dimming their lights and the city of Atlanta shutting off streetlights and closing nearby streets to ensure a huge crowd:

> In the early years, the lighting ceremony would be kicked off with the master of ceremonies, Welcome South Brother (WSB) Radio and TV announcer Bob Van Camp, reading the

---

[129] Sibley, *Dear Store*, 143

story of the birth of Jesus as told through scriptures. After his reading, the children's choirs, located on bottom level of the bridge to stories up, would be illuminated, and they would sing a hymn or popular Christmas song selection. After the children's choir had finished singing, each successive level of the bridge would be illuminated, and the choir on that level would perform until all four levels were ablaze and all the choirs had performed. Then, a switch would be flipped and The Great Tree would be lighted to the cheers of the crowd below. In later years, the tree would be lighted during the last few high notes of "O Holy Night," sung either by a lone soloist or with the accompaniment of one or more of the choirs. Under the glow of the tree standing atop the four illuminated levels of the bridge, the choirs along with the gathered onlookers would sing "Silent Night," ushering in what for many was the true start of the Christmas season in Atlanta.

That version of the tree lighting flourished when Atlanta was still a majority White city, controlled by a White city council, White police force, and a White mayor. Incidentally, Black police couldn't even arrest White people.

But there's something unsettling in all of this: why not just call it Rich's "Great Christmas Tree"; even now, under the Macy's brand, why not call it "Macy's Great Christmas Tree"?

It seems trivial, but then again, the reading of the story of the birth of Jesus is no longer part of the increasingly secular lighting of the Macy's Great Tree.

But just as community-building events like Trick-or-Treating or even Christmas Caroling are dependent on a high amount of social capital within the community to not only prosper, but exist, the lighting of the Rich's Great Tree required the assurance of safe streets for families to brave the Thanksgiving cold of Atlanta to watch the ceremony.

Sibley, writing in *Dear Store*, celebrated a long bygone era in Atlanta's history when White people felt safe going into what is now one of the nation's most crime-ridden cities:

> Down in the street, the crowd has been assembling for hours. Forsyth Street is roped off to vehicular traffic, and people pour into it from all directions, city people and their country cousins, rich people and poor people, the young, the old, crippled people in wheelchairs, blind people clutching their white-painted canes, clinging to the arms of seeing relatives. There are babies in their mothers' arms and toddlers riding fathers' shoulders. They jam the street, making it a vast lane of crowded bodies and uplighted faces.[130]

1967 Atlanta, when Sibley wrote this book, was experiencing high levels of White flight, largely from areas of the city that were increasingly areas with declining property value, increasing percentages of Black residents, and increasing crime.

As Tamar Jacoby notes in 1990s book *Someone Else's House: America's Unfinished Business Struggle for Integration*, the outcome of the 1970s in Atlanta—when Black people became the dominant population group in the city and took political control—was not integration, but an "uneasy coexistence":

> Even so, many whites used crime as an excuse to avoid downtown, and blacks and whites divided up the landscape like a battleground. Sometime in the '70s, localized shopping nodes eclipsed the old central hub, and by the end of the [Maynard] Jackson era, Atlanta had two downtowns: the deteriorating black downtown in the center city and the new white downtown, Buckhead, six miles to the north. With the city's upscale restaurants, its choicest hotels and newest office towers, Buckhead paid taxes to Atlanta and in an important way helped keep it alive, but its residents had less and less to do with the black on the south side of town.[131]

---

[130] Sibley, *Dear Store*, 142.
[131] Jacoby, *Someone Else's House*, 371.

With this in mind, the Rich's "Great Tree" would appear on the famed Crystal Bridge for the final time in 1990, with the down-town Rich's closed in 1991—largely due to White consumers no longer traveling to what was correctly deemed an unsafe part of town.

A new home for what seemed an antiquated event was needed in 1991, and Clemmons tells us in *Rich's: A Southern Institution* that the initial thought was to move the lighting to Buckhead. This, of course, would attract more White residents of metro Atlanta because it was located in one of the toniest parts of the Southeast:

> Initially, Rich's thought about moving the tree to its Lenox Square mall store, but many people protested the idea of the ceremony leaving downtown. As a result, the store worked out a deal with the owners of Underground Atlanta, a unique shopping district built around an on top of old street viaducts, and invested approximately $400,00 into the new 1991 event. Part of the $400,000 was for the purchase of the tree and new, clear lights for decorations, which would re-place the multicolored lights of years past. Other portions of the money were used to build a special platform on top of a parking deck at Underground Atlanta to support and an-chor the tree. . . .
>
> The Great Tree remained at Underground Atlanta through 1999. Unfortunately, over the nine years the event was held there, attendance had steadily decreased. By that last year, only about ten thousand people showed up for the tree-lighting ceremony, forty thousand fewer than the num-ber who had attended it eight years earlier when it had ini-tially moved there.
>
> For the start of the new millennium, Rich's finally de-cided to move the tree to its suburban Atlanta Lenox Square location in the fashionable neighborhood of Buckhead with the hopes of increasing attendance. The plan worked, as that year an estimated 75,000 to 110,000 people attended the tree-lighting ceremony at its new location, a place many

Atlantas felt was safer and more easily accessible than Underground Atlanta.

Rich's is no more, having merged with Macy's to stave off bankruptcy. But a tradition started in 1948 continues, though the trappings of being a "Christmas" celebration fall by the wayside each year. No longer held in the "Black" part of Atlanta that Whites long since abandoned, the Macy's Great Tree lighting is held in a highly secure area of Buckhead, where on Thanksgiving night 2012, a 60-foot White Georgia pine was beautifully illuminated just as *The Voice* contestant Chris Mann sang the tradition finale "O Holy Night."

Gone is the signing of "Silent Night"; gone is the reading of the story of the birth of Jesus; gone are the various choral groups signing traditional Christmas hymns, replaced with generic secular "holiday" songs; but still remains "The Great Tree," as it was named in 1948.

And the lighting of the Macy's Great Tree can only survive in an area of Atlanta where some semblance of social capital and social trust remains intact.

Fitting, though: the celebration of the lighting of the "Great Tree" couldn't survive in the Black part of Atlanta (Underground Atlanta, a failed revitalization of downtown Atlanta that cost the taxpayers $142 million—in 1989 money—to try and lure White people to new shops, restaurants, and clubs), it is now thriving in Buckhead.

What type of communities can White people create? What type of communities can Black people create? The former: one where commerce, caroling, and a safe tree lighting flourish; the latter, where dysfunction, crime, and low property valuations drive away commerce, caroling, and a safe tree lighting.

18

Atlanta Is the City Where Black-Run America Collapses

April 22nd, 2011

Whitopias around Atlanta formed because capable White people fled the Black Mecca, only to return in their metal coffins for employment at Georgia Power, Coca-Cola, SunTrust, Georgia Pacific, and other Fortune 500 companies based in a downtown area long abandoned for residential use to underclass Black people.

The Black crime in Atlanta made raising a family there an untenable proposition, and the cheap gas and cheaper land made fleeing to new White suburbs a winning idea. In "The Atlanta Youth Murders and the Politics of Race," Dr. Bernard Headley writes:

> Of all the things having the most disastrous impact on Atlanta's black poor and working class in the late 1970s, none was more serious and indeed more deadly—than ordinary street and domestic crime. In 1979 official crime statistics made Atlanta the nation's murder and crime capital. . . .
>
> Atlanta's homicide rates of 34/1 and 53.3 per 100,000 population in 1978 and 1979, respectively, were the highest for the forty largest U.S. cities, including many with far worse crime images.
>
> This upward swing in crime greatly concerned the city's white ownership class. The "horrifying" statistics would, in their view, scare away businesspeople, especially white con-

ventioneers. A more jaded fear was being expressed by middle and upper income white suburbanites. Media surveys reported them saying they believed that the rapes, robberies, and murders of inner-city Atlanta might soon be spilling over into surrounding white neighborhoods. Such a problem, they believed, would be of little concern to a black city administration that was already "insensitive" to the high level of personal crimes being perpetrated against the city's white minority—such as downtown merchants being held up in broad daylight.

Such fears were, of course, groundless. A crime-containment strategy of ghettoization (intended or not) was fully operational in Atlanta. Crime, especially violent crime, was being kept within the confines of the city's depressed areas. [132]

Flash forward to 2011. The suburbs of Atlanta are darkening. DeKalb County has been successfully sued for trying to create a "darker administration"; Clayton County has completely fallen apart under Black rule—remember that White police officers were fired and Black snipers were placed on the roof of the precinct by the new Black sheriff—after Whites fled from that once prosperous county; Gwinnett County, once the fastest-growing in America, has turned from all-White into a majority-minority county that is quickly disintegrating into public trust as Robert Putnam's studies showed it would.

Many of the college-educated White males who decided to raise families in the suburbs can no longer find employment. [133]

The suburbs of Atlanta are where Blacks from around the nation are seeking solace and community, having found northern cities unreceptive to their lifestyle.

It is important that everyone reading understand that Atlanta, "the city too busy to hate," perfectly encapsulates and represents the problems plaguing all of America. Horrible rates

---

[132] Headley, *Atlanta Youth Murders*, 28–9.
[133] Marin, "Can Manhood Survive the Recession?"

of Black crime go unreported in the news and Black-run school systems collapse amid one scandal after another.

But no scandal is as horrifying as the one brewing with MARTA. Atlanta's poorly run metro system, MARTA caters primarily to a Black clientele (76 percent of riders are Black) and serves as a jobs program for Black people who wouldn't have employment without such empowerment.

MARTA is broke, a poorly-run jobs program for Black people in the city (rumors persist that 97 percent of city employees in Atlanta are Black; being that Atlanta is almost 50 percent White, how can this disparity exist?) and is assiduously avoided by the White citizens of the city save when a sporting event requires cheap transportation.

The prospect of $6 or $7 gasoline makes MARTA a much more attractive form of transportation, though the presence of menacing, loitering Black people who shamelessly approach every patron and ask for spare change makes such a journey unpalatable.

Atlanta's newspaper, *The Atlanta Journal-Constitution*, has been publishing joyous pronunciations of the metro areas population changes. Whites are losing in the population battle; Blacks and their "supposed" non-White allies are winning, while Disingenuous White Liberals (DWLs) cheer on the righteous coalition of People of Color (PoC) against the hated conservative Whites.

No story captures that hate like this one, published today, that details plans for MARTA to expand into formerly all-White counties that voted down such proposals because, as we all know, MARTA stands for Moving Africans Rapidly Through Atlanta. The idea of MARTA was to contain the movement of Black people to within the city, thereby keeping intolerable crime rates where Black people live and White counties free of such unpleasant reminders of why they were created in the first place.

With former White suburbs now majority Black and facing crumbling infrastructure, MARTA is now needed:

Metro Atlanta is car country, but as cities and counties put together their transportation wish lists, there are signs that some in the suburbs, which rejected mass transit decades ago, are ready to embrace it.

Next year, voters will be asked to approve a 1-cent special sales tax to pay for a list of projects that could smooth their commute. It remains to be seen which road and rail projects state and regional officials will put before voters.

But if officials assembling the final list pick mass transit, will metro Atlanta voters say yes to the tax?

Recent polls and interviews with residents and business people show a mixed picture, but the metro area's decades-long opposition might be softening.

Sharon Fischer, general manager at the IceForum rink at Town Center, said personally she supports the idea of a light rail line, which is one proposal for the Cobb County corridor where she works. She thinks other Cobb residents may, too, although the county voted down MARTA in 1965.

The list includes at least $13.5 billion worth of mass transit—even though the final total for all of the projects probably can't exceed $8 billion.

On the wish list so far:

Commuters might travel 50 miles or more by rail, from Gwinnett

Arena in Duluth to Hampton near Atlanta Motor Speedway, passing through five counties at rush hour.

Or they could get from Acworth to a Turner Field MARTA station without ever touching a brake.

Or tool through neighborhoods on a streetcar or local circulator bus.

But some ask: Is the cost worth it?

"I don't know that it would be a priority if I had $1 billion right now," said Elizabeth Wright, who runs a business referral network in Lawrenceville.

She noted the "positives and negatives" of ways a rail line could change the county.

"You'd have to wait and see where the stations were go‑ing to be and what the proposals were," she said. "It totally depends on how it's sold or promoted."

Advocates originally hoped to build MARTA in Cobb, Gwinnett and Clayton counties, as well as Fulton and DeK‑alb. But at the time, only Fulton and DeKalb approved the tax, which is why MARTA doesn't serve Cobb, Gwinnett or Clayton.

Since then, growth has exploded in those counties—in‑cluding migrants from big cities who want mass transit.

Clayton County voters, who rejected a MARTA tax in 1971, asked to join MARTA and pay the MARTA tax in a nonbinding vote taken in November.

And just last month, MARTA found that 43 percent of the cars parked in its lots come from somewhere other than Fulton and DeKalb.

Who will support what?

Malaika Rivers, executive director of the Cumberland Community

Improvement District, said businesses in Cobb need roads and rail, and it's important in attracting developers.

That's why the CID, a self‑taxing business district, has paid to get preliminary studies for the rail line going.

It is still clear that a strong roads package will be key to winning support in those counties, and especially in more distant ones such as Cherokee County and Fayette County.

For some, it may not be possible.

Harold Bost, co‑founder of the Fayette County Issues Tea Party, is taking the lead coordinating tea party groups to oppose the referendum.

He says the burden of another tax is only one reason he opposes it; he also opposes mass transit because of the peo‑ple it would bring into the suburbs.

"Criminals catch that kind of transportation into our county," Bost said, "and I'm not going to support anything that works toward increasing our crime either."[134]

---

[134] Hart, "Mass Transit."

Public transportation should work. It does in Europe, just as it does in Portland. In Atlanta, public transportation is a night-mare because of the combustible elements of White flight mixed with Black indifference to committing criminal offenses and creating an unsafe environment on all forms of MARTA transportation.

Though completely broke, MARTA might try and expand into areas where White people once protested its expansion, but now are all-Black counties that have been fiscally misman-aged and ruined under Black governmental rule.

We are nearing the end of the experiment of Black-Run America (BRA). As Hunter Wallace of *Occidental Dissent* has shown, the commitment to placating a population representing 13 percent of the United States requires a misappropriation of tax dollars and federal funding through programs paid primar-ily through White and, yes, Asian tax dollars.

Jason Richwine of Heritage has produced a study showing that Black students receive far more in funding then their White counterparts.[135] The NAACP peddles an idea that edu-cation should get more funding than prisons, but spending per pupil is higher among Blacks than it is for Whites. What kind of return on investment do we get for this disproportionate spending?

An overburdened penal system.

If scientific inquiry into studying differences in federal ex-penditures directed toward different racial groups for subsi-dized housing, welfare, EBT cards, food stamps, free lunches at school and over-employment of Black people in the public sec-tor could be quantified—and were not taboo—the truth of what we call Black-Run America (BRA) would be startling.

As it is, we find it axiomatic.

Atlanta is a microcosm for all that is wrong with America. The creation of an artificial Black upper-class (ruling class) through taking over the day-to-day administration of Atlanta,

---

[135] Richwine, "Myth of Racial Disparities."

thereby Fulton County, allowed for a virtual monopoly of public jobs to go to employing (unemployable in the private sector) Black people.

No-bid contracts for minority-owned firms at Hartsfield Airport, the complete removal of all non-White judges from the Fulton County and Atlanta city court system (knowing a number of lawyers in Atlanta, SBPDL can confirm that courtrooms are staffed by virtually all-Black supporting employees), a school system on the verge of collapse under Black rule, and a city on the brink suffering from high rates of Black criminality point to Atlanta being the site of the major crackup of Black-Run America.

Indeed, we already saw that in 2010 when 30,000 Black people showed up to sign up for Section 8 Housing vouchers that won't be available until 2017.

We at SBPDL take no pride in reporting this news. Enjoying sports and popular culture, we wish we could return to the old # posts that helped our website grow and eventually led to Google blocking most of our entries on search results through manipulating search engine code.

However, Stuff Black People Don't Like is reaching unprecedented levels of traffic (3,000–4,000 visitors a day), so we must be doing something right.

It's coming though, the dissolution of BRA. Not through any actions of insurgents, no, but because of the complete ineptitude of those who receive the bulk of the goodies in this system of entitlement.

DWLs attempt to throw a disproportionate share of federal dollars at a seemingly insoluble problem. Why can't the Black underclass change? In the process, they augmented the Black underclass to the point where 75 percent of Black births are out of wedlock (and Daniel Moynihan was attacked for his piece on "The Negro Family" when that number was much lower) and have created an educational system that blames all Black failures on persistent White racism.

Most DWLs and *Stuff White People Like* White people walk around with the belief that their support of Obama and minority causes puts them above untouchable Whites who remain uncouth in their attitudes toward race.

Let this be known: Black criminality has no prejudice. You could have supported Obama, and dedicated your life to the cause of equality, but wanton criminality from flash mobs and Black gangs care little for your political predilections.

Crusading White pedagogues peddling lies of "White privilege" have enraged a generation of Black people who never made it to the NBA or the NFL.

Atlanta, "the city too busy to hate," is where BRA collapses.

19

Point of No Return

July 17th, 2012

Metro Atlanta is dying, the cancer known as the Black Un-dertow spreading from the containment zone of downtown At-lanta and ensuring that Clayton, DeKalb, Gwinnett, Rockdale, Newton, Cobb, and even Fayette County get an unhealthy dose of the very thing that once drove White people to flee for the suburbs to begin with.

Mike King wrote in the *Atlanta Journal* that one of Amer-ica's most affluent regions must become must another mediocre area of economic stagnation, inadequate school systems, and high-crime zones:

> The popular perception of metro Atlanta as an urban core of blacks surrounded by white suburban counties grew in-creasingly out of date during the 1990s, and has collapsed completely in the first half of the current decade.
>
> From 2000 to 2004, blacks, Hispanics and other racial minorities accounted for more than 80 percent of population growth in the 28-county metropolitan Atlanta area, accord-ing to a report issued this week by the Brookings Institu-tion. Fifteen years ago, whites represented 71 percent of the region's population; today, they make up 57 percent of the 4.7 million people in metro Atlanta.
>
> Think of the growth trend this way: Every year, the metro area adds about 100,000 people, the vast majority

moving into the suburban and exurban counties surrounding the city. Four of every five of the newcomers are minorities.

In the first four years of the decade, more than 183,000
blacks have moved into metro Atlanta, by far the largest in-
migration of blacks in the country. In 1990, metro Atlanta
had the seventh largest black population in the country. By
2004, its black population ranked only behind metro New
York and Chicago. At its rate of growth, there will be more
blacks in metro Atlanta than in metro Chicago by the end of
the decade, the Brookings report predicts.[136]

As Whites become the minority in places like Clayton County,
the fortunes of the latter grow dark as the minority population
rises. Now, all of metro Atlanta is headed in that ignominious
direction, while White people—long weary of traveling long, ar-
duous commutes to get to and from work—move into the downtown area.

But what awaits White people in downtown Atlanta is the
exact same thing that now is popping up in formerly crime-free
metro Atlanta White enclaves, a reminder that you can only
escape the Black Undertow for so long. . . .

Fayette County is being submerged by the Black Undertow,
and the culture being imported to the metro Atlanta county is
exactly that which White people fled from in the first place.
Reports *The Citizen*, a White family was the victim of a home
invasion by two Black males:

> Peachtree City Police are searching for two men involved in
> a home invasion Friday night on Woodland Drive near Rob-
> inson Road in Peachtree City. One of the residents suffered
> an injury from a shotgun blast as she fled the house in an
> attempt to escape and summon help.
>
> Peachtree City Police spokesperson Rosanna Dove said
> officers responded at approximately 10:24 p.m. Friday night

---

[136] AJC, "Racial shifts speak volumes."

to a possible home invasion with shots fired inside the Woodland Drive residence.

Dove said three residents were home at the time of the incident.

Dove said preliminary information pertaining to the home invasion indicates that two black males entered the residence through an unlocked door and once inside they ordered the female victim to relinquish money.

Statements indicate that the offenders carried shotguns and believed there was a sum of money inside the residence the victim had access to. The two offenders are described as African-American males, in their mid-twenties with dark complexions, both about 5'8" to 6' tall and medium to slender in build, Dove said.

Dove also noted that two male residents were at home during the incident.

"One resident was in an adjacent bedroom and came into the living room after hearing the commotion. As he did, he was confronted by one of the offenders who pointed a shotgun at him directing him to the living room floor," Dove said. "While this was taking place, the female victim fled from the residence but was pursued by one of the offenders. The offender fired a round from a shotgun at the victim. The victim was grazed on her head by a pellet as she continued to flee from the area."[137]

This is huge, huge news. Peachtree City is one of the top cities in America (especially for relocating and starting a family because of the excellent school system, a byproduct of being more than 90 percent White) and to have the type of Black criminal activity invade the city that once was the stuff of nightmares only shown on the 6 o'clock nightly news broadcasts . . . well, it's a reminder of the joy of diversity.

How do you think *The Atlanta Journal-Constitution* covered this Black home invasion of a White family? By completely ignoring the racial aspect of the story:

---

[137] Nelms, "Female Resident Shot."

A Peachtree City grandmother was beaten and grazed with a shotgun pellet during a home invasion Friday night, but she fought back and escaped the attack, according to a Channel 2 Action News report.

"I was not going to be executed in my own home," Cece Coffee told Channel 2. Coffee descried the harrowing experience she said she had with two suspects armed with a shotgun.

Coffee said the men were in their '20s and wearing all black, with black bandannas covering their faces. She said they left in a dark-colored pickup truck.[138]

So . . . what did those two men look like, *Atlanta Journal-Constitution*? Who should the fine residents of Peachtree City be on the lookout for?

The answer is the exact racial group of assailants that targeted an area near downtown Atlanta that is seeing a renaissance of economic activity (entirely due to White gentrification and a brush back of Black urban blight). You see, Black gunmen targeted a group of White people on the porch of their Cabbagetown home during a July 4th party. Of course, *The Atlanta Journal-Constitution* omitted this part from their coverage of the attack:

Gunmen robbed five people from their front porch in Cabbagetown Tuesday night and then kidnapped a man, Atlanta police said.

The robbery is the most recent in a series of crimes that have shocked and scared Cabbagetown residents, said Sam Gris, public safety chairman for the Cabbagetown Neighborhood Improvement Association.

"It just seems like people are getting more and more brazen," Gris said. "It's a frustrating time to be in town."

The robbery occurred at a house on Estoria Street around 11 p.m., said police spokesman Carlos Campos.

---

[138] AJC, "Grandmother Grazed with Shotgun."

Gris sent *The Atlanta Journal-Constitution* an excerpt of the preliminary police report detailing the robbery.

According to the officer's report, five people were sitting on the porch when they saw three men walk by. About ten minutes later, the men returned with handguns and ordered everyone inside the house.

Once inside, the assailants forced the victims to lie on the ground and took their phones, according to the report. The assailants remained in the home for about thirty minutes, going through rooms and collecting computers.

Then, one assailant suggested that a male victim might have money because he was dressed nicely. So, they forced him into a car waiting outside the home and made him to withdraw money from several nearby ATM's. The cash amount stolen was not disclosed.

According to the report, the assailants told the victim they would keep him until after midnight in order to withdraw more money. When the victim was unable to withdraw more money, one assailant suggested they kill him.

However, a female in the car advised them not to, and the victim was thrown out of the vehicle near Memorial and Columbia drives. A passerby noticed the victim looked disoriented and gave him a ride back to the scene of the robbery.

Gris said he received the excerpt from Valencia Hudson, public safety liaison for City Councilwoman Natalyn Archibong.

Campos said Homicide Unit investigators, who are handling the case even though no one was killed, were not available for comment. He said they were working to identify the suspects.

Gris, a former police officer, said the incident could have ended much worse. "A 30-minute home invasion and kidnapping—that's got all the making of someone being hurt and killed," he said.

In the past, Gris said, the worst crimes residents had to deal with were graffiti or car break-ins, but recently crimes have become more severe.

Campos said, "Crimes have started occurring in areas where we historically have not had problems."

The police spokesman said total arrests in Zone 6, which includes Cabbagetown, have increased by 44 percent this year. He said police have arrested individuals in 12 burglaries and seven robberies this month. He urged residents to report any suspicious activity to police.[139]

Southeast Atlanta was once one of the most violent places in all of America; now, many of those residents have matriculated into Clayton and Fayette County, pushed out by White gentrification and rising home values. They now seek areas with lower property value, which can readily be found in nearly all-Black Riverdale. But the problems that urban pioneers face when venturing into territory that has long been home to violent Black people, is that the violence will only go away when all Black people are removed. If not, then urban pioneers will become unwitting participants in this violence.

So what happened in the July 4th assault in Cabbagetown?

After seeing surveillance footage on Channel 2 Action News, parents drove their 15-year-old son to a police station to be arrested Thursday for his alleged involvement in the kidnapping of a man from a Cabbagetown porch, the TV station reported.

Investigators had released a crystal-clear snapshot of one of three suspects involved in the July 3 incident.

The victim was hanging out with four other friends on Estoria Street around 11 p.m. when three young men, brandishing guns, forced everyone inside the residence. After collecting their cell phones and ransacking the home for other valuables, the burglars— noting that one of the victims was well-dressed —drove him to several nearby cash machines, according to the Atlanta police incident report.

---

[139] Hong, "Gunmen Rob, Kidnap Man."

Surveillance footage captured at a Bank of America ATM showed one of the youthful suspects hovering over the captive as he withdrew money.

Atlanta Police Detective Paul Guerruci told Channel 2 that the footage is "extremely valuable to our investigation because it actually depicts the individual who committed this horrible, violent act."

The unidentified victim told police that one of the kidnappers suggested they kill him after he was unable to withdraw any more cash. Another advised against it and the thieves opted instead to throw him out of the car near Memorial and Columbia drives.

The kidnapping was just the latest in a series of brazen crimes that have unnerved the Cabbagetown community.

"It's a frustrating time to be in town," Sam Gris, public safety chairman for the Cabbagetown Neighborhood Improvement Association, told *The Atlanta Journal-Constitution* the day after the kidnapping.[140]

Gentrification might be changing the face of Atlanta, just as Black migration to the metro Atlanta is changing the face of formerly White suburbs.[141] But one face isn't changing, and that's the near monolithic face of crime.

It's Black, as it's always been in Atlanta.

Back in 2007, *Yahoo! News* published an article asking if Atlanta's gentrification was causing a new crime wave. The answer is a resounding no; it's just Black people committing the crime that White people won't, but now, White people live closer to it instead of watching it from the safety of their suburban home.

So, something must be done to stop it:

Many of Atlanta's historic areas look a bit different than they did about 5–10 years ago. In keeping with numerous

---

140 Boone, "Parents Turn in Suspect."
141 Dewan, "Gentrification Changing Face."

other cities in the United States, some of Atlanta's poorest neighborhoods are being completely overhauled into upscale communities. These "new" areas boast trendy boutiques, popular franchises like Starbuck's and Target and other pricey amenities. But there has long been controversy over the effect that gentrification has on these urban communities. City officials and lawmakers claim that cleaning up certain areas of Atlanta will help to reduce the amount of crime. In many cases, this is certainly true. But the proliferation of upscale businesses and residents in many of Atlanta's popular sections is causing concern that a new wave of crime may become more prevalent. [142]

John Henderson, who once worked as a bartender at *The Standard* in Grant Park, was one of those White urban pioneers who was gunned down by Black people.[143] His death in 2009 galvanized the Stuff White People Like (SWPL) Whites in the gentrifying areas that once were breeding grounds for the Black Undertow, but his memory is no longer invoked today.[144]

Metro Atlanta is the Black Hole of America, a region where a *Mad Max* mentality exists among a growing percentage of the Black underclass; a siege mentality exists among a growing percentage of the dwindling White population.

Not just in Cabbagetown, but even in Peachtree City.

So White flight is no longer an option, and gentrification isn't a viable option, either.

Now . . . we just might be getting to the point of no return for Black-Run America (BRA).

---

[142] Yahoo Voices, "Is Atlanta's Gentrification Creating?"
[143] Paul, "Jonathan Redding Sentenced to Life."
[144] Boone, "Suspect in Standard Bar Killing."

20

Urban Pacification: The Legacy of the 1996 Olympics

August 25th, 2012

The public housing units in Atlanta (which were populated with almost 99 percent Black people) are almost entirely gone, razed and replaced with mixed-income developments. The former Black inhabitants of these units have been spread throughout metro Atlanta, a bid to export the crime and misery that the city of Atlanta for decades exclusively enjoyed to the once all-White suburbs (where crime and misery was only spoken of when referring to Black-run Atlanta).

This is the legacy of the 1996 Olympics in Atlanta—and nationwide, cities where crime and poverty (Black people) are concentrated in public housing are aping the strategy employed in the so-called "city too busy to hate" to spread the Black Undertow to the suburbs.

It all starts with one of the world's biggest companies, Coca-Cola, and the use of this international conglomerate to pressure the city to change (we call this "Connected Capitalism"). Back in 1964, Martin Luther King, Jr. was awarded the Nobel Peace Prize, and the city of Atlanta wanted to throw a party in his honor. But the White business elite balked at this idea. Enter Coca-Cola CEO J. Paul Austin, who along with Mayor Ivan Allen:

[S]ummoned key Atlanta business leaders to the Commerce Club's 18th floor dining room, where Austin told them flatly,

"It is embarrassing for Coca-Cola to be located in a city that refuses to honor its Nobel Prize winner. We are an international business. The Coca-Cola Company does not need Atlanta. You all need to decide whether Atlanta needs the Coca-Cola Company." Within two hours of the end of the meeting, every ticket to the dinner was sold. [145]

Blackmail. Such a beautiful thing, isn't it?

Not a decade later, once Maynard Jackson had been elected the first Black mayor of the city, the same man who blackmailed the White business community of Atlanta would propose something quite different. Longtime Coca-Cola President Robert Woodruff had donated hundreds of million to the city of Atlanta for the construction of parks, education, and the arts, and now the peddler of sugar water (and one of the leading causes of diabetes) wanted something in return:

> From Coca-Cola's headquarters on North Avenue, CEO Paul Austin could look out on Techwood Homes, the nation's first public housing project, long occupied by white tenants, and watch it turning black. Once the transformation was complete, he believed, the crime rate in the neighborhood would triple, endangering his employees. He wanted to relocate the residents to a new facility on the outskirts of town and to fill the 50-acre site with middle-income housing, parks, a shopping mall, and a theater.
>
> Austin approached the mayor with his proposal, and Jackson initially agreed to help him. Once word of the plan became public, however, Jackson instantly backed off, fearing the black community would never forgive him for participating in another episode of "Urban removal." [146]

Techwood did go 100 percent Black; crime got out of control in this area. Paul Austin fears were correct, though he was the

---

[145] Young, *Easy Burden*, 127.
[146] Allen, *Atlanta Rising*, 180.

same man who had blackmailed Atlanta's White business establishment that Coca-Cola would leave unless they played ball with Black-Run America (BRA).

The concept of "Urban renewal" is quite simply to remove the Black people who have been concentrated in a certain area (like Techwood, where Coca-Cola CEO Austin correctly observed that crime would increase three-fold) to someplace else. Just get them out of sight, and immediately bulldoze the dilapidated dwellings upon their removal, and you'll see an instant decrease in crime.

Besides those Black people who were connected to the Black aristocracy of Atlanta (Mayors Jackson, Andy Young, and Bill Campbell) that was created when they took over the city, your average Black (indeed, the majority of Blacks in Atlanta) is engulfed in the muck of his own nature: the city has some of the highest concentrated Black poverty in America.

Thus, the need of the 1996 Olympics. *Chief Executive* magazine published this in 1992 concerning the "Urban Blight" that Black people had created in the heart of the city:

> Without exception, business leaders hope to share in the financial bonanza that will accompany the Olympic Games. But the black residents of downtown and midtown Atlanta also want a piece of the action, especially those in the Summerhill and Techwood Homes neighborhoods. Their situation concerns Atlanta, if only because the city's neglected areas could be a source of international shame when the Olympic spotlight shines in 1996.
>
> The main Olympic stadium will be in Summerhill, and Olympic athletes will be housed in a new village on the Georgia Tech campus. The school adjoins both Coca-Cola headquarters and the Tech-wood Homes, the oldest, if not the happiest, U.S. housing project.
>
> Buckhead, Sandy Springs and Chamblee. "Thousands of people new to Atlanta have never been downtown," the article continued.

"To many of them, especially white suburbanites, downtown looks unfamiliar." [147]

The job growth in the northern part of the city (strangely, it's
the part of Atlanta that will begin the secession movement—
just in case the city doesn't go White—starting in 2013) is entirely due to the ingenuity of the White people who live there,
and their ability to create self-sustaining communities that
outside investors feel safe in investing capital in.

The "Urban Blight" that seems to pop up wherever Black
people are the demographic majority isn't conducive to outside
investments and sustaining a strong business community is
entirely the fault of Black people.

Whites are safe in their suburbs for the same reason Coca-
Cola CEO Austin worried about the changing demographics of
Techwood—because Black people are responsible for virtually
all the crime in Atlanta.

Cue the 1996 Olympics and the ability to use the games as
a way to remove the "cancer" of "Urban Blight" from the city
and disperse it to the suburbs of Atlanta (Clayton County is the
prime example of what happens when concentrated Black poverty is imported to a majority White suburb). *The New York
Times* bemoaned the move in the early 1990s,[148] but changed
its tune in 1996 when Ken Edelstein wrote these words (A New
Mixed-Use Development for Atlanta):

> Techwood Homes and Clark Howell Homes were once con-
> sidered models of a new wave in low-income housing. In
> 1936, President Franklin D. Roosevelt dedicated the first
> units of what would quickly sprawl out into 54 acres of red-
> brick, garden-style apartment buildings.
>
> In recent years, however, civic leaders have bemoaned
> the crime, drug dealing and vandalism that crept across the

[147] Lacey, "Atlanta Games."
[148] Applebome, "Atlanta's Olympic Park Plan."

projects. At one point the authority declared 500 of the units unsuitable for habitation.

Business leaders fretted that Techwood and Clark Howell were eyesores nestled between downtown office towers, the Georgia Institute of Technology and the fortress-like headquarters of the Coca-Cola Company. The spotlight shone more harshly on the two projects in the 90's when Olympic organizers built their athletes' village on Techwood's northern boundary and constructed a new Centennial Olympic Park two blocks to the south.

Now, most of the 1,100 units have been razed and nearly all residents have been moved out. Some former tenants have been shifted to private housing and enrolled in a voucher program to supplement their rent.

Business leaders are viewing the new development as an anchor in a still unsteady downtown revival that has followed on the heels of this summer's Games. Centennial Olympic Park, small apartment complexes, a new 1.6-million-square-foot Federal office building, plans for a basketball arena and efforts to establish a new entertainment district have raised hopes that downtown's sterile west side will become a showcase on the doorstep of the city's 2.5 million-square-foot convention facility, the Georgia World Congress Center.

"Any time you clear out a blighted area you're certainly going to improve the areas around it," said Gerald L. Bartels, president of the Metro Atlanta Chamber of Commerce. But the new housing complex also makes the whole area easier to redevelop, Mr. Bartels said, because it creates a better link between downtown and

Georgia Tech. AND since it is a mixed-income development, it may help demonstrate that the downtown area is an acceptable place for middle-income people to live, he said.[149]

---

[149] Edelstein, "New Mixed-Income Village."

"Urban Blight" will always follow Black people wherever they go, be it via Section 8 Vouchers or through a migration shifts such as the so-called "Great Migration" of Blacks out of the south which turned Detroit, Chicago, Gary, St. Louis, Cleveland, and Baltimore into larger-scale versions of Techwood.

Coca-Cola's CEO Austin pressured the White establishment to capitulate to BRA in 1964; then, when he couldn't push the rising concentration of the Black Undertow out of the city (and from the view of his employees in the Coca-Cola high-rise overlooking Techwood), the 1996 Olympics was used as a cover for "Urban Pacification." Courtesy of a Georgia State research paper, we learn this:

> The poor African-American neighborhoods being displaced existed within the core of downtown Atlanta, in close proximity to the Olympic Village where athletes would be housed and other Olympic sites. Additionally, Techwood Homes was near two esteemed Games planners, Coca-Cola and Georgia Tech. The process of the tenant displacement and demolition of public housing and neighborhoods such as Summerhill lacked in "southern hospitality."
>
> While the result ultimately removed large concentrations of poverty and crime from the view of visitors to Atlanta, the opportunism that provided the impetus to break up this core of poverty did not actually provide resolve to the residents. Within Techwood Homes and Clark-Howell Homes, the Atlanta Housing Authority demolished these complexes without a mechanism to assist those that were being displaced in finding housing. Furthermore, the poverty concentrations were merely transplanted to the southern suburbs, beyond areas of business or tourism.[150]

Now, you should understand why 70 percent Black Clayton County (it was 75 percent White in 1990) would re-elect Victor Hill as sheriff; the "Urban Pacification" of the 1996 Olympics

---

[150] Lacoss, "Olympic Class."

enriched the county with the citizens who were once concentrated in public housing in Atlanta.

The Black Undertow always, always overwhelms.

This is the legacy of the 1996 Olympics in Atlanta—and now, other cities throughout the dying empire known as the United States of America will jettison the concentrated areas of "Urban Blight" within their city limits to the suburbs, utilizing the model set forth in Atlanta.

The end of the Black Mecca is upon us, though the White citizens of North Fulton County have doubled down (the creation of incorporated cities like Sandy Springs, Brookhaven, Johns Creek, and Dunwoody) just in case it doesn't happen in 2013.

21

Democracy in America

August 22nd, 2012

Recall that in 2008, 96 percent of Black people voted for Obama in the presidential election. Obviously, four percent of Black people made a huge error in the voting booth and were incapable of reading the ballot correctly; this is the only reasoning one can conceivably conjure when confronted with the latest NBC/ *Wall Street Journal* poll:

> Obama continues to lead Romney among key parts of his political base, including African Americans (94 percent to 0 percent), Latinos (by a 2-to-1 margin), voters under 35-years-old (52 percent to 41 percent) and women (51 percent to 41 percent).
>
> Romney is ahead with whites (53 percent to 40 percent), rural voters (47 percent to 38 percent) and seniors (49 percent to 41 percent).[151]

Yes, presumable GOP candidate Mitt Romney is currently polling at zero percent with Black people.[152]

Gotta love that, considering it was Valerie Jarret (senior adviser to Obama) who told Black journalists of all the wonderful things that he has done to specifically help Black people:

[151] Murray, "NBC/WSJ Poll."
[152] Howerton, "NBC/WSJ Poll Shows."

[T]he Obama administration's successes, among them fund-ing for historically black colleges and universities; health care reform, which she said will disproportionately help Af-rican Americans; and reducing disparities between penal-ties for possession of crack and for powdered cocaine.[153]

It was in an interview with *Black Enterprise* that Obama bragged about how his policies have successfully impacted Black entrepreneurs and small business owners, so no one can blame Black people for looking upon the tag team tandem of Mitt Romney and Paul Ryan with absolutely zero excitement.

But it is in another election that was held in Clayton County (Georgia) that we got to see how wonderful democracy is as a system of government. For those who have seen *Gone With the Wind*, you might recall that Scarlett O'Hara's beloved Tara was located in Clayton County. Once an almost all-White county (home to some of the first Chick-fil-A restaurants) as short as 30 years ago, Clayton is now almost 70 percent Black.

And it was the fine citizens of Clayton County who took to the polls on Tuesday, August 21 and cast their ballots in favor of Victor Hill for sheriff—a position that he first won in 2005 (and, as the first Black sheriff of Clayton County, promptly fired all White officers and had them led out with snipers on the roof)—despite having 37 felony counts pending against him:

Former Clayton County Sheriff Victor Hill has reclaimed the office he lost four years ago despite 37 pending felony charges that accuse him of using his government office and his 2008 campaign to enrich himself.

With only one precinct uncounted, Hill was ahead. But the charges he's facing make it uncertain whether he will take office in January because the governor could suspend him until he goes to trial.

---

[153] Taylor, "Valerie Jarrett."

"Don't be sorry for me. Be sorry for Clayton County," Kimbrough said. "I'll be fine but there are a whole lot of people's lives that will be affected by this and maybe they have to see this for themselves. It's something I've heard a million times; only in Clayton County. It is what it is."

Hill, in an emailed statement, thanked God and the voters for letting him "serve once again."

"As promised, I want to advise those who prey on others by breaking into homes, robbing businesses and drug trafficking to stop or leave Clayton while you still can. Your presence is not wanted and your lawlessness will not be tolerated," Hill said.[154]

Democracy in action. The embarrassingly leftist (almost openly communist) Atlanta alternative newspaper *Creative Loafing* published a hilarious look at life in the demographically changed Clayton County back in 2006. We have also targeted Clayton County for abuse—the concept of the Black Undertow was invented when thinking about how the new Black majority in the county remade Clayton into their image, which mirrored that of majority Black Atlanta—but it is this article from *Creative Loafing* which slams home what democracy actually means:

Bad news in Clayton ranges from the bizarre to the sordid. Aside from [Clayton County Commissioner Eldrin] Bell's self-inflicted wound, word came this morning that another lawsuit had been filed against Victor Hill, the controversial sheriff. This one, a discrimination suit filed by a white employee, contains explosive allegations that Hill misused funds seized from drug busts and vending machines he operated in the department's headquarters and jail. The suit alleges that he used the money to purchase provocative artwork for his office that depicted "African American cowboys" and "a lynch mob scene portraying Caucasian people with shotguns."

---

[154] Cook, "Hill Wins Another Term."

It's just another day in the headlines for Clayton County. The schools are on the verge of losing accreditation. The district attorney is a barrister who had little experience with criminal cases when she was elected. The sheriff fired 27 deputies on his first day in office, under the watch of snipers he'd dispatched to rooftops. And there's the irony that Bell was at a party thrown by Galardi, who had successfully sued the sheriff for setting up roadblocks almost every weekend near the newly opened Pink Pony South.

But shortly before the 1996 Olympics, residents noticed the face of the county beginning to change. Between 1990 and 2006, it underwent a dramatic shift in demographics— from 75 percent white to 64 percent black.

"Back in the 1950s, Forest Park was one of the fastest-growing municipalities in the country," Hatfield says. "Clayton County was growing dramatically. But that was a largely self-selected population that wanted to get out of Atlanta and the problems of the big city. Over the recent years, the population growth has been from those seeking lower-cost housing, and they've had relatively larger numbers of children."

Much as Atlanta faced a transition from white leadership to black in the '70s, Clayton County's new demographics brought a changing of the guard that began in the 2004 elections. It just happened less gracefully than it did in Atlanta.

And Victor Hill, a former Bell protégé, was elected sheriff.

Hill set the immediate tone when he fired 27 deputies on his first day in office, including four of the highest-ranking officers, all of whom were white. He called the officers in on the pretext of swearing them in; instead, they were relieved of their badges and service weapons and taken out of the sheriff's office inside inmate vans with police snipers posted on nearby rooftops.

Clark Talmage Stevens, chief of staff for the commission and a former adviser to presidents Carter and Reagan, told the *New York Times* it was "an embarrassment" and "blatant mass political firing." He added: "This is all over the country, like we're a bunch of goofballs."

It was also expensive. The firings wound up costing taxpayers $7 million in settlements and court costs.

Then, in 2006, Lee Scott made a run for county commission against a White incumbent, Michael Edmondson. He distributed fliers with Edmondson's face superimposed over a Confederate flag. Scott lost, but the changing of the guard was nearly complete. With the exception of Edmondson, the white Democrats who'd controlled Clayton County government were all cast out. The political leadership finally mirrored the demographics.

It's hard for an outsider not to notice the role the Scotts have played in Clayton County's political circus. They're close allies with Hill, often contributing to each others' campaigns. And Bell has openly bickered with Lee and Jewel Scott. But he reserves his harshest criticism for Hill, who was once his driver.

"If Victor Hill was [white], we would have already run him out of town, hung him in effigy, and we would've cussed his grandma out even if she were already dead," Bell says. "We would have not tolerated it. I'm worried about the fact that we vote for race over the ability to lead."[155]

Yes, the new Black majority in control of Clayton County are goofballs; they're also grossly incompetent. And yet, all those in seats of power were elected (or have benefited) from the racial demographic changes that have remade Clayton County from a majority White county into just another Prince George's County.

No Scarlett, there won't always be a Tara. And frankly, the new Black majority doesn't give a damn.

They re-elected Victor Hill, a man who upon seizing democratic power as sheriff fired all White officers and had snipers on the roof when they were escorted out of the building.

---

155 Wheatley, "Cover Story: Clayton County's Tribulations."

Black people support Obama 94-0 in the newest poll re-leased by NBC/WSJ, meaning Mitt Romney has zero Black support.

Democracy in America.

22

Success Used to Live Here:
What the Fall of Gwinnett County
Means for White America

September 11th, 2012

There's an apocryphal story involving Andrew Young, former mayor of Atlanta and President Jimmy Carter's ambassa-
dor to the United Nations, and an address he gave to the historically Black college Clark Atlanta University in the 1980s.
While addressing the subject of the eroding tax base in the city
and the fear of a diminishing amount of resources (funds) to
allocate, Mr. Young addressed White flight with this ominous
warning: "No matter where they go, we will follow. No matter
how far away they move, we will follow. They can't escape us."
  Andrew Young is correct. No matter where White people
fled—from the crime, crumbling business sector, private property devaluations, and poor school systems that accompany a
majority Black area, creating thriving communities in the process—the Black Undertow followed. DeKalb and Clayton
County went from being thriving majority White counties to,
well, majority Black counties that resembled the Atlanta that
Whites had fled from in the first place.
  The declaration of war set forth by Mr. Young proved true:
no matter where Whites went, Black would follow; importing
the same problems that Whites had tried to flee from when an
area went majority Black and eventually overwhelmingly the

social capital created in the community to the point of breaking all communal bonds that Whites had amassed.

Back in 1985, Oliver Thomas of *The Atlanta Journal-Constitution* tried to put his finger on why Gwinnett was excelling at such at rapid pace:

> To say that one of Georgia's 159 counties, Gwinnett, was the fastest-growing county in America during the first half of the 1980s is true, though not quite comprehensible. To say that a decadelong explosion of everything from new people, new housing, new offices and more cars has left Gwinnett staggering under its own good fortune, is also true but vague.
>
> So consider the implications of these very real numbers:
>
> In 1975, there were 115,400 people nestled quietly in Gwinnett, just northeast of Atlanta.
>
> Four years later, people were pouring into the county at the rate of 1,000 per month. By 1984, that migration surge had doubled.
>
> Twenty-three-thousand, five hundred new folks landed in and around Snellville, Lilburn, Lawrenceville and Duluth in the 12- month period ended this past April 1, pushing Gwinnett's population near the quarter-million mark.
>
> The reasons for this incredible growth are not hard to comprehend.
>
> While the chamber of commerce may credit leadership, and others may claim white-flight, one overriding reason that Gwinnett quickly mushroomed from rural to urban is its proximity to Atlanta and Hartsfield International Airport.
>
> When the Sun Belt migration began, Gwinnett benefited.
>
> Five years ago, a trailer park sprawled over the northwest quadrant of the I-85 and Pleasant Hill Road interchange. Fronting the park, a general store and a gas station serviced the trailer park's residents and those who motored down the little-traveled two-lane road.
>
> Across the street was a lonely diner, a Waffle House.

It was a heralded chamber-of-commerce event when a freight hauling firm built a terminal on the road between the interstate and

Highway 23 to the west.

Pleasant Hill today is a junk food addict's heaven, with McDonald's, Wendy's, Burger King and Krystal competing with Shoney's, Mrs. Winners and Red Lobster. They all compete against the once monopolistic Waffle House.

Today the Gwinnett Place mall, with its 150 stores, sits where the mobile homes once were, and an acre of land that cost $20,000 three years ago today brings around $218,000.

This area, around Gwinnett Place, is now considered the nerve center of the county, and residential developers fight to build as close to this mecca as possible. Hotels, office complexes, and more retail centers than imagined just a few years ago have sprouted up near the mall.[156]

Actually, it was the White people who fled to Gwinnett County and created a thriving community out of pasture land that deserve all the credit for the growth of the county; conversely, it is the departure of White people and the rise of the non-White population in Gwinnett County that are to be credited with its decline.

Such is the state of Gwinnett County now, which was 91 percent White in 1990, but is now majority-minority:

In 1990, Gwinnett was 91 percent white. Now, it is a different place altogether. "Gwinnett as a whole," says Bannister, "is becoming a majority-minority group of people." In fact, it already is one. In the U.S. Census Bureau's most recent American Community Survey, released this fall, the white population was down to 49.9 percent. Marina Peed, an affordable housing developer who works county-wide, says that "there's no lily white anymore anywhere in the county. I doubt if there's a single all-white subdivision in the whole county."

---

[156] Thomas, "Basic Reason Gwinnett Has Prospered."

Today, Gwinnett has large populations of blacks, Hispanics and (perhaps most surprisingly) Asians. The county
has substantial populations from Indian and Vietnam, as
well as people of Asian (especially Korean) descent who are
from elsewhere in the United States.[157]

Not only will immigration turn Gwinnett blue—from a solidly
Republican county—it will turn all of Georgia blue in a state
where Blacks vote in a monolith for Democrats:

In January 2001, Georgia's electorate was 72 percent white
and 26 percent black, while Hispanics made up less than
two-tenths of 1 percent, according to data compiled by the
secretary of state. As of Aug. 1, those numbers had changed
dramatically.

Blacks now make up 30 percent of active registered voters while whites are at 60 percent. Hispanics make up
nearly 2 percent of the electorate after seeing their registra-
tion numbers increase from just 933 in 2011 to 85,000 as of
Aug. 1.[158]

Thus, Gwinnett County serves as the perfect microcosm for
America: Whites were able to build a thriving community that
became the envy of the region, replete with crime-free streets,
schools (almost with almost all-White pupils) boasting average
standardized test scores that made the system one of the tops
in the nation, rising property values, and an abundance of the
type of social capital that makes opening and being successful
in business almost a guarantee. And just as Mr. Young said,
"we" (Black people) would follow, early attempts to break the
Whitopia in Gwinnett County with the public transit system of
MARTA were met with racial resistance:

---

[157] Goodman, "Will Immigration Turn Gwinnett."
[158] Sheinin, "Shifting Population Could Help."

David Chesnut, chairman of the board of MARTA, said Thursday he fears a regional transportation system is a long way off and "the reason is 90 percent a racial issue."

While Gwinnett and Cobb counties experienced their initial growth from the white flight from Fulton and DeKalb counties, said Chesnut, "I am very disturbed when I hear young professionals tell me they are going to form NNIG—No Niggers in Gwinnett."

Regardless of what politicians tell him, he knows such people are being honest, Chesnut told the Buckhead Business Association.

Chesnut also told the association:

"I don't think I need to call any names of politicians who, when asked to comment on the Bernhard Goetz verdict, say, 'I think it's awful that that man would have a gun and would with reckless abandon shoot at those poor black folks.'"

"Well, I agree, but I also think that it is terrible that there would exist any condition which would warrant somebody to carry a gun on a mass transit system. We at MARTA are doing everything that is humanly possible to eliminate not only someone carrying a gun on the system, but the cause that would warrant someone to want to."

During the recent deliberations over the MARTA fare increase, which took effect Sunday, Chesnut said the transit system needed to attract more white riders. About 75 percent of the system's riders are black, according to a MARTA study.[159]

MARTA never came to Gwinnett County, but a wave of Hispanics immigrants did. You see, White people want cheap housing, which requires cheap labor to keep costs down, so they had no problem having Hispanics build their new homes in areas devoid of Black people.

But guess what? Black people, following the prophecy set by Andrew Young, followed too:

---

[159] Schmidt, "Racial Roadblock Seen."

The last 10 years saw a boom in the number of black, Hispanic and Asian residents in metro Atlanta, while the number of white residents fell in four of the area's five biggest counties, according to U.S. Census figures released Thursday.

The surge in minorities as a percentage of the population also occurred at the state level. Georgia added 1.5 million people, an 18 percent increase. The Hispanic population grew 96 percent, followed an 81 percent increase in Asian residents and a 26 percent increase in black Georgians. The white population grew less than 6 percent statewide.[160]

Because Atlanta has no natural boundaries (save unsafe neighborhoods that are 100 percent Black), the spread of suburbs can continue in a 360-degree radius. And wherever Whites go and set up communities (remember, in 1990 Gwinnett County was 91 percent White after being nearly 100 percent White in 1980), Blacks do follow.

And the demands for political power won't be far behind:

Gwinnett long ago made headlines as a majority-minority county, a reality that is readily observed on the streets of the county's southern and eastern communities. Diversity is reflected in the faces of the men and women passing by. Among the children on school buses. In the signage lining some populous corridors. But there's at least one area in Gwinnett County where that cultural and ethnic diversity is noticeably absent: the county's leadership. The Gwinnett County Board of Commissioners is all-white and home-grown, and most county department heads are white as well. The same can be said for the county's Board of Education, many city councils and the various chiefs of police. "It's been a white club out there," said Harvey Newman, a Georgia State University professor of public management.

In theory, as the districts of all elected officials are redrawn to reflect the population shifts revealed by the 2010

---

[160] Schneider, "Blacks, Hispanics Lead Metro."

census, minorities should gain greater opportunities to elect the candidates they favor. The Voting Rights Act protects minorities from being disenfranchised by having their populations split among several districts. Where concentrations of minorities exist, political districts should reflect those concentrations.

"It would be a travesty that if after redistricting, the entire County Commission and school board is Caucasian—it would tell me that something went wrong," said state Sen. Curt Thompson, D-Tucker, who grew up in Lilburn. The math is complicated, however, by the fact that minorities often do not vote in proportion to their share of the population. Gwinnett looks to be no different. In 2010, white people made up 44 percent of Gwinnett's population but 59 percent its active voters; black people were 23 percent of the population and 22 percent of active voters; Asians were 11 percent of residents and 5 percent active voters; Hispanics were 20 percent of residents and 4 percent of active voters.[161]

It won't be long until the new majority-minority is permanently a Democrat stronghold, with the once all-White Republican county just another reminder of a past where racial socialism didn't reign. And not one White Republican (oxymoron, right?) will dare speak out on this, a tragic reminder that Gwinnett County is but a microcosm for the nation at large.

And with the drop in the overall White percentage of the population, the inevitable drop in the standard of living (a regression to the mean) has occurred in Gwinnett County:

Two decades ago, Rebecca Carlson's subdivision in Lawrenceville bustled with hard-working, middle-class families. At Christmastime, neighbors lit up their homes with colorful displays. At night, people could walk their streets without fear.

---

[161] AJC, "Face of Gwinnett's Leadership."

Then subprime mortgages flooded the market, and Quinn Ridge Forest changed. Some new residents let their grass grow 3 feet high, Carlson said. Others let broken windows stay broken. Many longtime homeowners have sold their properties and bolted.

Now, Carlson said, the house next door is filled with renters who come and go. The police have been called to two nearby homes, one for prostitution, the other for illegal drugs.

"I won't let the kids go outside by themselves," said Carlson, 45.

The decay of the neighborhood tracks closely behind the collapse of the housing market. Gwinnett County has become the foreclosure capital of metro Atlanta—44 percent of its 10,301 home sales in 2009 were bank sales—and that foul wave washed over Quinn Ridge Forest, too. At the moment, three of the 12 houses on the market there are bank sales.

The county looks no better in 2010: with 26,502 foreclosure notices for the year, Gwinnett surpassed Fulton, DeKalb, Cobb and Clayton counties, according to Equity Depot, which tracks foreclosure and other real estate trends in metro Atlanta.[162]

And yet, no one ever dares ask the important question: what are the costs associated with Andrew Young's declaration coming true? Well, here's your answer:

The notion that Gwinnett County is home to a population that's predominately white and affluent is as out-of-date as the idea that two painted water towers along I-85 in Norcross still proclaim: "Success Lives Here."

The 40-year-old towers were torn down two years ago. In the decade before their demolition, 40,000 whites had

---

[162] Blatt, "Atlanta Property Taxes."

moved out of Gwinnett. Now, the county's population is predominately non-white, and less wealthy and less educated than it was in 2000.

The demographic shift in Gwinnett speaks to the broader question of "Who are We?" That was the topic Wednesday, at the quarterly meeting of the Atlanta Regional Housing Forum.

Out of the entire two-hour program, the most stunning report was provided by Lejla Slowinski, executive director of the Lawrenceville Housing Authority.

Slowinski provided a snapshot of Gwinnett's population that gave some real heft to the demographic report on the metro Atlanta region that was delivered by Michael Rich, an associate professor of political science at Emory University who heads Emory's Office of University-Community Partnerships.

Slowinski prefaced her remarks by saying she would talk later about ways in which Gwinnett's civic and government leaders are leveraging the county's diversity. But first, she said, she wanted to provide a bit of context about Gwinnett.

Speaking without any visual aids, such as a PowerPoint slide show, Slowinski riveted the audience's attention with a cascade of nuggets derived from the 2000 and 2010 Census reports. The data shows that Gwinnett isn't just changing—it is a changed community:

- Per capita income has fallen by $7,000;
- The proportion of whites in the overall population has fallen to 49.3 percent from 67 percent;
- No single Census tract has a white population of greater than 90 percent;
- 32 percent of households speak a language other than English;
- 61 percent of students in the county school system are non-whites;
- High school graduation rates for non-whites rose to 70 percent from 50 percent;
- 25 percent of Gwinnett commuters spend at least 45 minutes a day in the car.

Sources other than the Census provide additional insights:

- 18 percent of Gwinnett's children live in poverty;
- The county's poverty rate rose from 5.6 percent in 2000 to 13 percent in 2009;
- The number of foreclosures in Gwinnett has topped Fulton since 2009 (Fulton formerly had the region's highest number of foreclosures). One relevant point is that Gwinnett's government and school board are trying to serve the human needs of this population with an ever-decreasing amount of tax revenues.

At the Piece by Piece annual meeting last week, Gwinnett County Commission Chairman Charlotte Nash said the county's digest has dropped 25 percent during the past five years. That decrease has reduced the amount of property taxes collected by the county and school system, which is the main source of funding for both governments.

"The population has continued to diversify," Nash said. "According to the 2010 Census, Gwinnett was the most diverse county in the southeast. That very different from what it was 20 years. It's created language considerations, and the demand for additional types of flexibility in terms of how we deal with the community."

Slowinski said the Gwinnett County Chamber of Commerce works diligently to reach out to, and serve, the minority business community. The number of firms owned by Hispanics and African Americans is still a small proportion of the overall mix, but it's growing, she said.[163]

Success no longer lives in Gwinnett County—diversity does. Those water towers that came crashing down in a controlled demolition boasted about the climate of the county when it was brimming with White families; now, the social capital is all but gone. The great social experiment in diversity continues unabated.

And a county created by "White flight" from Black people, now sees "White flight" from what silence on racial matters

---

[163] Pendered, "Gwinnett County's Dramatic Demographic."

(yes, it is White people that are responsible for "good schools," and "safe, crime-free subdivisions") will wrought:

> Mary James, an empty-nester from Snellville, craves the in-town bustle. Michelle Forren is tired of planning life around rush hour in Duluth. And Louise Stewart is fed up with the Spanish-language business signs, backyard chickens and overcrowded homes in her Norcross-area neighborhood.
>
> Though their reasons vary, all three women plan to join an emerging demographic: whites leaving Gwinnett County.
>
> In what might surprise metro Atlantans who remember the nearly lily-white county of old, Gwinnett's non-Hispanic white population declined for the first time last year, according to the latest estimates from the U.S. Census Bureau. The drop of about 1,500 whites came even as Gwinnett, the state's perennial growth leader, added more than 27,000 residents.
>
> One year doesn't make a trend. And some observers question the census estimates. But the figures offer more evidence that the number of whites is at the very least leveling off in Gwinnett,
>
> adding a new dimension to a lightning-fast demographic shift that has transformed a once-uniform suburb into what one Washington think tank called a "mini-Ellis Island."
>
> The number of Hispanics in Gwinnett is now more than 12 times what it was in 1990, according to the latest census estimates. The Asian population has increased more than sixfold. And the black population has grown sevenfold. Until recently, the white population was growing, too, just not as fast. The county is now 57 percent white, down from 90 percent in 1990.
>
> Louise Radloff, a member of the Gwinnett County school board for more than 30 years, said the additions have enriched her district between Norcross and Lilburn. It's the subtractions that hurt.
>
> Many schools in the area are now less than 10 percent white.

"It's called white flight," Radloff said. "There is a perception that with the diversity, there is low-income and there is crime. We need to learn to cope with these issues and decide that all men are created equal."

Bart Lewis, chief of the research division at the Atlanta Regional Commission, said any "white flight" from Gwinnett is limited. It's a far cry, he said, from what happened a generation ago in parts of Atlanta and DeKalb County, where neighborhoods changed practically overnight as white families moved to outlying areas such as Gwinnett.

In fact, Lewis finds it hard to believe that the number of whites isn't still rising in Gwinnett. Accurate racial breakdowns are difficult to estimate, particularly at the county level, he said.

Lewis sees the shift in Gwinnett as driven more by economics than race, anyway. Lower-income families scouring metro Atlanta for an affordable house or apartment are landing in the aging neighborhoods of western Gwinnett. Most of them happen to be minorities, Lewis said.

"What I think you're really seeing is an evacuation of more-affluent households of one race replaced by less-affluent people of another race," he said.[164]

For those paying attention, Gwinnett County is the apt metaphor for modern America. And, wherever White people go, wherever they create thriving communities, the warning set forth by Andrew Young remains: "No matter where they go, we will follow. No matter how far away they move, we will follow. They can't escape us."

Success can't live again in America until people dare say the reason Gwinnett County was once the fastest growing county in the nation, and why it now is failing.

Four letters. One word. Race.

---

[164] Feagans, "'White Flight' in Gwinnett?"

23

On the Beach: The Fall of America's Best County as a Microcosm for America's Future

July 11th, 2012

Sure, Whites can flee to states (metro Atlanta suburbs) far away from the racial chaos that afflicts other states (think downtown Atlanta), but eventually the Black Undertow will come. Today, news broke that one of the top counties in all of America—Fayette County, Ga, home to one of former best small cities in America to grow up in, Peachtree City[165]—has seen its White population drop from 84 percent in 2000 to 67 percent today:

> It has often been said that the only constant is change. And that is true of Fayette County as reflected by estimated U.S. Census figures for 2011.
>
> Compared to 2000, the 2011 figures show Fayette with a population that is aging, with the number of households with children shrinking and one that is becoming much more diverse in terms of race and ethnicity.
>
> Fayette County in 2011 had an estimated population of 107,784 compared to a population of 91,263 in 2000, according to census.gov.
>
> The 2011 data showed 25 percent of Fayette residents under age 18, down from 29 percent in 2000.

---

[165] CNN Money, "Best Places to Live 2009."

Meantime, the 2011 data also showed 13.9 percent of residents are age 65 and over, up from 8.9 percent in 2000.

While on the surface those numbers might not seem significant, a look back at the 2000 census begins to show a different story. Here's how.

Fayette County in 2000 had a population with a median age of 38.2 years. In 2011 the median age had increased to 43.3 years, an average age increase of more than five years in just over a decade.

Back in 2000, Fayette County households that included children totaled 43.1 percent but by 2010 that figure had dropped to 36.3 percent. That's a telling decrease of numbers of children, including—most ominously for the Fayette County School System—school-age children. But there is more to the story.

Recession notwithstanding, there is a projection by the Atlanta Regional Commission from a couple of years ago that showed Fayette with the third fastest growing senior population in the 10- county metro Atlanta area. Combined with the aging population in general, the projection was that Fayette's senior population is expected to increase by 450 percent by 2040.

Those aged 65 and older already account for 13.9 percent of the county's population, so if the projection is anywhere near accurate it will mean a much larger senior population relative to other age groups in Fayette in the coming years.

That increase in Fayette's aging population will likely have an impact on property tax revenue for the Fayette County School System. The reason is that at age 65 the homeowner is eligible for a 50 percent exemption on school taxes. Also at age 65 the homeowner or couple is eligible for a 100 percent school tax exemption if the Georgia taxable income is $15,000 or less.

That might not seem like much income, except that Social Security and up to $35,000 of retirement income per person plus regular deductions are not counted in the taxable income equation. The slope for school tax revenues continues to be downhill.

Another adjustment in Fayette County demographics is in terms of race and ethnicity.

A breakdown of census figures in those categories showed a population that was nearly 84 percent white in 2000. Eleven years later, the percentage of whites relative to all other races in Fayette had fallen to 67.2 percent white, a decrease in relative numbers of nearly 17 percent.

During the same period all other race and ethnic populations categories showed increases. The black population in 2000 was 11.5 percent, though by 2011 the black population had increased to 20.8 percent, a relative increase of more than 9 percent.

Similarly, the Hispanic population of 2.8 percent in 2000 more than doubled in relative terms to 6.5 in 2011 percent while the Asian population increased from 2.4 percent in 2000 to 4.1 percent in 2011. [166]

The Black Undertow swept aside businesses, wealth, and prosperity in Clayton County (which borders Fayette), a county that went from 90 percent White in 1980 to less than 20 percent today; it is coming for Fayette County. There is no escape for White people.

Fayette County has one of the top school systems in all of America,[167] boasting students whose combined test scores far exceed those posted in the state [168] (even those fraudulent scores from the Atlanta Public Schools system) and the national average. Its school system is but a reflection of the abilities that the sons and daughters of the predominately White community there produce, just as the poor Clayton and DeKalb County school systems are a byproduct of abilities of the Black children whose parents reside there.

As the Fayette County attracts more Black residents, the school system will go the direction of Clayton County. The

---

[166] Nelms, "Census: Fayette Getting Grayer."
[167] Walker, "NAACP Places Race."
[168] US News, "Fayette County."

same can be said for the business community, with once thriving shopping complexes boarded up or the new home of Title
Pawn shops and hair accessory stores.

To illustrate this change, as more Black people call Fayetteville (a city that borders Clayton County), Fayette County High
School has switched from having an enrollment that was
nearly 80 percent White (class of 2000) to just 29 percent White
in 2011–2012. The school is now 47 percent Black, and rising.
[169]

Large corporations from around the world have settled in
Peachtree City, knowing that their employees will be able to
send their children to safe, productive schools that reflect the
community at large. All of this will change with the advance of
the Black Undertow from Atlanta (2010 Census: Minorities
gain in Fayette, Cal Beverly, March 23, 2011, The Citizen):

> The demographic change in Fayette is dramatic, compared
> to decennial censuses for the past 30 years, with big in-
> creases in the Hispanic and black population and an actual
> net decline in white residents.
>
> The white population of Fayette County has fallen by
> 2,789 persons over the past decade—a decline of 3.7 per-
> cent—while the black and Hispanic populations have dou-
> bled and tripled respectively, according to figures from the
> 2010 U.S. Census released Friday by the Atlanta Regional
> Commission.
>
> Fayette County has a 2010 counted population—not an
> estimate—of 106,567 persons. Neighboring Coweta has an
> official count of 127,317.
>
> According to just-released reports, Fayette saw a jump of
> 16.8 percent over the 2000 population count, while Coweta
> exploded by 42.7 percent.
>
> Fayette's black population doubled in 10 years to its cur-
> rent level of 21,117, nearly 20 percent of the total county

---

[169] Find Good School, "Fayette County High School."

population. That's an increase of 102.2 percent, according to the Census. The black population in 2000 was 10,446.

Fayette's Hispanic numbers also have increased dramatically—from 2,582 at the beginning of the decade to the current count of 6,760, an increase of 161.8 percent.

Coweta has experienced a growth in all segments: an increase of 34.3 percent in the white population, 36.2 percent in the black numbers, and 203.6 percent in Hispanics, the ARC says.

What is striking is that Fayette and Coweta now have nearly identical numbers of black residents—21,117 in Fayette and 21,744 in Coweta.

In raw numbers, Fayette has 6,760 Hispanics, while Coweta counted 8,493 Hispanics.

Fayette is not alone in its declining numbers of whites. Neighboring Clayton County saw a decline of 46,468 whites; Cobb lost 32,986; DeKalb dropped 13,352; Douglas was down 5,198; Gwinnett lost 41,985; and Rockdale declined 16,279, the ARC report said.

Picking up the most in numbers of incoming white residents were Cherokee (46,314), Coweta (23,643), Forsyth (49,962), and Paulding (33,444).[170]

Fayette County emergence as one of the top counties in all of America (and Peachtree City's ascendance to the top of CNN Money and US News and World Report's lists of best places to live, raise a family, etc.) are the result of White flight from Atlanta, the thriving business districts and school systems, coupled with safe, virtually crime-free communities are a direct representation of what White people can create in but a generation.

Clayton County, which went from 90 percent White in 1980 to 20 percent White today, represents what Black people are

---

170 Beverly, "2010 Census."

capable of creating, lacking the ability of sustaining any semblance of a business district, property values, or a quality
school system.

And when the Black Undertow arrives, so do the demands
from Organized Blackness:

> The Georgia and Fayette County chapters of the NAACP
> have joined 11 Fayette County voters in a lawsuit against
> the county's board of commissioners and board of education,
> alleging that its practice of at-large elections is disenfran-
> chising black voters.
>
> The federal lawsuit was filed Tuesday also lists as de-
> fendants the Fayette County Board of Elections. According
> to the 2010 Census, Fayette County is nearly 73 percent
> white and 21 percent black. The lawsuit says that because
> of the practice, no black candidate has ever been elected to
> the county's board of commissioners or board of education.
>
> "Plaintiffs assert that Fayette County's at-large method
> of electing members to these boards, given the levels of ra-
> cially polarized voting, guarantees precisely this result," the
> lawsuit reads.
>
> "Elections in Fayette County show a clear pattern of ra-
> cially polarized voting. Although black voters are politically
> cohesive, bloc voting by other members of the electorate con-
> sistently defeats black-preferred candidates."
>
> Ryan Haygood, director of the NAACP's Legal Defense
> Fund's Political Participation Group and the lead attorney
> for the plaintiffs in the case, said the group has been ana-
> lyzing the latest Census data and how that growth coincides
> with what they consider to be potential voting schemes. He
> said the Voting Rights Act is the best vehicle for addressing
> the issue.
>
> "Fayette County's at-large election method is a struc-
> tural wall of exclusion that guarantees that black voters, in
> spite of having tried in election after election, cannot elect

their candidates of choice," Haygood said. "There's no benefit to any system that weakens the voting strength of a ju-
risdiction's voting rights. That catches our attention."[171]

So start the demands. The eternal question of "and then?" to
each concession by Whites will never, ever cease. Fayette
County will be submerged by the Black Undertow; property
values will plummet and charming subdivisions will become
the breeding ground for poverty, crime, and desperation, where
only a decade early White parents snapped photos of their children on graduation day, the only crimes committed then the
occasional toilet papering of a yard.

Were restrictive covenants still constitutional, Fayette
County could have insulated itself from the onslaught of the
Black Undertow (the growth in Hispanic population in metro
Atlanta is directly correlated to the need for extra construction
workers to build new homes for White people to move into as
they flee a city/county that has fallen to the Black Undertow).
Actually, the county wouldn't have existed as a White flight
refuge, because Whites would have been able to maintain the
integrity of their neighborhoods in Atlanta.

The point is simply this: metro Atlanta is the microcosm for
all of America. Whites can flee areas that go majority-minority
and set up thriving communities that are implicitly White
(though everyone will say they moved there for the "good
schools," an explicitly White comment masquerading in egalitarian terms), but the diversity they fled will find them.

And the process will have to start again.

Idaho, Montana, North Dakota . . . yes, these sound like
great options, but the storm clouds reside on horizon. Just like
in the Cold War story *On the Beach* in which a nuclear war
between America and Russia devastates the planet, making
Australia the last inhabitable place on earth (though a nuclear

---

[171] Haines, "NAACP Suit."

winter cloud heads their way which spells imminent doom), Whites who flee to these states only delay the inevitable.

Fayette County and Peachtree City ... once the best place in America to call home, are prepared to become just another Clayton County.

The Black Hole of Atlanta grows, pushing Whites further and further out, destroying property value (real wealth) and uprooting businesses at the same time.

Meanwhile, the instruments of our liberation reside in North Fulton County.

There's a reason you should be paying to Atlanta; the Gordian Knot for a true American Renaissance is there.

24

They Will Come for Stone Mountain

April 18th, 2012

But not only that; let freedom ring from Stone Mountain of Georgia!

— Martin Luther King, 1963

Georgia's Racist Past Demolished at Stone Mountain Park
July 14, 2016
 Byline: Racially ambiguous graduate of an Ivy League college/university
 It will be completed soon. Freedom will ring from sea-to-shining-sea finally, just as Martin Luther King prophesied in his angelic "I Have a Dream" speech from 1963. Stone Mountain Park's divisive Confederate Memorial carving of Robert E. Lee, Jefferson Davis, and Stonewall Jackson will be demolished today.

 One of the last vestiges of public, prominent racism left in America (after the White House in Washington D.C. was renamed "The People's House"), Stone Mountain Park—located in predominately Black Stone Mountain, Georgia—will see a new mural erected in place of the three most prominent leaders of the white supremacist Confederate States of America.

 The new mural, selected by the presidents of America's leading Historically Black Colleges and Universities (HBCUs) will depict Martin Luther King giving his fabled address in the shadow of the Lincoln Memorial.

"This is a powerful day in our nation's history, with true racial reconciliation coming to a state whose history is replete with the stain of white bigotry," said President Barack Obama.

"It is only by removing every white stain of bigotry that we can move forward with creating a more powerful union," he said.

The Army Corps of Engineers will supervise the demolition. Pieces of the memorial will be distributed across the nation as part of the Department of Education's Teaching Tolerance program.

•   •   •

It's not such a far cry that such an article could be published in *The Atlanta Journal-Constitution* in the no-so-distant future.

Not far from downtown Atlanta sits Stone Mountain, one of the more awe-inspiring geological sites in all of the world. I was young when I was first went to Stone Mountain Park, and each time I've climbed to the top of the mountain since, that first trip still lingers in my mind.

When you see the huge carving of Lee, Jackson, and Davis on horseback (the largest bas-relief in the entire world) it leaves a lasting impression upon you. But for how much longer?

How can America—governed by the concept and principles of Black-Run America (BRA)—allow a monument to those traitors remain on Stone Mountain? *The Los Angeles Times* made a huge deal out of this mountain of hate in 1995, just before the Coca-Cola Olympic Games were held in Atlanta:

> When Tyrone Brooks was a child growing up in rural Georgia, he learned from his elders that the freakish outcropping of granite east of Atlanta known as Stone Mountain was a frightful—even evil—place.
>
> The Ku Klux Klan marked its rebirth early this century by torching a cross upon its peak. And in olden times, his grandmother told him, black people had been lynched and thrown from the mountaintop. "I did not grow up with a good feeling about Stone Mountain," Brooks said. "I still don't have a good feeling about it."

A year from today, when Atlanta hosts the 1996 Centennial Olympic Games, 2 million visitors will be expected to feel good about Stone Mountain and the numerous other reminders that the city known as the cradle of the civil rights movement also has a vivid historical flipside.

From the grandiose Confederate memorial carved into the mountain to the ever-present evocations of "Gone With the Wind" to the contentious Rebel emblem that dominates the state flag, Atlanta's Civil War and antebellum history will be much in evidence during the Games. Many visitors will find it charming.

But with various groups threatening protests and lawsuits over the flag, and with lingering resentments swirling around the other symbols, the stage is set for a momentous—or at the least loud—clash over how the South's past should be remembered and portrayed.

Three Olympic events will be held at Stone Mountain, a Southern Mt. Rushmore that since 1958 has been a state-owned park commemorating the Lost Cause of the Confederacy. While park spokeswoman K Thweatt said she knows of no lynchings ever taking place at the site, the land was owned by a family with a long history of klan involvement and was a frequent site of cross burnings.

A gigantic carving of Robert E. Lee, Jefferson Davis and Stonewall Jackson graces one side of the mountain, and on weekends and every night from May through Labor Day the park puts on a laser light show featuring Lee and the Confederate flag and accompanied by Elvis Presley's rendition of "Dixie."

Brooks, a black 49-year-old state legislator, said he can't bring himself to visit the park except for official state functions. But despite criticism of the show, Thweatt said it will not be changed before the Olympics.

When Atlanta launched its underdog bid to become the first Southern and first predominantly black city to host the Olympics, much of its appeal rested on its image as spiritual capital of a modern, harmonious South. But the road to 1996

has been marked by collisions between conservative Southern traditions and the new.

To his way of thinking, Atlanta was awarded the Games
because of the legacy of Dr. Martin Luther King Jr. Former
Mayor Andrew Young, who was an aide to King, is one of
the local people most responsible for bringing the Games to
Atlanta and is co-chairman of the organizing committee. He
and other organizers have made it no secret that they employed King's image to sell Atlanta to the International
Olympic Committee as the cradle of the civil rights movement.

For that reason, Brooks argued, the city should strive to
portray itself as a racially enlightened New South metropolis. "It puts Atlanta in a whole other category in terms of
world image, but my feeling is that the Olympics would not
be here if it was not for the legacy of Martin Luther King Jr.
and the actions of Andrew Young."[172]

Since this article was published in 1995, Georgia did change its
state flag. Gone is the Confederate Flag.

More importantly, we are nearing the point where the gradual deracination—which turned into a full-fledged sprint (courtesy of Black athletes like Hershel Walker and Bo Jackson)—
of Southern Heritage and Roots has been completed. Why
should this monument remain on Stone Mountain anymore?
Who cares about the past?

Jackson, Lee, and Davis were nothing more than evil White
men, right? This memorial must come down.

After all, Stone Mountain is a majority Black city (though
NBC's *30 Rock* imagined the city as some hayseed White dump)
that already exonerated itself of racism by electing a Black
mayor back in 1997. Courtesy of *The New York Times*:

---

[172] Harrison, "Mountain of Racist History."

The 20th-century Ku Klux Klan was born here in 1915, and for half a century afterward this quaint town on the out-skirts of Atlanta played host to an annual rally of cross-burning Klansmen.

Until his death in 1993, the town was home to James R. Venable, the hate-spewing imperial wizard of the National Knights of the Ku Klux Klan. Even today, the granite mon-olith that gives the city its name is revered as a Confederate Rushmore because of its giant relief sculpture of Robert E. Lee, Jefferson Davis and Stonewall Jackson.

Now Stone Mountain has elected a black mayor. What is more, it has elected a black mayor who happens to live in the same house where Mr. Venable, himself the mayor in the 1940's, lived for most of his life.

"Tell me," said Chuck E. Burris, the Mayor-elect, "that God doesn't have a sense of humor."

In a low-turnout election on Nov. 4, Mr. Burris defeated the incumbent, Pat Wheeler, by 278 votes to 260; a third candidate won 30.

Neither the small turnout—16 percent of the town's reg-istered voters—nor the narrow margin of victory has stopped Mr. Burris and his wife, Marcia Baird Burris, from proclaiming the election a landmark in the racial evolution of the New South.

"There's a new Klan in Stone Mountain," Mr. Burris said in an interview, "only it's spelled with a C: c-l-a-n, citizens living as neighbors. And I guess I'm the black dragon."

Mr. Burris's election to the part-time, $300-a-month po-sition is a tribute to his years of public involvement, both in Stone Mountain, where he has served two terms on the City Council, and in nearby Atlanta, where he worked as a budget analyst for that city's first black Mayor, Maynard H. Jackson. It is also a testament to the gradual easing of racial politics in some Southern communities.

But perhaps above all, it reflects a remarkable demo-graphic shift in the suburbs of cities like Atlanta, where cer-tain middle and upper-class neighborhoods, once exclu-sively white, have seemed to integrate almost overnight.

In 1980, white voters were 94 percent of the electorate in the city of Stone Mountain. By 1990, the figure had slipped to 85 percent. Only seven years later, half the registered voters in this town of 35,000 people are black.

As a scholarship student at Morehouse College in 1967, he sat in on several Saturday seminars led by Dr. King, and once told Dr. King that he did not think he could respond to violence with nonviolence. Dr. King replied, "You will always be a slave if you let other people control your behavior."

To Mr. Burris's thinking, as to many here, Stone Mountain's image has been distorted by the activities of a few locals, an annual pilgrimage by outsiders and some distant history (the Klan had been largely inactive for decades before its rebirth at a 1915 rally on the mountain).

Of course, the Confederate carving on the mountain, which rises from a state park abutting the city, remains. The huge sculpture, depicting Lee, Davis and Jackson on horseback, was commissioned in 1916 by the United Daughters of the Confederacy as a memorial to their Civil War dead, but, with work proceeding in fits and starts for decades, it was 1970 before it was dedicated.

Mr. Burris says the sculpture does not bother him as much as the need to pour new sidewalks, reduce property tax appraisals on the elderly and cleanse the city of crack houses.

"Maybe things are getting a little better," he said. "If nothing else, hopefully my election will make people know that the city of Stone Mountain is a good town, that everybody is welcome here, that there are no bars to anyone moving here and finding friends and neighbors."[173]

Stone Mountain today is still home to crack houses and crime, courtesy of its 89 percent Black population. But on the north

---

[173] Sack, "Birthplace of Klan."

face of the nearby quartz monzonite dome monadnock commonly known as Stone Mountain rests a mural honoring three
White men who aren't warranted that honor in BRA.

It will come down. It will be replaced with a more acceptable
bas-relief. Probably MLK.

And then, the only thing left to demolish will be Mount
Rushmore. After all, Thomas Jefferson was an individual who
didn't believe in racial equality: Lincoln wanted to send all
Black people back to Africa, Teddy Roosevelt was a progressive
racialist, and George Washington—the father of a nation that
no longer exists—was a slave-holding White male.

25

Chick-fil-A vs. Coca-Cola:
The Strange Trajectory of Two Southern Companies

August 3rd, 2012

A random Facebook post by the bloated, turgid Gov. Mike Huckabee has enabled Chick-fil-A to have record one-day profits with an outpouring of support for the embattled privately held company:

> Chick-fil-A said it set a one-day sales record Wednesday after thousands of diners poured into the chain's stores from coast to coast.
>
> "We are very grateful and humbled by the incredible turnout of loyal Chick-fil-A customers on Aug. 1 at Chick-fil-A restaurants around the country," Steve Robinson, the company's executive vice president of marketing, said in a statement. "Chick-fil-A Appreciation Day was not a company promotion; it was initiated by others."[174]

HW correctly nailed the euphoric atmosphere surrounding the fast-food franchise that asks you to "Eat Mor Chikin," with those who still put their faith in backing Conservatism, Inc. declaring victory—over a chicken sandwich:

> In order to get White Christians off the couch and into the streets, the only thing it took to start a resistance movement

---

[174] Stafford, "Chick-Fil-A Says."

(remember, this is the second time, as Rick Santelli started the Tea Party on CNBC in 2009) is for our so-called conservative leaders (i.e., people on FOX News and talk radio) to start acting like leaders, and not be intimidated by insults like "racist" and "bigot" and "homophobe" hurled at them by the liberal media.

Civilization didn't have to collapse. We didn't need a Second Great Depression. Mike Huckabee, a "respectable" and "mainstream" face on television, simply had to make one post on Facebook about "National Chick-fil-A Appreciation Day," and Rush Limbaugh, Sarah Palin, Rick Santorum, and Glenn Beck had to back him up.

If our conservative leaders would speak out more forcefully about the evils of black-on-White crime, multiculturalism, political correctness, and Third World immigration, close ranks and refuse to be intimidated by the liberal media, what do you suppose the result would be among the White Christian conservative masses?[175]

Interestingly, the *New York Times* has written an attack on Chick-fil-A for being grounded in "Southern roots."

Another company, also started in Atlanta, cut all ties to those Southern roots and then poured pesticide on what remained: Coca-Cola.

As I noted in a post at *VDARE* the so-called "cultural wars" that Pat Buchanan spoke of are over. Paul Gottfried over at *TakiMag* nailed it, writing:

I feel sorry for the multicultural left, which has triumphed so completely in the Western world that it doesn't have any real enemies to fight anymore. Can one really take organizations such as Focus on the Family, which advocates heterosexual marriage, as a grave neo-fascist threat? Things aren't looking up for the warriors against Christian bigotry because most of the opposition has now melted into putty. The only thing progressives can do these days is portray

---

175 Wallace, "National Chick-Fil-A Appreciation Day."

quasi-wimps such as Cathy as would-be Grand Inquisitors, even though he runs around oozing affection for the left's protected classes.[176]

Remember, this was all prompted by Dan Cathy, the president of the Atlanta-based Chick-fil-A, telling a Baptist Web site that the fast-food chain is "guilty as charged" when it comes to supporting the biblical definition of marriage.

"We are very much supportive of the family—the biblical definition of the family unit," Cathy was quoted in article published Monday by the Baptist Press. "We are a family-owned business, a family-led business, and we are married to our first wives. We give God thanks for that."

But what if there's another angle to this entire debate that few dare discuss?

•   •   •

The Coca-Cola Bottling Company, also headquartered in Atlanta, has been one of the most vocal organizations in promoting marriage equality, receiving a perfect ranking in the 2011 Corporate Equality Index as one of the most "gay-friendly" corporations in America.[177]

Back in the dark days when "gays" were still in the closet and the struggle for human rights was defined in stark black and white, Coca-Cola was one of the companies in the vanguard of pushing for a colorblind world. (Think back to Robert Woodruff, the Atlanta Chamber of Commerce, and integration.) In 1986, Coca-Cola would provide a huge boost to the anti-apartheid movement in South Africa by divesting from the nation entirely:

In a major victory for opponents of apartheid, Coca-Cola Co. said Wednesday that it plans to withdraw from South Africa

---

176 Gottfried, "Chick-Fil-A Eats Crow."
177 Smith, "More Businesses Than Ever."

and will attempt to sell its operations to black investors there.

Coca-Cola, the dominant soft-drink marketer in South Africa and a major symbol of U.S. corporate involvement there, thus will join a growing list of U.S. firms pulling out of that nation amid mounting furor over its apartheid system of racial discrimination.

Coca-Cola also is believed to be the first American company to at least publicly express plans to sell its South African operations to black investors. And it is also one of the first to acknowledge political as well as economic reasons for its withdrawal. Most U.S. companies have said they were withdrawing solely because of deteriorating business conditions.

"We have been reducing our investment in South Africa since 1976, and we have now decided to sell our remaining holdings in that country," Donald R. Keough, Coca-Cola's president and chief operating officer, said in a statement. "Our decision to complete the process of disinvestment is a statement of our opposition to apartheid and of our support for the economic aspirations of black South Africans."[178]

How'd that work out for South Africa? (Chick-fil-A opened three locations in South Africa and all have closed now.)

Despite bending over backwards to accommodate a Jesse Jackson shakedown in 1980, despite paying a record $156 million out-of-court settlement in a racial discrimination lawsuit in 2000, [179] despite bragging about winning "diversity" awards[180] and being one of the most diverse in the world in terms of employment, despite donating $10 million worth of land[181] for the future location of the Center for Civil and Human Rights in Atlanta, despite dropping monetary support of

---

[178] Sing, "Coca-Cola Acts to Cut."
[179] Winter, "Coca-Cola Settles Racial Bias Case."
[180] Coca-Cola, "Our Progress."
[181] USA Today, "Civil Rights Museum Location."

the American Legislative Exchange Council (ALEC) (the Conservatism, Inc. non-profit that backed Voter ID laws)—despite all of this, Coca-Cola is associated with those hate-mongers: Chick-fil-A.

This will have to end, because "gay" is the new "Black." Coca-Cola has an exclusive contract for providing their soft drinks and Simply Orange Juice (replacing PepsiCo's contract for Tropicana in 2011) with all of Chick-fil-A's franchises.

In 2011, the Republicans in the House of Representatives hired King & Spalding—a law firm that is based in Atlanta which has worked closely with Coca-Cola—to defend the constitutionality of the Defense of Marriage Act.

In 2010, Chick-fil-A donated two million dollars to organizations that publicly defend DOMA, including donating $1,188,380 to the Marriage & Family Foundation; $247,500 to the National Christian Foundation, and smaller donations to the Family Research Council and Exodus International.

The New York Times reported that gay rights had fiercely criticized the law firm and said that it would hurt "its ability to recruit and retain lawyers."[182]

A King & Spalding lawyer and solicitor general under President George W. Bush, Paul Clement, who was hired to lead the Republican case in defense of DOMA resigned from the firm over this bowing to pressure from homosexual advocates, saying, "I resign out of the firmly held belief that a representation should not be abandoned because the client's legal position is extremely unpopular in certain quarters." He wrote, "Defending unpopular clients is what lawyers do. I recognized from the outset that this statute implicates very sensitive issues that prompt strong views on both sides. But having undertaken the representation, I believe there is no honorable course for me but to complete it."

---

[182] Shear and Schwartz, "Law Firm Won't Defend."

A number of news outlets, including the *Washington Post*, speculated that Coca-Cola pressured King & Spalding to remove itself from the DOMA case.[183]

Gay rights groups have long targeted Chick-fil-A for standing against homosexual marriage, with *Time* reporting in 2011 that a Pennsylvania operator (operating independently from the privately held business) had offered free sandwiches to the Art of Marriage seminar put on by one of the states most right of center organizations.[184]

Equality Matters, an organization that seeks to promote full LGBT equality, reported in 2011 that Chick-fil-A has a long history of working with organizations that promote traditional marriage, lumping any Christian charitable organization with what they label an "anti-gay" group.

"The company's charitable division has provided more than $1.1 million to organizations that deliver anti-LGBT messages and promote egregious practices like reparative therapy that seek to 'free' people of being gay," Equality Matters wrote.

With more than 1,500 restaurants in 38 states and Washington, D.C. Chick-fil-A is a nationally recognized brand and one of the few that closes its doors on Sunday. In essence, Chick-fil-A is more concerned about the morality of the community it serves than accumulating profits at the expense of the community.

In response to the reaction to Cathy's column—both positive and negative—the corporate page for Chick-fil-A on Facebook had this message posted:

> "The Chick-fil-A culture and service tradition in our restaurants is to treat every person with honor, dignity and respect—regardless of their belief, race, creed, sexual orientation or gender. We will continue this tradition in the over 1,600 Restaurants run by independent Owner/Operators.

---

[183] Rubin, "King and Spalding Plot."
[184] Webley, "Controversial Chicken."

Going forward, our intent is to leave the policy debate over same-sex marriage to the government and political arena.

"Chick-fil-A is a family-owned and family-led company serving the communities in which it operates. From the day Truett Cathy started the company, he began applying biblically-based principles to managing his business. For example, we believe that closing on Sundays, operating debt-free and devoting a percentage of our profits back to our communities are what make us a stronger company and Chick-fil-A family.

Our mission is simple: to serve great food, provide genuine hospitality and have a positive influence on all who come in contact with Chick-fil-A."

•   •   •

Interestingly, it is that tradition of treating every person with honor, dignity, and respect that came crashing to the ground at one of its first stores, as in January of 2012, the first Chick-fil-A in all of America had to close at The Gallery at South DeKalb Mall because of falling sales:

> After almost 42-years in business, the Chick-fil-A at South DeKalb Mall closes this week. This location opened just three years after the first mall store opened at Greenbriar Mall in 1967. At that time, enclosed malls were growing in popularity. In fact, Greenbriar was only Atlanta's third such shopping facility.
>
> Brenda Morrow, a spokesperson for Chick-fil-A, says, "We had a great run at South DeKalb Mall." She cites "declining sales over the years" as the reason for the closure. When a location underperforms, "for financial reasons, it is difficult to run a store in the caliber which we run the stores."[185]

---

[185] Turknett, "Chick-Fil-A Closes One."

Hilariously, The Gallery at South DeKalb Mall brags about be-ing a Black mall that caters to Black people:

> We've carved out a unique niche by constantly asking our community how we can better serve them. This non-tradi-tional relationship with our trade area makes for a success-ful commerce-meets-community business model.
>
> The Gallery at South DeKalb caters to a close-knit com-munity of African-American consumers with more than 600,000 potential customers in the primary and secondary market area.[186]

When the Chick-fil-A opened in 1970, DeKalb County was roughly 80 percent White. Today, DeKalb County is touted as one of the top counties for Black people to live in now 56 percent Black/35 percent White), in all of America. Yet for some strange reason the new Black majority is unable to maintain the busi-nesses and economy that fell into their laps like ripe fruit when the White population fled. Case in point, the complete collapse of Memorial Drive:

> Driving along Memorial Drive from its humble beginnings in warehouse world in downtown Atlanta to its monumental end at Stone Mountain isn't so much a glory story as it is a cautionary tale. And in many ways, some people say, it could be the story of Atlanta. The road has all the city's elements. There are shadows of Atlanta's Old South—magnolia trees, Margaret Mitchell's final resting place at Oakland Ceme-tery, the tribute to slain Confederate heroes carved into Stone Mountain.
>
> There, too, are signs of Atlanta's more recent history and its present—neglected intown neighborhoods, white flight and boarded-up businesses decorated occasionally by the blaring orange signs of check-cashing establishments. Some say Memorial Drive also could reveal the future of a city that

---

[186] Gallery at South DeKalb, "Mall Information."

went through nearly promiscuous growth in the '70s and whose suburbs now keep stretching to the next frontier whenever things get a little too messy or congested.

Now, what was once a model for both middle-class life and suburban affluence—with the first suburban Rich's and the world's first Home Depot store—is largely a picture of decline. Income levels of residents in some areas along the road have dropped, even before adjusted for inflation. For example, the average income in 1980 for Census Tract 220.02, a section north of Memorial to Lawrenceville Highway, was $20,337; for 1990, the average income for that tract was $17,695. Now, retail vacancy rates along Memorial are 14.9 percent, nearly double the metrowide average of 7.7 percent, according to Jamison Research Inc.

During the '80s, the demographics of DeKalb County, including the Memorial Drive area, also changed dramatically. In 1980, of the 12,053 residents of Census Tract 220.02 along Memorial, only 22 were African-American. By 1990, 8,614 African-Americans lived in that tract, out of a total population of 14,319.

Memorial Drive snakes 16 miles through two counties, Fulton and DeKalb, and four municipalities, Atlanta, Decatur, Avondale Estates and Stone Mountain. And while it has one name, Memorial Drive actually seems like two different roads, with two distinct personalities—the 10-mile urban stretch inside the Perimeter and the remaining six, suburban miles heading to the "big rock" at Stone Mountain.

The history of the road is replete with irony and contrast. It was a vital artery for suburban growth in the '50s and '60s, home to a shopping center—Belvedere Plaza—that was as stylish for its time as Lenox Square. Now the Rich's that once anchored the shopping center has closed. Boarded up, too, is the historic Home Depot, the first store in the Atlanta-based chain. The site is now a flea market, with its next-door neighbor boarded up from lack of business. It's emblematic of the fate of much of Memorial Drive, now a confusing array of traffic, pawn shops, boarded-up houses and fast-food joints.

And how's this for irony? Memorial Drive draws its name from the Confederate Memorial at Stone Mountain, where the Ku Klux Klan held meetings earlier this century. Now African-Americans predominate in the area around the road, a popular boulevard for thousands of young African-Americans who cruise it on weekend nights, and, during Freaknik, block traffic for miles.[187]

That is the reality of the Black Undertow that swallowed DeKalb County. That is the reality of what happens when White flight transpires and the new Black inhabitants of a city that had no hand in building it are tasked with sustaining high rates of residential real estate value and with maintaining the business districts and economy they inherit. Where commerce and community once thrived, a reflection of its White inhabitants, now only boarded-up businesses and crime remain—a stunning reminder of the unrelenting power of the Black Undertow.

The first Chick-fil-A to ever open was the one at Greenbriar Mall in South Fulton back in 1967. Opened at a time when the area was roughly 90 percent White (as well as the clientele), Greenbriar Mall and the surrounding area have undergone a cultural (racial) shift, with the area now roughly 90 percent Black and fighting to survive:

Marva Kenny may be Greenbriar Mall's greatest booster. She had the funeral procession of her husband, John, the mall's maintenance chief, pass through Greenbriar's parking lot.

"The mall is part of my family," she said.

So she is apologetic when speaking about the 44-year-old Greenbriar, one of the city's first enclosed malls.

"When I moved to this neighborhood [in 1970], Greenbriar Mall was a flourishing mall with several good stores," she said. "But the mall is going down. When nicer stores do

---

[187] Anderson, "Lessons of Memorial Drive."

a study [of the area], they don't come. There's a lot of low income."

Increasingly, the mall's offerings are not her style. "Greenbriar is predominantly urban wear; the five-inch heels and little skirts aren't my bag," she said with a laugh, but added that she still shops there and still is pulling for its revival.

Greenbriar has endured some blows recently: the AMC Magic Johnson movie theater, once seen as a boost to the Southwest Atlanta community, closed in October; a clothing store suffered a smash-and-grab robbery this month, and merchants here, like those everywhere, complain about a dearth of shoppers.

Greenbriar Mall has been counted out many times since opening in 1965. And it has witnessed as many rebirths. It's history is almost a microcosm of that of an ever-changing city.

Designed by famed architect John Portman, Greenbriar was one of the region's first enclosed malls and the birthplace of the modern food court concept, with Chick-fil-A opening its first store there in 1967.

But white flight in the surrounding southwest Atlanta neighborhoods cut deeply into its white clientele, contributing to many fits and starts through the years. In 1985, J.C. Penney, one of the mall's two original anchors left, bringing protests from residents and black leaders, including then-Mayor Andrew Young. "There is as much income in this neighborhood as there is in any other neighborhood in the city," he said at the time.

A blossoming black middle-class population in the area caused developers to keep bringing improvements to the mall because, as has often been noted, metro Atlanta's south side is underserved in shopping capacity. In 1993, grocer Cub Foods opened a 63,000-square-foot, free-standing store on the property and in 1996, the Magic Johnson's Theatre complex opened.

But a decade later, Cub Foods pulled out of the region. This fall, the 60,000-square-foot theater closed. Both remain vacant.

Greenbriar Mall has also gained a place in black popular culture consciousness. It was here that Jermaine Dupri discovered the two members of the platinum-selling group Kris Kross. And rap artists ranging from Ludacris to T.I have mentioned the Greenbriar in song.[188]

There exist no signs of hope. The Greenbriar Mall Chick-fil-A was the first Chick-fil-A in all of America. Built in 1967, when the area around the mall (and the clientele) was nearly 100 percent White, the now 100 percent Black Greenbriar Mall (with even a Tyler Perry movie studio nearby) represents a stunning example of the real purchasing power of the Black community as well as the type of social capital present in an all-Black community, even one that has absorbed so much commercial infrastructure, built long ago by a people who participated in massive White flight.

How much longer does the first Chick-fil-A location have before it goes the way of so many other businesses at Greenbriar Mall? And how much money are the Cathy family pumping into the mall to keep it alive, knowing full well the psychological defeat that closing the first store would have?

Chick-fil-A is interested in investing in communities; Coca-Cola, on the other hand cares little for the community as long as the consumers there have the ability to purchase their sugar water. (Tell us again how that's working out in South Africa, now.)

Greenbriar Mall is the type of mall about which Chris Rock jokes, the one that has gone all Black; thus, stores start to close.

Even one of the oldest Chick-fil-As isn't immune from shutting its doors once a community that once reflected its primarily White population goes Black.

---

[188] Torpy, "Greenbriar Mall Boosters Hope."

In a country ruled by Connected Capitalism and a Minority Occupied Government, good citizenship can no more be tolerated than individual citizenship. The Establishment actively works to the benefit of those who hate the country the most. Chick-fil-A is a company that puts the community first, holding fundraisers for families in need of help paying medical bills; the operators of independent franchises expected to integrate their business into the very fabric of the community.

Chick-fil-A is a company that truly stands athwart history yelling "stop." The more than 1,500 communities served by Chick-fil-A restaurants are a reminder of the real America, the one that the combined actions of Connected Capitalism (basically sociopathic capitalists more concerned with enlarging profits for shareholders than sustaining the community where they were raised) and the Minority Occupied Government is busy trying to tear down and replace through mass immigration.

Now Dan Cathy has kicked dirt in the face of the powerful homosexual lobby. (There's no social stigma in coming out as a homosexual anymore; just try coming out publicly as a "racist," though, and see true social ostracism.)

The values that drive Chick-fil-A and the values that drive Coca-Cola are diametrically opposed, the latter representing the culture-leveling goals of the managerial elite who push for open borders and higher profit margins (with pandering to minorities a general operating procedure); the former more interested in building strong communities, knowing that strong values and high moral character are the bedrock of perpetuating a business with long-term aspirations.

Which way will Chick-fil-A go? Our hope at SBPDL is that we are witnessing a watershed moment at which point the culture wars finally see a counterthrust from the real America that we all seek to preserve.

26

The Connected Capitalism of the DWL:
Let's Have a Coke Party

May 22nd, 2012

Tea Party is so 1770s. Coke Party will be the new vogue in the coming years.

While reading *Inside Coca-Cola: A CEO's Life Story of Building the World's Most Popular Brand* by former Coke CEO Neville Isdell, a story from the chapter "Connected Capitalism" stood out and slapped me clear across the face.

It tells the story of a biracial gathering of Atlanta's civic and religious leaders to honor Martin Luther King's receiving of the Nobel Peace Prize. To be held in late January 1965, Coke patriarch Robert Woodruff "politely persuaded" Atlanta's White business community to attend the event, for the event would have represented a "worldwide embarrassment for Coca-Cola and for Atlanta" had they no-showed:

> The night of the dinner, King delivered to a standing-room only, integrated audience what would become one of his most famous quotes: "If people of good will of the white South fail to act now, history will have to record that the greatest tragedy of this period of social transition was not the vitriolic words and then the violent actions of the bad people but the appalling silence of and indifference of the good people."

All segments of Atlanta society were there: churches and synagogues, government, private universities and business, all working together, as [Sam] Massell (Atlanta's last white mayor) recalled, for their "mutual interest." That is Connected Capitalism.[189]

Connected Capitalism.

A perfect term for the actions of the Managerial Elite (Disingenuous White Liberals in perfectly tailored suits) who preside over Black-Run America, who no longer have any allegiance to a nation-state (any) that they have so busily deconstructed.

No, Mr. King, history will not judge those "people of good will" you excoriated to get on their knees so as to allow Black people to jump on their backs, pocketing the loose change that falls from this noble gesture in the process.

After all, isn't that what Connected Capitalism is?

We saw what Connected Capitalism was capable of in 1981, when the then stewards of Coca-Cola capitulated to Jesse Jackson (one of MLK's right-hand men) over a threatened boycott. The late Lewis Grizzard, a columnist for *The Atlanta Journal-Constitution*, wrote these words on the surrender:

> When the Rev. Jesse Jackson of Operation PUSH took on Coca-Cola, I figured he had written a check his admittedly considerable power as a black leader couldn't cash.
>
> You might take on 7Up, but Coke is the big dog in the soft drink market. I fully expected Coke to flip Jesse Jackson off its back with one sweep of its powerful tail.
>
> Either I underestimated Jackson or I overestimated Coca-Cola. The word came the other day that Coke had made a $30 million deal with Jackson to do more business with blacks.
>
> Coke denied that Jackson's threat to lead a black boycott of its products had anything to do with the deal. "We were going to do this all the time; we're just no getting to around to it," said a cokesperson.

---

[189] Isdell and Beasley, *Inside Coca-Cola*, 213–215.

Sure.

What Jesse Jackson did was as simple as a liquor-store heist: He blackmailed a huge American company into giving him what he wanted. Meet my demands, or I'll snap my fingers and my loyal subjects won't even say the words "Coca-Cola" until I tell them to. What Jackson did to Coke was essentially the same: Come across, or else.

Coca-Cola kept paying Mr. Jackson tribute and sought his advice during the 1999–2000 racial discrimination suit against the company. *The New York Times* reported on November 17, 2000:

> In the largest settlement ever in a racial discrimination case, the Coca-Cola Company agreed yesterday to pay more than $156 million to resolve a federal lawsuit brought by black employees.
>
> The settlement also mandates that the company make sweeping changes, costing an additional $36 million, and grants broad monitoring powers to a panel of outsiders—an unusual concession in employment discrimination cases.
>
> The lawsuit, filed in April 1999, accused Coke of erecting a corporate hierarchy in which black employees were clustered at the bottom of the pay scale, averaging $26,000 a year less than white workers. As redress, the settlement provides as many as 2,000 current and former black salaried employees with an average of $40,000 in cash, while the four plaintiffs whose names are on the lawsuit will receive up to $300,000 apiece.
>
> "It sets a new standard for corporate settlements," said the Rev. Jesse Jackson, referring to Coke's agreement to tie executives' salaries to how well the company meets its diversity goals. "The internal cultures of companies have been built on patterns of exclusion based on gender and race. This is a step in the right direction."

Despite the short-term costs, a negligible amount for a company with about $20 billion in sales last year, Coke officials and plaintiffs' lawyers characterized the settlement as a "business necessity," particularly because minorities in the United States drink a disproportionate share of its sodas.

"This company had a credibility gap between the image that it cultivated with the African-American community on the outside and how African-Americans were treated on the inside," said Cyrus Mehri, a plaintiffs' lawyer who negotiated a $140 million cash settlement in a discrimination suit against Texaco in 1996.

While efforts by disgruntled Coke employees in Atlanta to start a boycott never crimped the company's bottom line, the lawsuit has troubled Coke for 18 months and, company officials acknowledge, tarnished the image of one of the world's best-known brands.[190]

History will judge that the greatest tragedy of that period of social transition that Mr. King bemoaned was the capitulation of Connected Capitalism to BRA. Coca-Cola fell in line behind the pied piper who touted a society where "content of character" mattered above all else, but a society based firmly on the promotion of Blackness was erected in its place. Well, that, and the promotion of Whites to the Managerial Elite who bow in delirious obsequiousness to this objective.

David Greising wrote about these types of White people in his biography of former Coke CEO Roberto Goizueta, in the book *I'd Like the World to Buy a Coke: The Life and Leadership of Roberto Goizueta.*

The wasted capital that could have gone to building infrastructure, research and development, cure diseases, and further space exploration instead was diverted to uplift a segment of the American population who remade Detroit into their image.

---

[190] Winter, "Coca-Cola Settles Racial Bias Case."

And Birmingham. And Memphis. And Baltimore. And Cleveland. And New Orleans.

Atlanta, the city too busy to hate, represents a gaping black hole that continually sucks in more and more resources and misplaced capital that is diverted from projects that could see an actual Return on Investment (ROI). In fact, a sales tax referendum on July 31 will see if a 10-year plan to collect taxes from ten counties passes, which would result only in marginally reducing the worst traffic in America—all due to White people trying to escape Black people.

The ecological impact to the continued need to build new suburbs (and infrastructure to support this in terms of roads, sewage facilities, etc.) to escape the ever-widening reach of the black hole that is Atlanta is incalculable. The misplaced capital and investments (and opportunity costs) involved in this process fall in the same category.

No, Dr. King, it is the appalling silence of and indifference of the good people now to the totality of the failure of BRA and the horrible consequences of those "people of good will of the White South" who did act on your behalf that history will record as the great tragedy.

We could have been on Mars, but instead, we have Detroit, circa 2012, and hundreds of other US cities well on their way to being Detroit-ed.

They represent the sunk cost of BRA. The ruins of Detroit represent actual manifestation of the goodwill of the White South's failure to act now.

This is the real legacy of the Civil Rights movement.

This is the shame of "people of goodwill of the White South" whose legacy is the complete collapse of Birmingham and the turning of Atlanta into a Black Mecca that has been completely subsidized by White tax dollars.

Freedom failed.

Tea Party is so 1770s.

Coke Party will be the new vogue in the coming years.

27

The Death of Public Housing
(The Law of Unintended Consequences)

July 9th, 2012

"Public housing." Two words that, when uttered separately, have a far different meaning than when they're combined, eliciting a predetermined response of dread if approaching near one such place in your car. More to the point, the mere thought of public housing conjures up visions of crime, misery, neglected children, a massive police presence, drugs, prostitution . . . basically a level of Dante's *The Inferno* that makes you understand hell is on earth.

And it's in a place called "public housing."

In the city of Atlanta, gradual White flight to the suburban (metro) area created a black hole of poverty directly in the heart of the New South's capital city. This black hole of poverty resided in "public housing" that one out of every ten Atlanta residents called home.

The Atlanta Housing Authority's Olympic Legacy Program: Public Housing Projects to Mixed Income Communities by Harvey K. Newman documents the concentration of poverty in "public housing" in Atlanta—which no one dares points out looks oddly like the current state of 90 percent Black Detroit:

> While many of these blacks moved to northern cities such as Chicago, Detroit, and Cleveland, others left rural areas in the south for Atlanta. Sensing the change, many whites fled

Atlanta, so that by 1970, a majority of the city's residents were black. This process of white flight from the City of Atlanta and its housing projects hastened the decline in the city's population as more than 100,000 people left Atlanta during the twenty years after 1970. From a peak of 496,973 in 1970, the city counted only 394,017 residents in 1990. At the same time, the suburban area outside the City of Atlanta added more than 1.5 million people, creating a metropolitan area of almost 3 million by 1990.

There were several important consequences of this change in the city's population. First, the expansion of public housing left the City of Atlanta with one of the highest concentrations of public housing residents per capita of any city in the nation. While cities such as New York and Chicago had larger numbers of citizens living in public housing, Atlanta had a higher ratio of public housing residents compared to those not living in public housing. Almost one out of every ten residents of the City of Atlanta lived in public housing. The presence of other poor residents in the city gave Atlanta the second highest concentration of poverty (behind Newark, New Jersey) of any city in the US.

Yes, during the height of Atlanta's reign as the Black Mecca of America, one out of every ten residents of the city lived in public housing. And, as Howard Husock of *City Journal* wrote in *The Washington Times,* 98 percent of the occupants of public housing in Atlanta were Black.[191]

It was this concentration of Black people in public housing that vexed police (Black people in public housing helped contribute to Atlanta's vice on being the most dangerous city in America for years), befuddled Crusading White pedagogues attempting to find the magic formula to stop the *Waiting for Superman* and close the racial gap in learning, and helped keep the Atlanta Black political machine moving forward.

---

[191] Husock, "Husock: Reinventing Public Housing."

What do we mean by that latter statement? Well, on July 14, 2001, *The Atlanta Journal-Constitution* published a story that basically lamented the end of the Black political machine, which included this hilarious anecdote:

> Public housing voters accounted for much of Mayor Bill Campbell's 4,191-vote margin of victory in 1997. But his second term as mayor has scattered that once-accessible constituency to the far reaches of the metro area.
>
> Public housing edge gone.
>
> In a close race, those votes could make a winning difference as they did for Campbell in his re-election race against Marvin Arrington. But candidates will have to look for many ways to reach voters, political observers say.
>
> Louise Watley has been a public housing leader committed to politics in the black community all of her adult life. She has been registering black voters and taking them to the polls since the 1960s.
>
> "It used to be very easy and very simple," said Watley. "You knew who the registered voters were and you could just send a letter out" telling them who to vote for.
>
> Angelo Fuster, a political strategist who began his career with Jackson in the 1970s, said public housing was an essential element in turning out black voters.
>
> "It used to be that Techwood Homes was a prime place. You could go and hustle up 1,000 people just like that," he said, snapping his fingers in the air.
>
> Since 1995, though, Watley has watched as six of the city's largest public housing projects have been redeveloped and most of their residents dispersed to places as far-flung as Stockbridge. Where thousands of voters with identical political leanings once lived within effortless reach of transport vans and a day's worth of door-to-door greetings, mixed-income communities of highly transient newcomers with no particular political loyalties now dwell.

Watley said public housing contained as many as 20,000 registered voters a decade ago. Now, only about 4,000 of those voters remain, she said.[192]

Wait a second? What in the world happened to public housing in Atlanta? 20,000 registered voters prepared to vote on pertinent matters, if only a van can drive them to and from the polling place . . . down to less than one quarter of its political power!

Now, this number is in the hundreds since public housing was completely removed from Atlanta. NPR decried the breakup of concentrated Black poverty in public housing in the 2008 article *Atlanta Housing Demolition Sparks Outcry*:

> The Atlanta Housing Authority has already demolished 11 complexes since 1994 and plans to get rid of another dozen in the next two years. In most cases, mixed-income housing was built on those sites, and some of the homes were set aside for low-income residents. Residents got vouchers that they could take anywhere to find rental housing.
>
> Renee Glover, CEO of the housing authority, says there are "a lot of good choices" for families to find housing.[193]

One of the primary considerations a White family must consider before moving into an area is the ability to safely raise a family, the quality of schools near said house for kids to be sent, and the ability for that home to appreciate in value. None of this is possible in a city with a large population of Black people, hence the need to for White flight. At one point, the metro Atlanta suburbs boasted schools with some of the highest standardized test scores in all the land, property values that seemed destined to only head north, and crime-free cities whose police force spent their time merely handing out speeding tickets.

---

[192] Hairston, "Black activists change vote tactics."
[193] Lohr, "Atlanta Housing Demolition Sparks Outcry."

The *HOPE VI and Mixed-Finance Redevelopments: A Catalyst for Neighborhood Renewal: Atlanta Case Study* made clear the severity of the Black criminal problem that once existed in Atlanta public housing and served as a reminder of why White flight transpires:

> Fifty years after being unveiled as the nation's first slum-clearance public housing development, Techwood Homes and its sister development, Clark Howell Homes, were urban nightmares. In 1993, over one-third of the 1,195 barracks-style units were vacant and another third were occupied by overcrowded households. Despite $15 million worth of repairs in 1981, the units had outdated heating, sewer, and plumbing systems as well as lead-based paint. More than 1,000 emergency work orders—nearly one per unit—remained to be completed at the two developments. Crime was rampant; in 1992, there were a total of 8,670 police and security field responses—an average of one every hour for the entire year. The 913 serious crimes reported at the developments in 1992 represented an average of more than one per household.

Because of the Law of the Visible Black Hand of Economics, Black people who inherited Atlanta were unable to thrive without government-mandated minority contracting and affirmative action programs; levels of poverty for Black people whose lives weren't enriched by the spoils of the Atlanta Way were drenched in the muck of avarice to the tune of some of the highest poverty rates in all the land.

Now . . . many of these same counties reflect the majority Black population that calls them home, while Atlanta attracts a renaissance of White people (and thus, a rebirth of tax revenue instead of having a population largely incapable of producing wealth).

They, in turn, are prepared to enact laws that deprive the dwindling White populations stranded there (primary due to a loss of personal wealth, directly tied to the home they own: its depreciation correlated tragically with the demise of the White population and rise of the Black population) of the same ability to generate wealth that the Black political structure in Atlanta once did to Whites who weren't connected to the capitalist elite—all the while relying on the sturdy Black vote from public housing! An editorial by Mike King in *The Atlanta Journal-Constitution* published in June of 2007 addressed the important subject of Blacks leaders being concerned about losing power:

It's rare when Atlanta politicians talk frankly, especially in public, about race and power.

So, Mayor Shirley Franklin's candid assessment last week that African-Americans are in danger of losing their Atlanta political base marks an important threshold in the evolution of one of the first American cities to be governed almost exclusively by black leaders.

It suggests that the demographic changes happening within the growing city population portend a time, very soon, when blacks will have to share much more power with whites—not unlike the reversal of fortune the city's white politicians faced when a young Maynard Jackson was elected mayor 35 years ago.

And on a base level, it might explain, in part, the motivation behind the radio ad last year by Franklin, U.S. Rep. John Lewis and former Mayor Andrew Young, exhorting Fulton County residents to vote for black county commission candidates or risk bringing back the days when fire hoses and attack dogs were turned on black Americans demanding voting rights.

The images conjured up in the radio ad—that the days of Jim Crow might return in Fulton County if blacks surrender power to whites—were reckless and irresponsible.

The mayor's most recent assessment of Atlanta politics was much more subtle. But the theme was similar.

Franklin, speaking at an urban affairs symposium in Washington, noted that "there are concerns" about the loss of African-American political dominance in the city, which once had a minority population that was pushing 70 percent. Blacks still represent 58.6 percent of the city's population, but much of Atlanta's growth over the last 15 years—when it went from less than 400,000 people to more than 470,000—has been fueled by whites. With nearly all the city's public housing demolished and its population dispersed around the metro area, the two races could reach a rough parity in the next five to 10 years.

Since Jackson's rise to power, political decisions in Atlanta, and to some degree in Fulton County and DeKalb County as well, have been measured by whether they benefit whites or blacks most. Everything—how the airport is run, who is chosen police chief, school superintendent or chief executive for Grady Hospital, who gets government contracts—has been weighed against whether blacks are getting their fair share or whites are attempting to regain control.

"African Americans of the city of Atlanta have been the most progressive on issues of inclusion of anyone," Franklin told the group. "In our metropolitan area there have been traditions of exclusion, so we are concerned that the loss of political power might undermine the progression of these social policies."

To paraphrase: When we got the power, we set the rules. If we lose power, the rules might change.

Sound familiar? If you're older than 50, you may remember white politicians saying essentially the same thing after the Voting Rights Act was passed in 1965.

Franklin wasn't specific about what she means when she says the city is "progressive on issues of inclusion," but the current debate in Clayton County—which may be the largest recipient of Atlanta's dispersed black population—might provide some indication.

There, blacks represent 62 percent of the population, but only in recent years has the county elected black leaders, including County Commission Chairman Eldrin Bell and County Sheriff Victor Hill. The NAACP president and other

black leaders in Clayton are demanding that the county implement an affirmative action plan designed to award more
contracts to minority-owned businesses.

If Clayton takes that step, it will be the first metro government to do so in years. Under Jackson, Atlanta was
among the first cities to enact rules requiring set-asides in
major contracts for minority subcontractors. But those rules
were weakened as a result of a lawsuit in the 1990s. Bill
Campbell, then mayor, famously likened the plaintiffs in the
lawsuit to the Ku Klux Klan.

It didn't seem to matter that the set-asides were consti-
tutionally questionable and cost the city millions. They also
played an important role in Campbell running the most corrupt administration in the city's history. Under his watch
contracts were awarded not based on whether they might
help a struggling business, but how they might help Bill
Campbell and his cronies.

As Atlanta's white politicians learned years ago—and its
current band of black leaders may soon discover—it's hard
to give up the power to make the rules.[194]

Five years later, DeKalb County is in economic chaos, Clayton
County the foreclosure capital of America. Those White politicians who warned about the passing of the Voting Rights Act
of 1965 and the consequences therein . . . their voices can be
heard echoing through the ruins throughout metro Atlanta.

Husock, writing in the Autumn 2010 of City Journal,
bragged about the wonders of Atlanta tearing down its public
housing without mentioning the crisis that is brewing: what
happens to the areas where the former residents of Atlanta
public housing—99 percent of whom were Black—use their
vouchers to call home?

---

[194] King, "Blacks leaders concerned about losing power."

Crime rates, moreover, are consistently high in and around public housing, and voucher units have been widely implicated in the spread of social problems to formerly safe areas. The problem is financial, as well: housing vouchers alone, which didn't even exist until 1974, now cost taxpayers $18 billion, more than the $16.9 billion that we spend on welfare. And it's a policy that disproportionately affects the African-American poor. Nearly 45 percent of public-housing tenants are black, as are 42 percent of voucher recipients.

All this makes what Renee Glover is doing in Atlanta so important. Since 1994, Glover, a child of Jim Crow–era Jacksonville, Florida, has led the Atlanta Housing Authority (AHA)—the nation's fifth-largest public-housing system, with 50,000 tenants and voucher recipients, 99 percent of them, like her, African-American. She has drawn national recognition for the fact that during her tenure, Atlanta became the first city in the United States to tear down virtually all its projects.

But Glover's plan is far more ambitious than demolition: she has set out to transform the dysfunctional behavior that condemns people to languish for years in public housing. Her approach is the most dramatic change in any city's public-housing system since Franklin Roosevelt created the program in 1937.

When Glover first took charge of the AHA, just 18.5 percent of household heads in the city's bleak projects held jobs. At a time when Atlanta overall had the nation's highest murder rate, crime was six times higher in the projects than the city average. Lawlessness prevailed in these campus-style complexes. Drug gangs had their own apartments for conducting business, such as grisly initiation ceremonies (in one, teenagers performed oral sex on a six-year-old boy to prove that no act was too horrible to commit). Calls to 911 were so numerous, Atlanta police lieutenant Scott Kreher recalls, that reports of anything but the worst violent crime had to wait, sometimes for more than eight hours. "It was very common to start the night shift with 50 or 60 calls pending," he says. In part, that's because the projects came alive at night, especially during the summer. With so few residents working, most slept during the heat of the day and came out after dark. "You'd think it was midday at midnight. Everyone was out barbecuing, partying on the porches. And you were always hearing gunfire."

All this was happening in places built to eradicate slums, whose immorality had so shocked progressives a century ago. Not surprisingly, real-estate development in the neighborhoods surrounding the projects was essentially nonexistent for decades, though the rest of the city boomed, say Atlanta development officials.

For Glover, the projects were clearly a "toxic environment" to be leveled—and she proceeded to do it. Starting with grants from the Clinton-era Department of Housing and Urban Development (HUD), and then using private financing, she reduced the city's 14,000 public-housing units to 2,000, most of them in complexes for the elderly. Gone were crime-ridden projects like Bowen Homes—immortalized in a rap lyric by the Shop Boyz: "My hood I love them ladies, / My hood I love them babies, / I can't forget my niggas, / Bowen Homes we love you baby!" Glover then leased the land to private developers, who built apartment and townhouse complexes there; in return, the developers agreed to dedicate 40 percent of the new units to tenants who qualified for public housing. Two-fifths of the projects' residents relocated to these "mixed-income" complexes. The remaining three-fifths received housing vouchers and used them to move into other private apartment buildings.[195]

The course of history can change quickly. It just requires people being granted another option outside of the continued direction of narrow political thought and debate.

Public housing units nationwide are being torn down, the concentration of Black crime and poverty no longer contained.

---

[195] Husock, "Atlanta's Public-Housing Revolution."

Your government is actively dispersing public housing residents throughout major metropolitan areas like Atlanta, Memphis, and Chicago.

It seems our government is intent on spreading *The Inferno* of public housing, by redistributing the poverty (Black people) to areas lacking the enrichment of diversity.

White America owes Black America nothing, especially those living who once lived in public housing or who now have "vouchers."

28

Black Lawmakers in Congress, DeKalb County, and Training Day: The Ethics Behind Black People in Power

August 2nd, 2012

Alonzo Harris is a character who utilizes a philosophy that has been mimicked and consumed by virtually every elected Black official in Congress and by Black officials who run major cities throughout the United States.

The fictional antagonist in the 2000 film *Training Day*, Harris is a police detective in Los Angeles who believes he owns and runs the city he is sworn to protect. Denzel Washington portrays Harris and, interestingly, he is the same actor that plays Frank Lucas in the 2007 film *American Gangster*.

It is with these two fictional characters in mind that we consider the implosion of the Black Congressional Caucus and the ethics violation that threaten to bring down many long-standing Black Congressman, whose hubris cemented their downfall:

> The House ethics committee is currently investigating seven African-American lawmakers—more than 15 percent of the total in the House. And an eighth black member, Rep. Jesse Jackson Jr. (D-Ill.), would be under investigation if the Justice Department hadn't asked the committee to stand down.
>
> Not a single white lawmaker is currently the subject of a full-scale ethics committee probe.

The ethics committee declined to respond to questions about the racial disparity, and members of the Congressional Black Caucus are wary of talking about it on the record. But privately, some black members are outraged—and see in the numbers a worrisome trend in the actions of ethics watchdogs on and off Capitol Hill.

"Is there concern whether someone is trying to set up [Congressional Black Caucus] members? Yeah, there is," a black House Democrat said. "It looks as if there is somebody out there who understands what the rules [are] and sends names to the ethics committee with the goal of going after the [CBC]."

African-American politicians have long complained that they're treated unfairly when ethical issues arise. Members of the Congressional Black Caucus are still fuming over Speaker Nancy Pelosi's decision to oust then-Rep. William Jefferson (D-La.) from the House Ways and Means Committee in 2006, and some have argued that race plays a role in the ongoing efforts to remove Rep. Charles Rangel (D-N.Y.) from his chairmanship of that committee.[196]

Undeniably, the fate that awaits Rangel and Waters—who have both been long-serving representatives of their community—is extraordinarily politically charged:

The politically charged decisions by veteran Democratic Reps. Charles Rangel of New York and Maxine Waters of California to force public trials by the House ethics committee are raising questions about race and whether black lawmakers face more scrutiny over allegations of ethical or criminal wrongdoing than their white colleagues.

The controversy over the cases and the prospect of the first simultaneous ethics trials for multiple members in more than 30 years mark the biggest challenge for the ethics committee's and the House's ability to police its own mem-

---

[196] Bresnahan, "Racial Disparity."

bers since the mid-1990s, when then-Speaker Newt Gin-grich (R-Ga.) and leaders from both parties found them-selves hauled before the secretive panel.

The question of whether black lawmakers are now being singled out for scrutiny has been simmering throughout the 111th Congress, with the Office of Congressional Ethics a focal point of the concerns. At one point earlier this year, all eight lawmakers under formal investigation by the House ethics committee, including Rangel and Waters, were black Democrats. All those investigations originated with the OCE, which can make recommendations—but takes no final actions—on such cases.

There's a "dual standard, one for most members and one for African-Americans," said one member of the Congres-sional Black Caucus, speaking on the condition of anonym-ity. [197]

Corruption is a common theme that plagues the major cities of the United States, many of which coincidentally are run by Black people. Atlanta, Birmingham, Baltimore, Washington D.C., Memphis, Newark, Detroit, etc. The list is long and dis-tinguished, regrettably for reasons that usually deal with one city's attempt to out-corrupt the others.

Once labeled the Black Mecca for enterprising young Black people, [198] DeKalb County has lost the entire luster from its shine as of late. *USA Today* ran a story promoting DeKalb County as a place to raise close-knit Cosby-like Black fami-lies. [199]

However, DeKalb County is a virtual mirror-image of Clay-ton County in Georgia, steeped in corruption both morally and economically bankrupt. Black people love DeKalb County so much, they have bestowed the government, school system, and prison facilities there with the same enthusiasm and results that every other city in America with a large Black population

---

[197] Allen and Bresnahan, "Ethics Cases Raise Racial Questions."
[198] Whitaker, "Is Atlanta the New Black Mecca?"
[199] Copeland, "Black Youths Learn."

can observe. The only problem is that DeKalb County is supposed to be the county with the most educated concentration of Black people in America.

In DeKalb County, those Black people in power enrich themselves, while the lower-level public employees are soaked in a combustible mix of low morale and anger.

DeKalb County shows us what diversity endgame is, with the elimination of White city employees' positions and the replacement of them with Black people (unlike in Clayton County, no Black snipers were positioned on the roof as fired White cops were escorted out of the building).[200]

Some of the worst performing schools in America are filled with the sons of daughters of the Black elite of DeKalb and Atlanta, who flocked to the county when Oprah said it was a great place to raise Black families.

DeKalb County was to be the subject of a study by a University of Georgia professor, who was awarded $500,000 for a four-year research project on Black adolescent development in the county (though results of the search started in 2005 have not been found yet):

> A University of Georgia education researcher hopes a new, four-year study of the experiences of African-American adolescents in a predominantly Black Atlanta suburb will help explain the reasons behind a persistent achievement gap between African-American and White students.
>
> "Adolescence is a period of time when young people are attempting to gain an integrated sense of self," said Jerome Morris, an associate professor of social foundations of education in the College of Education and a research fellow at UGA's Institute for Behavioral Research (IBR). "For African-American youth, this process can be further complicated by race, gender and class status."
>
> Morris has received a $505,000 grant from the Spencer Foundation to investigate issues of identity formation and

---

[200] Rankin, "$2 Million Verdict Sought."

negotiation in a project beginning in January 2006 called, "African-American Adolescents in a Black Suburb in the U.S. South: A Social Study of Schooling, Identity, and Achievement."

Based in DeKalb County—considered "the heart of Black Mecca" because of its burgeoning predominantly Black population—Morris' study will employ sociological and anthropological research methods to follow adolescents over a four-year span as well as evaluate the school district and county.

"By studying the school district, it will help us to understand how district policies and practices shape African-American schooling and will allow us to see the factors that surround academic engagement and promote students' success, shape identity formation and inform teachers' perceptions of African-American students," said Morris.

DeKalb County is 80 percent Black, and has a predominately African-American school board as well as an African-American superintendent. The county is at the center of the largest growth spurt of any Black community in the United States and has outpaced other Georgia counties in "Black buying power."[201]

Incredulous as what is about to be written may seem, a Black parent filed a Civil Rights complaint against the DeKalb County school system for alleged racial discrimination against Black children, though Black children comprise 85 percent of the students enrolled in the school system[202] (the dropout rate in DeKalb County is shockingly high, one of the highest in the nation for Black students in the purported Black Mecca):

A parent has filed a federal civil rights complaint against the DeKalb County School System, alleging discrimination against black students.

---

[201] News Wire Report Staff, "University of Georgia Professor."
[202] Matteucci, "Civil Rights Complaint Filed."

The parent and In My Shoes-The National Parent Education Center filed the complaint Friday with the U.S. Department of Education's Office for Civil Rights.

"The complaint is under evaluation to determine if the allegations are appropriate for OCR investigation and resolution," said Jim Bradshaw, a spokesman for the U.S. Department of Education.

The complaint alleges DeKalb's International Baccalaureate program for middle school students, which is for high-achievers, is geared toward white children, Bradshaw told *The Atlanta Journal-Constitution* on Wednesday.

"Specifically, the complaint alleges that during the 2009–2010 school year, only one middle school, located in the northern section of the DeKalb County School System, has an IB program," Bradshaw said, "and, that the predominantly non-African-American students who live in that school's attendance area were given first priority to the IB program."[203]

Even in a county like DeKalb—that professes to be home to so-called Black Mecca—do the sons of daughters of those who work in big corporations in Atlanta and pull down large salaries underperform academically as compared to the sons and daughters of White parents unable to move out a county that is now dominated by Black people.

Schools are closing there, because of large budget cuts (the children of the people who made the Black Mecca obviously couldn't expand the tax brackets there), though crime is an area of constant expansion:

"In the '80s and '90s, you said you lived in DeKalb and it was beloved," the 25-year resident said. "Now when you hear DeKalb, you say 'Oh Lord, what happened now?' "Ann Brown, president of the Belvedere Civic Club, rarely sees officers and feels crime has spiked.

---

[203] DeKalb County School Watch, "Dropout Crisis Is Statewide Problem."

"In my immediate community, we had three people mur-
dered right here; it was the most heinous thing—an infant
was killed," said Brown, a resident for 28 years. "My neighbors, the majority of whom are seniors, are afraid to be out
at a certain time after dark because of the one-on-one crime.
They're locked in."[204]

Why compare the Black United States Congressman's ethical
violations to DeKalb County?

Even in Black-Run America (BRA), the levels of abuse and
unethical activity by those in power cannot go unhidden. Every
municipality—save the heroic Newark where any drop in the
Black murder rate is cause for applause—that is run by Black
people is awash in corruption and dishonesty.

Though Black government officials do not have a monopoly
on fraud in office, it seems to accompany them in droves.

And though the belief in Black infallibility is strong, this
hubris is grounds for a cataclysmic earthquake to wipe away
the very foundations that BRA was built upon. "My nigga," as
Harris affectionately said in the film *Training Day*, will quickly
become "King Kong ain't got shit on me," as Black people turn
their backs on each other.

It is imperative that people understand the lessons that Detroit, Baltimore, Atlanta, Birmingham, and Clayton County
(let alone DeKalb County) provide, for we inch closer and closer
to the film *The Second Civil War* daily.

A cursory glance at *The Drudge Report* will provide ample
evidence as to why the conversation about race should never
begin: making White people think honestly and openly about
the racial implications of their displacement through massive
immigration and federally-mandated diversity in every corporation, government agency, ivory towers of Wall Street, and
major university (both staff and enrollment) in the nation

204 Within the Black Community, "Dekalb County Ga Sees."

means the gradually cohesion of this long-splintered group will occur.

They might live in Whitopias, but they don't think and act in those Whitopia's best interests. This is changing at a rate that should alarm those in power, for like the pivotal scene in the film *Edge of Darkness*, we at SBDPL do believe that the people in this country deserve better.

All of those in power in Black-Run America believe like the characters of Alonzo Harris and the real-life Frank Lucas that they can't lose. In areas where the ideas that are omnipresent in BRA are replaced with actual Black-dominated local governments, the belief that "we are in power and we will do what we want" is pervasive.

In the end, King Kong does have shit on you, Mr. Rangel, DeKalb County, and BRA.

29

A Man in Full: Obama's New Campaign Slogan
"We Got Your Back" Directly from the Pen of Tom Wolfe

June 2nd, 2012

The Blaze brings us a report on Obama's new campaign out-
reach to Black America (no, we aren't talking about *African
Americans for Barack Obama*, the hilarious website that is
part of the official 2012 Barack Obama campaign site), which
appears to a song straight from music catalogue of the early
2000s hit *Arrested Development*—paging Franklin Delano
Bluth.

Using the (no homo) phrase, "We got your back," the new
Obama campaign phrase would seamlessly integrate with
McDonald's 365Black campaign or Coca-Cola's pitching of
Sprite to Blacks. *The Blaze* dog whistles:

Imagine a Soul Train soundtrack combined with politics and
you have the start of President Obama's new ad targeting
blacks.

The new spot, which is set to air nationally on Tuesday,
is based on the phrase "We got your back." The phrase is
repeated several times throughout by a group of singers as
quotes form the president and Barry White-like music play
in the background.

Thegrio.com has some quotes from the ad:

"Four years ago we made history," a male announcer
says. "Now it's time to move forward and finish what we
started together. We have to show the President we have his

back." The spot is intercut with audio from President Obama's speeches, touching on familiar political and campaign themes.

"I refuse to pay for another millionaire's tax cut by kicking children off of Head Start programs; asking students to pay more for college; or eliminating health insurance for millions of poor and elderly and disabled Americans on Medicaid," the president can be heard saying in the ad.[205]

"We got your back." Don't forget to say "no homo."

All of this would be beyond parody if it hadn't already been parodied in Tom Wolfe's 1998 novel about the city too busy to hate, with *A Man in Full* providing a scene that has the exact same phrase uttered by Black people in defense of a fictional Black candidate (like Obama always hoped to become, a former National Basketball Association player) for mayor of Atlanta.

Adam Taxin, who is a writer in Philadelphia (a three-time *Jeopardy!* Champion), pointed out in a YouTube video that "We got your back," is ripped from the pages of Wolfe's (incredibly honest) look at race relations in Atlanta.

To make the plot easy to digest, let's quote from Wendy Brandes of CNN's review of the book:

> Meanwhile, Fareek "the Cannon" Fanon, a black football star at Charlie's alma mater, faces accusations of date rape after an encounter with the gorgeous daughter of one of Charlie's [Croker, the protagonist of the story] rich white pals during the Spring Break madness known as Freaknic. One of his lawyers is Roger White II, who obsesses about being called "Roger Too White" during his college days at Morehouse. White is a corporate lawyer, called in because his old frat brother, Wes Jordan, is mayor of Atlanta. Jordan has his reasons for taking interest in the plight of an inner-city black athletic star; he's facing a re-election campaign against Andre Fleet, who is urging African Americans to

---

vote for their "first black mayor" and against the "high yella" political establishment.[206]

In this scene, our light-skinned Morehouse educated lawyer (a rib by Tom Wolfe at the first Black mayor of Atlanta, Maynard Jackson?) is attending a church service in the south side of Atlanta, a predominately poor and dangerous (thus authentic) Black section of the city:

> Roger Too White expected to see Andre Fleet emerge from one of the two wings of the stage, as the choir and Isaac Blakely had. But Blakey gestured toward the very rear of the church, and everybody, including Roger Too White, turned about in his seat. There, in the aisle, level with the very last row of seats in the hall, was Andre "Blaq" Fleet. In the ranks of the National Basketball Association he had been anything but a tall man. He had played point guard for Philadelphia and the New York Knicks. He was known as a good playmaker and a good but not great outside shooter. . . . He was built in a V, from the extraordinary width of his shoulders down to his narrow waist. And he was dark. Oh yes; no question about it. He had the good looks of a Sidney Poitier, and his flawless teeth fairly gleamed against the deep chocolate of his skin. The man had good looks and then some.
>
> No sooner had Roger twisted about to take a look than Sister Sally Blankenship had plunged her two amazing hands into the Curland, and the stirring Toreador Song from Bizet's *Carmen*, that rousing refrain, was roaring forth, vibrating in every gizzard in the church and making Andre "Blaq" Fleet seem like even more of an invincible champion. He was working the crowd, reaching deep into each row, on both sides, to touch the hands that reached toward him. He wasn't the sort of politician who materialized elevated about you onstage, having just departed some unseen VIP room. Oh no; he was here among you, starting with

---

206 Brandes, "Out of Step."

the very last row, yours to see up close, to touch and hear from. Blaq Fleet had something to say to everybody, although it was doubtful that anybody could hear a word of it. Quite in addition to the organ's triumphal anthem, the cries had begun. At first: *Andre!... Andre!... Fleet!... Blaq!... Blaq! Gotcha Back! Blaq!... Gotcha back!... Fleet!... Gotcha back!...* Then cries from every quarter of the audience: *Gotcha back!... Gotcha back!... Gotcha back!...* from here, from there, from way over there and the other side: *Gotcha back!...* until it became a single, unified chant springing forth from hundreds of gullets: *Gotcha back, gotcha back, gotcha back!*

It took a few moments, but then It dawned on Roger that *gotcha back*—"got your back"—was an Atlanta street expression meaning "I'm behind you—I am your follower—and I'll protect you against attacks from the rear."

Roger wouldn't have believed it possible, but the chant continued to swell in volume as Blaq Fleet made his way down the aisle: "Gotcha back! Gotcha back! Gotcha back!"

Life in Black-Run America (BRA) is beyond parody. We just have one task before us: endure. This age will end.[207]

---

[207] Wolfe, *Man in Full*, 358.

30

Reverse the Polarity

The United States of America is nothing more than a loose confederation of present-day South Africas, with tax-paying serfs (White people) keeping alive once-thriving metropolises that, were they left to stand on their own devices, would die overnight.

Down in Atlanta, Georgia, the reality of this situation became glaringly apparent, with the overall fragility and health of the system being on full display:

In a case that rings alarm bells about race and politics in upper tiers of the Fulton County government, a federal jury has found that county officials snubbed an applicant for a director's job because he is white and male.

It ordered Fulton to pay $300,000 in back wages to former Human Services Deputy Director Doug Carl, who sued five years ago.

The sum could triple next month when a judge decides whether to add in future lost wages, pension benefits and attorneys' fees, according to Carl's attorney, A. Lee Parks.

But Fulton County Attorney David Ware said, in a written statement after the verdict last week, that Carl lost the job because he "completely blew the interview" and he expects the verdict to be overturned on appeal.

"The only reason Mr. Carl alleges that race played a part in the selection process is because the person chosen happened to be an African-American female," the county attorney's statement said. "Mr. Carl was incredulous that a black woman would be chosen over him and thus decided to accuse the county of a race-based decision."

Carl, who said he retired in 2010 after his position was eliminated, told *The Atlanta Journal-Constitution*, "I just think people should be employed based upon their merit, and not on their race.

Discrimination is wrong, period, and discrimination has no color bounds."[208]

White boys? Merit? These mean little in Black-Run America (BRA), especially in the epicenter of where many of the policies that other municipalities copied and duplicated originated. But what if Fulton County has participated in "reverse-racism" at a scale that makes Doug Carl's claim look like chump change?

A story published in early August of 2012 exposed the depths of discrimination present in the city too busy to hate:

> WND acquired the breakdown of 2012 employment for Fulton County and found that of the 4,851 full time county employees, 3,980 of them are black (82 percent). Fulton County has a population that is only 47 percent black. Of the 916 county employees who are classified as "other than full-time employees," 787 are black (85 percent).
>
> A quick breakdown of certain departments shows a trend of exclusion in Fulton County public jobs, with 86 percent of the Arts and Culture Department personnel black; 93 percent of 140 people in the Behavioral Health Department black; 81 percent of the 98 people in the County Managers Department black; 90 percent of the 65 people in the Emergency Services black; 89 percent of the 118 in the Finance Department black; of the 353 in the Health and Wellness Department, 306 are black; of the 37 people in the Purchasing Department, 100 percent are black; of the 19 in the Registrations and Elections Department, 100 percent are black; of the 150 employed in the Tax Assessor Department, 84

---

[208] Edwards, "Jury: Fulton Discriminated."

percent are black; of the 185 employed in the Tax Commissioner Department, 94 percent are black.[209]

A city like Atlanta is kept alive because of White tax dollars;
remove them, and you have the conditions that are present in
2012 Detroit. Emma Darnell is no stranger to antagonizing
White people, having behaved in the 1970s (when Mayor
Maynard Jackson was elected the first Black mayor of Atlanta)
much as the African National Congress (ANC) acted when they
took control of South Africa:

> As the mayor's administrative services commissioner, Dar-
> nell had become Jackson's battering ram on affirmative ac-
> tion, and an admired figure in black Atlanta. A graduate of
> Howard Law School, Darnell monitored city contracts to
> make certain white contractors compiled with joint venture
> requirements.
>
> Devoted in her task and headstrong in her style, Darnell
> told white contractors hoping to land city contracts, "If you
> want to do business with us I've got to see who you're hiring.
> Are you hiring minorities?"[210]

Darnell was too aggressive in her push for affirmative action
and White dispossession, and she was forced out:

> Emma Darnell, Jackson's commissioner of administrative
> services, was removed from office in 1976 and her depart-
> ment abolished, according to her statement, because white
> business leaders had viewed her as overly aggressive re-
> garding the airport's joint venture program. She claimed
> that the mayor fired her because of complaints from the
> white business community. [211]

---

[209] WND Staff, "Taxpayer Smackdown."
[210] Pomerantz, *Where Peachtree Meets Sweet Auburn*, 465.
[211] Colburn and Adler, *African-American Mayors*, 187.

But don't think that the changeover of power from White to Black (and the South African-like actions of the new Black political class) is germane to only Atlanta. Just prior to Hurricane Katrina's arrival in New Orleans, the story of mass firings by the first Black District Attorney resulted in a lawsuit against the city:

> The jury, made up of eight whites and two blacks, returned the unanimous verdict in the third day of deliberations in the racial discrimination case against District Attorney Eddie Jordan.
>
> Jordan acknowledged he wanted to make the office more reflective of the city's racial makeup, but denied he fired whites just because they were white. He said he did not know the race of the people fired.
>
> Under U.S. District Judge Stanwood Duval's instructions, jurors had to find Jordan liable if they concluded the firings were racially motivated. The law bars the mass firing of a specific group, even if the intent is to create diversity.
>
> "We thought the facts as well as the law favored us. I still maintain that I did not use race as a factor in my hiring practices," Jordan said.
>
> Jordan said the district attorney's office, which is liable for the award, cannot afford to pay the verdict. It was not immediately clear whether state or city, or both, would be responsible for paying the money.
>
> Plaintiffs' attorney Clement Donelon said he was elated. "The plaintiffs' civil rights, every single, solitary one of them, were violated," he said.
>
> The judge could order that the fired white workers be reinstated, but lawyers consider this unlikely. Such mandates are rare, as they require continuing court supervision.
>
> The whites' lawyers argued that many of those who were fired had far more experience and scored higher in job interviews than blacks who were either hired anew or kept on.

The whites testified that they found themselves jobless in late middle age, after years of working in law enforcement agencies, including the New Orleans Police Department.[212]

Were an enterprising lawyer prepared, a cottage industry for so-called "reverse-discrimination" lawsuits exists in Black-Run America (BRA). Birmingham, Atlanta, Memphis, Baltimore, New Orleans, Chicago, Philadelphia . . . the list of mini-South Africas in America is long and particularly undistinguished. They limp along on the redistribution of White tax revenue to support a Black political class (the only way to create a Black middle class is through government jobs) ensconced in power because no one dares challenge them in court.

Remember, there are no "double standards" or "reverse racism/discrimination" in BRA, only "the Standard."

Reverse the polarity.

---

[212] Associated Press Staff, "Jury Says Official's Mass."

31

Know Your Role and Shut Your Mouth:
The Coming End of Black-Run America

It will never end. No matter how many concessions one makes, no matter how many attempts to rectify racial inequities from the past (largely made-up or exaggerated), there will always be an "and then?"

Case in point in Fulton County, Georgia (home to Atlanta), where 56 percent of the residents are non-Black—44 percent being White. At 44 percent of the population, Black people will not tolerate any reductio in the public workforce that negatively impacts their seat at the position of power:

> A coalition of civil rights and attorney groups says African-American judges are being replaced by white appointees in one of Georgia's most heavily populated black counties and called Thursday for Georgia's governor to fill vacancies with judges who reflect their communities' diversity.
>
> The coalition, led by the Rev. Joseph Lowery, said black representation on the bench has decreased from 44 percent in 2002 to 30 percent. They say every African-American judge who has resigned or retired from Fulton County Superior Court replaced by gubernatorial appointment since 2002 has been replaced by a white appointee.
>
> Fulton County is 44 percent African-American, according to the latest Census figures.
>
> "We need fairness," said Lowery, head of the Georgia Coalition for the People's Agenda, as he stood on the steps of

the courthouse. "Do the right thing. We're not here to ask them for favors. We're asking them for justice."[213]

Fairness? What percentage of Fulton County public employees is non-Black? Does anyone have that information? What about City of Atlanta public employees? MARTA? Are these numbers available? What about employees over at Hartsfield-Jackson International Airport?

It wouldn't be surprising to learn that of the aforementioned public entities, 75 percent or more of the employees of each are Black.

Fairness. These words only apply to Black people in Black-Run America (BRA). Just look at this article from *Ebony* in 1989, written by Renee Turner:

> AIR travelers to Atlanta witness a spectacle that bolsters the city's image as the jewel of the New South and a showcase of Black achievement. Airplanes fly over fields of emerald pines that encircle a bustling metropolis run by Black politicians. They glide over some of the $300,000 homes of the Black elite, and land on runways built by Black firms before depositing passengers at a high-tech airport that some call America's greatest monument to affirmative action.
>
> A quarter-century after the signing of the Civil Rights Act, the city that was the setting for Margaret Mitchell's famed Civil War novel, *Gone with the Wind*, is a city that the book's heroine, Scarlett O'Hara, would not recognize. Gone with the winds of change are the Jim Crow-era "Whites Only" signs, segregated lunch counters, and laws that prevented Blacks from voting.
>
> Today, Atlanta is the benchmark of Black political and economic success—a mecca for Blacks seeking and often finding fulfillment of the American dream. Blacks and Whites exercise and network at the Downtown Athletic

---

[213] WSB-TV, "Atlanta Implements Curfew for Teens."

Club. Everything from T-shirts to coffee mugs bearing the logo of Underground Atlanta, the city's new downtown $142 million retail and entertainment attraction, are produced by a Black-owned firm, the Logo Depot. The city of nearly a half-million people is run by its second Black mayor. In fact, African-Americans, who comprise almost 70 percent of the city's residents, hold the majority of city council and county commission seats.[214]

Fairness.

How many of those glittering homes that belong to a manufactured Black elite—all due to the pernicious machinations of radical affirmative action—are now in foreclosure? Judging by the fact that a Section 8 riot erupted in South Fulton County when thirty thousand Black people overwhelmed an event to sign forms for housing vouchers *that won't be valid for years*, it should be obvious that the Black Mecca is more like . . . Africa.[215]

With great power, comes great responsibility, right? In the PBS documentary *Eyes on the Prize*, there is an episode called "Keys to the Kingdom" that profiles Mayor Jackson and what happened in Atlanta after his election in 1973. Political power, in his eyes, was about redistributing wealth (and jobs) to his community, in a move that would benefit Black people and Black people alone:

> First of all, start with exaggerated black expectations, that overnight Valhalla will be found, heaven will come on earth and it's all because the black mayor's been elected. And things just don't work that way. The obligation that I felt was to try with everything in my power and every legal and ethical way that I could to move things as quickly as possible in that direction.[216]

---

[214] Turner, "Atlanta: Gone with the Winds."
[215] Joyner, "Housing Crisis Reaches Full."
[216] PBS, "Keys to the Kingdom."

To Black people, the only responsibility of government (and elected officials) is how its actions will improve their lives. More importantly, every action, every bill, and every legal decision must be made to improve the quality of life of Black people only, even if it is to detriment of White people (and increasingly, a non-White, non-Black population).

The Blacks have abused the power that connected capitalism ceded to them in 1973. Atlanta is on threshold of a battle that will forever alter the landscape of America, if the predominately White North Fulton cites of Sandy Springs, Milton, Johns Creek, Chattahoochee Hills, and Dunwoody (potentially even Buckhead) were to push for secession, predominately Black South Fulton turns into Detroit overnight.

The ability to create a Black middle class—based on redistributing wealth to Blacks via public jobs and contracts that stipulate unfair quotas toward Black firms—would end.

You see, in Detroit, White people fled Wayne County. Though many White people fled to other metro Atlanta counties, enough wealth stayed in Fulton County since 1973 to keep the whole unfair system chugging along.

But now, that is ending. *The Atlanta Journal-Constitution* reported this on May 17, 2012:

When the Legislature passed new maps for the state House and Senate last year, Republicans gave themselves extra slices of certain counties. [217]

Earlier this month, House Speaker pro tempore Jan Jones of Milton bluntly explained the merits of the tactic to a group of North Fulton voters. From *Neighbor Newspapers*:

In January, according to Jones, there will be a north Fulton majority in both the House delegation and the Senate delegation.

Which means, "we can cut Fulton County down to size until we get Milton County," she said.

---

[217] Galloway, "House GOP Leader."

"My goal is that we reduce the thumbprint . . . of Fulton County on your lives and your pocketbooks such that in a very few years, Atlanta and south Fulton will not fight us on recreating Milton County because Fulton County will be insignificant," she said. "We will begin that process next year."

Jones said she actually thinks splitting Fulton into three counties would be in the best interest of all citizens.

"My goal is not to re-create Milton County. My goal is to end Fulton County and bring government closer to the people," she said. "But it will take convincing." [218]

Jones' comments, reported last week, are only now circulating within the city of Atlanta. They explain the motives behind HB 1052, which would have given the power to appoint two of three Fulton County representatives on the MARTA board to municipalities in north Fulton, said state Rep. Rashad Taylor, D-Atlanta.

This means the end of Actual Black-Run America (ABRA) Fulton County and Atlanta.

It was in a discussion on a proposed MARTA Bill that we begin to learn that when given great power, the Blacks will do everything possible to keep it:

Vice Chair Emma Darnell said the bill would disenfranchise the Southside. She also brought up the forming of new north Fulton cities, which she called "segregation based upon race and income."

Since 2005, three communities north of Atlanta voted to incorporate, a backlash against a perception of lackluster services and poor representation by the county government. One effect has been a higher tax rate on unincorporated south Fulton, the only area still under direct county governance.

---

[218] Kellogg, "Lawmakers Still Optimistic."

"In my district, from Bankhead to Buckhead, we have no intention of going back [to segregation]," Darnell said. "There's too much blood back there."[219]

South Fulton is one of the most violent places in America. Consequently, it's almost all Black.

For too long White people in America have been told to know their role and shut their mouth. Pay taxes that go directly to fund the proliferation of a people whose only contribution to Atlanta (and America) has been crime, increased poverty, and the degradation of formerly great cities like Memphis, Birmingham, Baltimore, and Detroit.

Now, rumblings are being heard in the city too busy to hate. A fissure is developing of catastrophic potential.

With great power came the belief that the Blacks would forever play the race card and never expect "blowback" for race-based policies that require high taxation of the private sector (White people) to pay for an almost all-Black public sector.

With great power comes great responsibility.

The Blacks have reneged on this in Atlanta. Though it might not seem that obvious yet, the coming political war in Fulton County is the start of a series of clashes around the nation, as White people begin to slowly understand the burden of high taxation goes directly to pay for public jobs and services that go toward their dispossession.

It might seem like a tax revolt, but it's the start of something much more important: the repudiation of Whites knowing their role and keeping their mouths shut.

---

[219] Edwards, "Marta Bill Blasted as Racist."

32

The Implicit Whiteness of Chick-fil-A

August 1st, 2012

The Atlanta-based Chick-fil-A fast food company is in the news today, with supporters around the nation flocking to the more than 1500 locations nationwide to show their support for the embattled organization.

"Chick-fil-A Appreciation Day" is August 1, set for "conservatives" (who confuse Christian theology as axiomatically conservative principle) to show those radical liberals pushing gay marriage a thing or two about collective consumer power from the "right."

In reality, Chick-fil-A is company that is entirely wedded to a business model completely reliant on serving communities with strong social capital and a thriving middle class. Yes, the religious aspect is important, but it is the concept of community that is fundamentally at the heart of the Truett Cathy's enterprise. As Harvard sociologist Robert Putnam begrudgingly told us, communities can only thrive when trust and high social capital are present (i.e., a lack of diversity).

Cathy, whose family lived in the first public housing unit in America (Techwood Public Housing, built in 1936 in Atlanta), was and continues to be the driving force behind the incredible rise of Chick-fil-A.

Interestingly, once Techwood Public Housing integrated (and the Whites fled), it became the poster child for "urban blight" and one of the highest crime areas in Atlanta. Of course, it was 99 percent Black—luckily, it was torn down and the Black residents scattered across metro Atlanta to alleviate the problem of centralized criminality, but do you expect an entrepreneur of the caliber of Truett Cathy ever came from 99 percent Black Techwood Public Housing?

An article from the St. Petersburg Times in 2002 points out the driving force behind Chick-fil-A's growth, but also points that three stores in the Nelson Mandela's rainbow nation of South Africa had been forced to close:

> Their company, Chick-fil-A Inc., is the country's No. 2 fast-food chicken chain, with 1,055 restaurants and $1.2-billion in revenues last year. Another 500 stores are planned by 2006. Even Warren Buffett stopped by the Atlanta company's offices recently for a chat.
>
> But Chick-fil-A has a higher calling than just chicken. "We're here to glorify God," said president Dan Cathy, who was in town this week to celebrate the opening of a $2-million store in Oldsmar.
>
> Since 1967, Chick-fil-A has juggled profit and prayer. Founder and CEO Truett Cathy, Dan Cathy's 81-year-old father, makes no bones about the fact that it's a company built on Christian principles. Chick-fil-A is the only major fast-food chain that is closed on Sundays. It spends millions each year on foster care homes, college scholarships and summer camps. Prayer is not unwelcome at the company's headquarters or stores.
>
> "I see no conflict between biblical principles and good business practice," Truett Cathy told NBC Nightly News in July.
>
> Ethics and charity are not the only arrows in Chick-fil-A's quiver. QSR Magazine recently ranked its drive-through service No. 1 in the industry. It is using cash, not loans, to finance its current growth plan, though it still has some bank debts left over from the 1990s. It possesses one of the better known icons in the fast-food world: a cartoon cow who

humorously tries to save his own skin by encouraging cus-tomers to "eat mor chikin'." (Chick-fil-A does not serve ham-burgers.)

Except for a couple hundred licensed stores in airports and on college campuses, Chick-fil-A owns its restaurants. Each one is run by a separate operator who shares the prof-its, but not the equity, with the chain. Operators like Gus Mir, who runs a store in Lakeland, put up a refundable $5,000 investment and are guaranteed a minimum income of $30,000 per year. The chain takes 15 percent of the gross revenue and half the profit. The average operator of a mall store earns roughly $70,000 a year, Dan Cathy said, while operators of stand-alone restaurants typically earn double that. Cathy said his opposition to franchising is simple. He'd rather do business with a hungry entrepreneur than a wealthy investor who is unwilling to "interview 16-year-olds."[220]

In Cathy's book, *Eat Mor Chikin: Inspire More People*, we learn quickly what type of operator of a restaurant he hopes to work with:

> Truett Cathy's loyalty to Chick-fil-A restaurant Operators is evident in the selection process. "We don't select or even seriously consider an Operator unless we want the individ-ual to be with us until one of us dies or retires," he says.

On page 97–98 of that book, we learn this:

> We expect our Operators to abide by several tenets that we adhere to:
> • People want to work with a person, not for a company.
> • Each new Operator is committed to a single restaurant.
> • Operators will hold no outside employment or business interest.

---

[220] Barancik, "Chicken with a Conscience."

- We choose Operators for their ability and their influence, so we want them in their restaurants.
- We expect quality interaction between Operators and team members.
- We expect quality interaction between Operators and customers, both in the restaurant and in the community.

Finally, on page 111–112, Mr. Cathy explains:

Most (Operators) . . . feel that this is more than just a job. They feel either a divine call or the satisfaction of a desire to make a difference in the world. They contribute greatly to the development of teenagers who work in our restaurants, creating a wholesome atmosphere in which to work and modeling positive leadership traits that teenagers will take into their adult lives. Our Operators consider themselves to be mentors to the next generation.

Chick-fil-A isn't McDonald's. It isn't Burger King. It certainly isn't Coca-Cola, which has no problem with what a community looks like that it peddles it products in, as long as the consumers there can purchase an abundant amount of Coca-Cola. Chick-fil-A owners/operators are the type of people who are instrumental in building solid communities and as serving as leaders and uniting their towns.

Whereas McDonald's is one of the world's largest owners of real estate, the surrounding values of the neighborhood (and strength of those communities) and overall property value is nothing compared to the locations where Chick-fil-A carefully selects to move into and serve.

Interestingly, Chick-fil-A corporate Web site actually has a store locator function where you can look up the location of restaurants.

Texas has the most locations (263). Naturally, Georgia has the second most Chick-fil-A locations (196), with North Carolina, Florida, South Carolina, Alabama, Maryland, California,

Tennessee, Virginia, and Pennsylvania all having more than fifty stores.

Looking at the location of Georgia's 196 locations is striking how those "thriving communities with high social capital" that Chick-fil-A Owners/Operators invest are incredibly and overwhelmingly White. Those that were first opened in Clayton County when it was 90 percent White in the 1980s are outliers, with Riverdale, Jonesboro, Morrow, and Forest Park heavily Black and those that were "grandfathered in" in East Point— the restaurant, in some cases a fabled "Dwarf House," being remnants of past civilization while the surrounding area becomes littered with liquor, title loan stores, and pawn shops.

By controlling for certain variables, it became a comedy of errors in seeing where Chick-fil-A decides to open up stores. Hospitals weren't counted, nor were malls, considering that they have a tendency to go from catering to a majority White clientele to a majority Black clientele in a matter of years.

Some highlights:

- Small Dawsonville, Georgia (population 619 according to the 2000 census) can have a Chick-fil-A; of course, the city is 97 percent White and zero percent Black.
- Georgia's population breakdown is 55.9 percent White and 30.5 percent Black.
- 137 restaurants were located in majority-White areas.
- 16 restaurants were located in majority-Black areas, with 75 percent of those in cities that were majority White when the restaurant was constructed.
- Despite the famed Historically Black Colleges and Universities (HBCU) located in Atlanta, only one Georgia HBCU has a Chick-fil-A—Albany State. Georgia Tech (62 percent White, 6 percent Black); UGA (80 percent White, 8 percent Black); West Georgia (78 percent White, 20 percent Black); Valdosta State (76 percent White, 20 percent Black; Berry College (92 percent White, 1 percent Black); Kennesaw State (69 percent White, 13 percent Black); and Mercer University in Macon (72 percent White, 17 percent Black).

- Hiram, Georgia, a town that is 60 percent White and 40 percent Black, has a Chick-fil-A location opened in zip code 30141—which is 91 percent White and 7 percent Black.
- A Chick-fil-A location opened in zip code 30341 (which is 85 percent White and .84 Black), is located in Clayton County . . . a county that is roughly 70 percent Black.
- The majority of the Fulton County Chick-fil-As (outside of hospital or one at Georgia State University) are in North Fulton; an area that is overwhelmingly White.
- Chick-fil-A locations thrive in Alpharetta (72 percent White, 11 percent Black), with four separate locations; Peachtree City (87 percent White, 6 percent Black) with three locations; McDonough (76 percent White, 19 percent Black) with three locations; Roswell (81 percent White, 9 percent Black) with two locations; Kennesaw (64 percent White, 22 percent Black) with three locations; Flowery Branch (80 percent White, 10 percent Black) with two locations; Fayetteville (77 percent White, 20 percent Black) with two locations; Snellville (89 percent White, 5 percent Black) with two locations; Suwanne (84 percent White, 6 percent Black); and Newnan (84 percent White, 12 percent Black) with two locations.
- The Chick-fil-A in majority Black Madison, Georgia is located in a zip code (30650) that is 64 percent White and 34 percent Black).
- Strangely, few majority Black areas (virtually none in South Fulton County, and only one—Lithonia—in a majority Black zip code in DeKalb County) have Chick-fil-As.

The question has to be asked now: based on the empirical evidence we have garnered from a look at the 196 Chick-fil-A locations in Georgia (wait, we forgot the one at Greenbriar Mall in DeKalb County, one of the oldest Chick-fil-A locations that closed because the mall went all-Black. When it opened in the late 1970s, the county was roughly 75 percent White . . . now it's only 35 percent White), is the business model of Chick-fil-A . . . racist? Does it conform to the methodology that Steve

Sailer laid out in his concept of the Affordable Family Formation (cities with Chick-fil-As tend to actually have thriving communities)? Should the Department of Justice look into the locations of Chick-fil-As because of some sort of disparate impact in where they open, considering that the clientele that owners/operators tend to cater too is overwhelmingly White?

Chick-fil-A is reliant on strong communities (which, coincidentally, means White communities) to exist and prosper. Outside of Chick-fil-As in areas that went from majority White to majority Black (thus, grandfathered in), the company has a business model that can be accurately described as "racist" (using modern parlance) and shouldn't just be under assault because of the company's stance on homosexual marriage.

As noted in Chick-fil-A, Coca-Cola, and Cobb County over at *VDARE*, the cultural wars were already over in the 1990s, largely because people didn't realize the importance of the so-called "right" needing to actually fight back.

Seeing how "conservatives" have rallied around Chick-fil-A today is interesting, because it showcases how they could actually win—and win quickly if they dared defend their interests.

But it is the inherent racial reality of Chick-fil-A that will becoming increasingly important to recognize in the coming years—those cities and communities with Chick-fil-As are the ones that have an abundance of social capital, precisely because trust and cohesion (low crime, good schools, clean streets—all things that White America produces) exist.

The tenets that Cathy expects Chick-fil-A owners/operators to live by are not the same values of Coca-Cola, McDonald's, Burger King, Arby's, or other fast food companies that peddle poison to consumers and who care little for the community they serve.

Coca-Cola versus Chick-fil-A . . . it is the values that drive these two companies that underscores the battle against Black-Run America (BRA).

A true defense of Chick-fil-A is a defense of the communities that the owners/operators choose to do business in; based on the analysis of the 196 locations in Georgia, they look like an America that is quickly dying; replaced with communities that have virtually no social capital.

33

White People Are the Real
"Walking Dead" in Atlanta and America

February 13th, 2012

It is in *The Walking Dead* web episodes (based on AMC's immensely popular *The Walking Dead*) that tells the tragic story of how Hannah—the iconic half-eaten "walker" from the first episode—met her demise that I realized the zombie phenomenon means much more than meets the eye. Hannah, the divorced White mother of two children, lives in Cumming and ultimately sacrifices herself to a swarm of zombies so that her children might reach a safe zone.

There are six, two-to-four-minute web episodes that detail the first moments after the zombie outbreak begins to break down civilization around Atlanta. One can only imagine that the horror, fear, dread, and false sense of hope that the characters felt in these *Walking Dead* Web episodes was the exact same mixed of emotions that White residents of Detroit felt in 1967, when Black people waged a war on the city that they still haven't quite finished.

In the duration of the episodes, we learn that the emergency broadcast is heard on every channel, the power eventually goes, a hopelessly Disingenuous White Liberal (DWL) relies on his untouchable White neighbor for guns to protect his family, a military helicopter is seen overhead advising all citizens to get to the "green zone" and make it to Atlanta for safety. But it is in the harrowing episode six that we see Hannah sacrifice herself so that her children can survive.

In real life, it is every White parent who moved to the suburbs of Atlanta (and out of every major city where the Black Undertow makes raising a healthy family an unlikely—and expensive—task) that has ultimately sacrificed their happiness and well-being for the safety of their children.

No one wants to spend two hours of every one of their working days commuting up and down 400 North and South, I-85 North and South, I-75 North and South, I-20 East and West, or spend deadening hours circle Atlanta on I-285. But White people do, and for one simple reason: to live and die in communities free of the Black Undertow.

Every suburb of Atlanta owes its existence to the Black Undertow in Fulton County, whose government sits uncontested in a city that the *New York Times* dubbed "the center of Black entertainment."

It is in Atlanta that we see the true power of the Black Undertow effect, as suburbs that rest close to the heart of Fulton County—the first, like Clayton, Gwinnett, DeKalb (the Prince George County of the South), Rockdale, and Newton County, to enjoy the fruits of White flight—are now undergoing real "climate change."

Atlanta's "climate change" accelerated after a Black riot in 1966, one that *Taki Mag*'s Jim Goad discussed in *Blight of the Living Dead*:

> When Atlanta blacks rioted in 1966 and chanted things such as "black power," "white devil," and "kill the white cops," MLK described it as "the desperate language of the unheard." When Vine City blacks smashed windows in white-owned stores in 1967, apparently egged on by a "crudely lettered handbill" claiming that "White peope [sic] own our stores. White people own the housing we live in" and urging rioters to "Clean up Atlanta tonight," the remaining white residents in The Bluff heard the "desperate language" loud and clear—nearly all of them left. A "civil-rights" movement

ostensibly aimed at desegregation merely resulted in reseg-regation—this time both racial *and* economic. The Bluff is now 97 percent black. A pie chart of its racial breakdown looks like Pac-Man eating the world. It is also overwhelm-ingly poor.[221]

It was not only Atlanta that suffered when Black people nu-merically took over the city; the Great Migration of Black peo-ple from South in the 1910s–1930s brought the same problems to Detroit, Cleveland, New York City, Philadelphia, Chicago, and other Northern cities. Now, their failed descendants, hav-ing economically burdened these cities, head back to the South, primarily to the suburbs of Atlanta.

Those lily-White suburbs, the ones that Black elected offi-cials in Fulton County wish to see declared "illegal," have the highest property value. Those majority Black ones, like Riverdale (only 20 years ago a majority-White drifter colony in Clayton County) have the lowest property values in all of Geor-gia. It was in Clayton County where we saw a glimpse of what happens on the Day the EBT Card Runs Out.

It was in another former drifter colony that we saw a thirty thousand-person Black riot over Section 8 Housing Vouchers (College Park).

If you've ever wanted to understand why Atlanta's suburbs almost reach Tennessee (head up 1-75 North); Alabama (head down 1-85 South); or South Carolina (drive up 1-85 North), it's all due to a desire to avoid living near Black people.

During the past ten years, a trend has emerged of young White people moving back into the city, while Black people flock to Black Undertow areas in metro Atlanta where property value has begun to depreciate, because of the steady demo-graphic replacement of the White people who made the suburb prosperous in the first place. As we saw in the collapse of three Atlanta-area school systems, whenever Black people are the

---

[221] Goad, "Blight of the Living Dead."

majority of a school district, you'll inevitably have to wait for Superman to appear if you want to see academic success:

> Atlanta itself has actually grown whiter in the past decade while its suburbs have gotten blacker, according to Frey's analysis. Atlanta's population in 1990 was 67% black and 30% white; the suburbs were 71% white and 25% African American. By the end of the decade, non-Hispanic whites made up 39% of the city and 53% of the suburbs while blacks were 51% of the city and 31% of the suburbs.
>
> "You have the young, white, single professional who's willing to take a new job in the city, live in a condo or apartment, and walk or take the bus to work," says Doug Bachtel, a demographer at the University of Georgia. "The growth of the African-American population in the suburbs is due to changing policies associated with housing discrimination. It's not a matter of race, it's social class. There are some gated black communities in (suburban) Cobb County."[222]

Property value is intrinsically tied to the academic performance of the children in the school system. The Whiter the school district (think Fayette County), the higher the property value. The Blacker the school district (think Fulton County), the lower the value. Inner-city Atlanta property value is, well, embarrassing. It is only the Northern (nearly all-White) suburbs where value continues to increase.

The story of Hannah from *The Walking Dead* takes place off of Old Mill Road in Cumming. Were it safe to raise a family in Fulton County, living way out in a Whitopia wouldn't be necessary. But people's experience of living in areas with high concentrations of Black people have helped remove the dogmatic teachings of equality. When you see "climate change" transpire, all illusions of racial equality die.

---

[222] Copeland, "Georgia's Black Population Outgrows."

Fayette County, which borders Clayton County (perhaps only rivaled by Wayne County in Michigan for its sorrowful nature), is on the chopping block next.

Where will White people flee next? Considering that Atlanta is one of the worst metro areas for construction growth, its apparent that little capital remains for new drifter colonies. Or little demand, as metro Atlanta has also seen some of the highest job loss in the nation. Worse, Atlanta had some of the worst housing depreciation in America during 2011.[223]

All of this is happening as Black people (replicating the Great Migration) move back South from Northern cities they ruined. Inevitably, housing prices will continue to fall in Metro Atlanta as the school systems become Blacker. Many have wrongly placed the hopes of Atlanta's resurgence on White people moving back into the city, but the recent Atlanta Public Schools fiasco (where Black principals and Black teachers knowingly conspired to cheat and raise Black test scores) makes this unlikely.

But one recent story highlighting the collapse of commercial real estate shows why the hope for an economic revitalization of Atlanta is misguided. The iconic Bank of America building's recent foreclosure, the South's tallest building, tellingly shows us the future of Atlanta:[224]

With the forced public auction yesterday of Bank of America's signature 55-story office tower in Atlanta, the U.S. foreclosure crisis—commercial division—just got significantly worse.

Atlanta's troubles and those of other cities, say experts, are the result both of overbuilding and of the issuance of commercial mortgage-backed securities (CMBS) that inflated office building prices. Nationwide, some $5.8 billion worth of five-year office loans, bundled into CMBS, must now be refinanced. With all that debt coming due, experts

---

[223] ABC, "Zillow: Atlanta Home Prices."
[224] Trubey, "Bank of America Plaza."

predict, more distressed properties will soon come to market, and the price per square foot of commercial office space will continue to fall.

"It's a fine building, a beautiful building, and still very much a landmark," Atlanta real estate expert Kirk Diamond, speaking to Bloomberg News, said of the former Bank of America Plaza. "It just needs to be recapitalized."

The tallest tower in the U.S. Southeast went for $235 million at auction, after landlord BentleyForbes had missed mortgage payments. BentleyForbes bought the building from Bank of America Corp. in 2006 for $436 million.

More than 25 percent of loans on commercial buildings in Atlanta that were bundled into bonds are delinquent, the highest rate of the largest U.S. metro areas, according to data compiled by Bloomberg.[225]

Atlanta's fate is sealed. The suburbs will get Blacker as Black refugees from cities they (and their ancestors) helped ruin return back South. Crime will rise, corrupt city officials will get elected (primarily on the promise of shooing away White people), and school systems will collapse into the miasma of all-too-frequent Black failure when compared to White standards.

Considering that it is largely White taxpayers being fleeced via taxation to support the overwhelmingly Black government of Fulton County (and the many publicly-funded Black job programs, like MARTA) it is no wonder that secession movements are afoot. And yes, they are 100 percent racial.

The Walking Dead is about a zombie apocalypse set primarily in Atlanta. In the first season, we learn that the outlying metro Atlanta citizens were told to seek safety in downtown Atlanta. As real-life crime figures show us, heading into downtown Atlanta is one of the worst ideas imaginable, regardless of if a global zombie apocalypse is occurring or not.

Atlanta is the city where the full force of Black-Run America (BRA) is being played out. Unlike Detroit, where Black people

---

[225] Farnham, "Bank of America Tower Foreclosed."

have largely remained in the inner city, Black people are filter-ing out into the Metro Atlanta suburbs, laying economic waste to every city they become the majority population in. Those same suburbs that once opposed MARTA's expansion because it would bring shiftless Black people into their midst know are majority-Black Undertow cities (Clayton County).

White people—like Hannah in the Web episodes of *The Walking Dead*—are the real walking dead of Atlanta, in all of America. They exist to be taxed to pay for entitlement pro-grams that primarily benefit the expansion of a class of people who have been at war with them for sixty years.

Add the growing Hispanic population into the equation, and you begin to see that the days are numbered for Whites. Or so it would seem.

It has long been my belief that Atlanta will be the city where we see the unraveling of Black-Run America (BRA). How that happens is anyone's guess, though the continued drumbeats for secession by majority-White cities and suburbs from Fulton County is a positive sign of what is coming.

White homeowners in counties quickly going majority-Black—whose mortgage is now underwater thanks to this Black migration—might decide to just walk away from their home, and move away from the South. Time will tell.

Until then, those White people who spend wasted hours of their lives commuting to and from their Whitopia homes, will continue being *The Walking Dead*. It is pronounced in Atlanta, but this goes for any drifter colony citizen in America.

You are the walking dead, and the federal government of the United States is out to ensure that your future is like that of the zombie menace in *The Walking Dead*.

34

The Funeral Pyre Has Been Built:
Effects of Minority Mortgage Meltdown Become Clear

June 11th, 2012

In his review of my book *Escape from Detroit: The Collapse of America's Black Metropolis* at AmRen, Gregory Hood notes this:

> Dreary as this all is, I believe it is cause for optimism. As Mr. Kersey says, "History is about to begin again." In some of the largest cities in the country, the system is beyond salvation. This offers new opportunities for changing the debate and starting a new movement that might just save the white race—and keep the streetlights on. Detroit is hopeless—and that should give us hope.[226]

Hope. In 90 percent Black Detroit, there is no hope. As noted in a PK column at *VDARE* today, acceptable public debate has been incapacitated on the subject of the real reason behind Detroit's monumental collapse: to even broach the racial correlation to Detroit's demise in the public sphere would allow the genie to escape from the proverbial bottle that has been sealed shut by the most effective example of bipartisanship in the history of American politics.[227]

---

[226] Hood, "End of an Illusion."
[227] Kersey, "Robert Putnam, The Detroit Corollary,."

One of the main inspirations behind the launch of SBPDL was Steve Sailer; I've long hoped he would finally get around to writing the book on his concept of the Minority Mortgage Meltdown (MMM) and was upon looking at *The Drudge Report* today that the reality of the folly of the MMM hit. *The Washington Post* reports:

The Great Recession wiped out nearly two decades of Americans' wealth, according to government data released Monday, with middle-class families bearing the brunt of the decline.

The Federal Reserve said the median net worth of families plunged by 39 percent in just three years, from $126,400 in 2007 to $77,300 in 2010. That puts Americans roughly on par with where they were in 1992.

The biggest drops occurred among middle-income Americans, whose wealth was inextricably linked to the housing market boom and bust. Meanwhile, the wealthiest families actually saw their median income rise slightly.

"It's hard to overstate how serious the collapse in the economy was," said Mark Zandi, chief economist for Moody's Analytics. "We were in freefall."

The survey, conducted every three years, painted a portrait of consumers still under significant duress: Though Americans made progress in paying off their credit cards, the median value of family debt did not change between 2007 and 2010. The percentage of families saddled with debt greater than 40 percent of their income also stayed the same. More families reported being behind on their bills.

The implosion of the housing market inflicted much of the pain. The value of Americans' stake in their homes fell by 42 percent in those three years to just $55,000. The poorest families suffered the biggest loss of wealth from the drop in real estate prices. But middle-class Americans rely on housing for a larger part of their net worth. For some, it accounts for just over half of their assets.

That means every step downward is felt more acutely.[228]

Forty percent of their wealth is gone. Middle Americans. White people. Hard working, honest, law-abiding people who do most of the living and dying in this country; who pay the brunt of the costs (and lost opportunity costs) of real "climate change"; who commute long distances just to give their children the chance to attend schools that are located in safe, orderly Whitopia's; who have now seen a 40-percent drop in equity in their homes.

It was in 1988 that *The Atlanta Journal-Constitution* would publish Bill Dedman's first part of *The Color of Money* a multi-part series that purported to show evidence of discrimination by banks in lending to the Black community.

In 2000, the U.S. Department of Housing and Urban Development published a study called "Unequal Burden in Atlanta: Income and Racial Disparities in Subprime Lending," describing the Dedman's study this way:

> a series of Pulitzer Prize winning articles about the geographic disparity in mortgage lending between black and white neighborhoods in Atlanta. *The Atlanta Journal-Constitution* series revealed that in 1986, Atlanta lenders originated six times more home purchase loans per owner-occupied housing unit in predominantly white as in predominantly black neighborhoods. A recent study concluded that although there had been improvements during the 1990s, disparities in lending between black and white neighborhoods continue to persist in Atlanta.

Wait, so all *The Color of Money* showed was that White people actively sought home loans in greater numbers than Black people did in Atlanta? Well, yes. Somehow, this equals discrimination, even though Atlanta's Black community was (and still is) perhaps the poorest in the nation. Banks have a responsibility to lend money (which was deposited by individuals) that will

---

[228] Mui, "Americans Saw Wealth Plummet."

have the greatest potential of being paid back—to make money for the bank and its shareholders.

Black people always were (and always will be) a huge credit risk.

Here's what Dedman wrote in *The Color of Money*:

"We're talking about disinvestment, capital flight from the Southside," said Sherman Golden, assistant director of the Fulton County Department of Planning and Economic Development. "When the banks disinvest, the governments also find themselves disinvesting. To accommodate the growth on the Northside, all the public funds flow north. Southside residents put money in the bank and pay taxes, but their money is spent on the Northside."

Although the Journal-Constitution study focused on middle-income neighborhoods, the results concern groups working to solve Atlanta's shortage of decent housing for the working class and the poor.

"As long as they won't lend in Cascade Heights, I don't know how we'll get them to lend in Cabbagetown or Ormewood.

Whites receive five times as many home loans from Atlanta's banks and savings and loans as blacks of the same income—and that gap has been widening each year, an *Atlanta Journal-Constitution* study of $6.2 billion in lending shows.

Race—not home value or household income—consistently determines the lending patterns of metro Atlanta's largest financial institutions, according to the study, which examined six years of lender reports to the federal government.

Among stable neighborhoods of the same income, white neighborhoods always received the most bank loans per 1,000 single-family homes. Integrated neighborhoods always received fewer. Black neighborhoods—including the mayor's neighborhood—always received the fewest.[229]

---

[229] Kovach and McCutchen, eds. *The Color of Money*, 1.

Basically, what Dedman wrote here is this: Black people didn't seek out loans, but they should get them anyway. To make mat- ters worse, banks in Atlanta pooled money together to offer low-income people (Black people) low interest loans. The AJC would proudly report:

Last summer, after a series of newspaper articles about ra- cially unequal patterns in home mortgage lending, several black real estate agents and five white bankers met one morning to discuss what could be done.

The bankers, shaken by the bad publicity, were eager to reach out to the black community. But what struck Miller Johnson Jr., a broker with Citywide Realty Associates Inc., was that they had very little idea how to do it.

"They didn't know where the Atlanta Daily World was. Now, how were they going to reach blacks without advertis- ing in a black newspaper? I told them (it was on) Auburn Avenue, and one asked where that was," Mr. Johnson said. The street, historically the spine of black commerce in At- lanta, was a block from where they were sitting, in the First American Bank's Peachtree Street office.

The past year has been an education for Atlanta's lend- ers. Since May 1988, when *The Atlanta Journal-Constitu- tion* reported that whites received five times as many home loans from Atlanta's banks and savings and loan associa- tions as blacks of the same income, lenders have taken a number of steps toward better serving the black community.

Through four special lending programs, nine banks have lent nearly $45 million to more than 850 homebuyers in tar- geted low-and moderate-income areas. The $20 million At- lanta Mortgage Consortium (AMC), one of the largest lend- ing pools, has hired a black-owned public relations firm. Several of Atlanta's majority-owned banks have had their first meetings with the all-black Empire Real Estate Board and have acted on some of its recommendations. One bank sent its employees on a guided tour of the mostly black

Southside and adopted a blighted neighborhood, Pitts-burgh.[230]

Later that year, Dedman would pen an article titled "Federal study finds bias in lending across nation" that purported to doc-ument discrimination in lending in not just Atlanta, but all of America. It wouldn't be until 1993 that this study was released (Dedman's article appearing in 1988, citing an "unreleased" federal study), and it would take two enterprising journalists from Forbes to quickly squash the already entrenched notion of "discrimination." Peter Brimelow noted in a column at Mar-ket Watch in 2008:

> I really did co-write the first one, for Forbes magazine on Jan. 4, 1993. The Federal Reserve Bank of Boston had just published a study purporting to prove definitively that mortgage lenders were discriminating against minorities, the hot cause of the day.
>
> But when my brilliant co-author, Leslie Spencer, asked the Boston Fed's research director, Alicia H. Munnell, what minority default rates were, she said proudly that census tract data showed that they were equal to whites. When Leslie pointed out that this actually proved there was no discrimination, because the lenders had somehow weeded out the credit risks down to the same acceptable level, Mun-nell was dumbfounded and had to concede (on tape) that she did not, in fact, have definitive proof of discrimination at all. (here's a link to the actual *Forbes* article, The Hidden Clue)[231]

Flash forward to 2012: North Fulton has been paying 80% or more of the taxes to support South Fulton County (home to the Southside of Atlanta, perhaps the collection of the poorest Black people in all of America—a reflection of their innate abil-ities to operate in either a white or blue-collar world) for scores

---

[230] Kovach and McCutchen, eds. *The Color of Money*, 62.
[231] Brimelow, "Another Case of Collusion?"

of years. Now they are on the verge of trying to secede and form their own county.

That same US Department of Housing and Urban Development study would report that in the 1990s, some pretty drastic measures went into effect to ensure Black people in Atlanta got a piece of the American Dream:

The importance of subprime lending to minorities and low-income Americans, which is documented in what follows, demonstrates how important it is to these communities that subprime lending not include any lenders engaging in predatory practices.

1. From 1993 to 1998, the number of subprime refinance loans originated in Atlanta increased by over 500 percent. The number of refinance mortgages reported under HMDA by lenders specializing in subprime lending in the Atlanta metropolitan area increased from 1,864 loans in 1993 to 11,408 in 1998.

2. Subprime loans are three times more likely in low-income neighborhoods in Atlanta than in upper-income neighborhoods. In low-income neighborhoods, subprime loans accounted for 21 percent of all refinance loans originated during 1998—compared with only 11 percent in moderate-income neighborhoods and just 6 percent in upper-income neighborhoods. In the poorest communities, where median family income is 50 percent or less of the area median income, subprime refinances accounted for 43 percent of all refinance loans.

3. Subprime loans are almost five times more likely in black neighborhoods in Atlanta than in white neighborhoods. In predominantly black neighborhoods in Atlanta, subprime lending accounted for 33 percent of home refinance loans originated during 1998—compared with only 7 percent in predominantly white neighborhoods.

4. Homeowners in moderate-income black neighborhoods in Atlanta are almost twice as likely as homeowners in low-income white neighborhoods to have subprime loans.

In 1998, only 9 percent of homeowners in moderate-income white neighborhoods have subprime refinance loans while 27 percent of homeowners in moderate-income black neighborhoods have subprime loans, which is almost double the 14 percent of homeowners in low-income white neighborhoods who have subprime loans.

In addition, a recent study by Abt Associates of foreclosures in Atlanta found that foreclosures of mortgages originated by subprime lenders have substantially increased since 1996—while the overall volume of foreclosures in Atlanta declined by 7 percent between 1996 and 1999, the volume of foreclosures started by subprime lenders grew by 232 percent. As noted earlier, this increase in foreclosures in the subprime market occurred amidst a trend of rapidly increasing subprime lending.

What does all this mean? It means that Bill Dedman's reporting helped usher in the Minority Mortgage Meltdown, because no one bothered to challenge him. The nobility of the Black person who wasn't even seeking a home loan was far superior to the bank or S&L, which wasn't even aware it needed to lend to this borrower.

Now, more than 50 percent of the mortgages in metro Atlanta are underwater. The AJC reported:

For the fifth year in a row, metro Atlanta home prices are down—way down, according *The Atlanta Journal-Constitution*'s yearly analysis of home prices and sales.

The median sale price dropped nearly 15 percent across the region in 2011, to $115,000 from $135,000, the data shows. By a separate measure, Atlanta's price index has now dropped almost 40 percent from its peak, to the same level it was in 1996.

And in a further sign of the region's dysfunctional housing market, the price drop came even as overall home sales rose sharply in 2011, the most recent full year of data, and inventory fell.

Prices typically rise with stronger sales. But metro Atlanta's prices are being pushed lower in part because foreclosures and low-end homes dominate sales, accounting for
about half of all transactions in some areas.[232]

And as the percentage of Black people living in metro Atlanta
counties rises, the market will see even greater drops in home
values, eventually rivaling Detroit. Just look to Clayton and
DeKalb County for a glimpse of this future.

The funeral pyre has been assembled for what we have
dubbed Black-Run America (BRA): fittingly, it rests in a city
that General William T. Sherman once burned to the ground.

One can only guess what the net worth of your average
metro Atlanta White family has plummeted to over the past
three years as Black people flock to live in the Black Mecca,
attracted by minority contracting positions mandated by both
Fulton County and the City of Atlanta (not to mention Hartsfield International Airport)?

White America owes Black America nothing. Nothing.

Policies enacted by the federal government and mandated
for compliance by big mortgage lenders (lowering income re-
strictions, down payments, and credit-worthiness for a home
loan) to ensure that Black (and other non-White) home buyers
got a taste of the American Dream has ended in what Sailer
calls the Minority Mortgage Meltdown.

That bipartisan refusal to talk about race is about to end.

---

[232] Quinn, "Home Sales Up."

35

Real American Hero:
Billy Corey's War Against Black-Run Atlanta

June 15th, 2012

Alright, let's now look back to 2010. *The Atlanta Journal-Constitution* reported this:

A federal jury on Monday awarded $17.5 million in damages to an Atlanta businessman who claimed the City of Atlanta and Hartsfield-Jackson International Airport illegally steered a lucrative indoor advertising contract to a competitor with deep political connections.

The verdict, which came after nearly eight hours of deliberations, called for Billy Corey and his company, Corey Airport Services, to receive $8.5 million in compensatory damages, to be paid in thirds by the city, Clear Channel Outdoor Inc. and businesswoman Barbara Fouch.

The jury also awarded Corey $9 million in punitive damages. Clear Channel was ordered to pay $8.5 million and Fouch $500,000.

The verdict was an embarrassment for Hartsfield-Jackson and City Hall that recalled the political maneuvering and outright corruption that came to symbolize the operation of the airport during the 1980s and 1990s.

The city said it will appeal Monday's verdict.

Corey charged the city violated his rights and its own bidding rules in awarding the contract to Clear Channel and

Fouch, its minority partner, whose business interests at the airport go back to 1981.

Cronyism. It will always be part of the human experience. But racial cronyism, of a variety that deprives a city (even the Black Mecca) of additional revenue . . . well, only in BRA would this be tolerated. The AJC reported during the trial:

> The former general manager for Hartsfield-Jackson International Airport testified in a federal trial Monday that former Mayor Bill Campbell barred her from bidding out an airport advertising contract because he didn't want his politically connected friend to lose it.
>
> Angela Gittens, airport general manager from 1993 to 1998, said Campbell rebuffed her attempts to solicit bids for the lucrative indoor billboard contract and the two got into a "heated" argument over the issue, she said in a videotaped deposition.
>
> The mayor's friend, Barbara Fouch, is a minority partner with Clear Channel, which still controls indoor billboard advertising at Hartsfield-Jackson.
>
> "At some point, the mayor told me not to bid it out, not to tender it," Gittens testified, recounting a 1996 conversation with Campbell. "She was a friend of his and he did not want her hurt."
>
> Fouch, Clear Channel, the city and the airport are defendants in the federal lawsuit filed by Corey Airport Services in 2004. Gittens was the plaintiff's final witness.
>
> Owner Billy Corey charged that Fouch's cozy relationship with Atlanta City Hall led to the woman securing the contract when it was rebid in 2002.
>
> Campbell, who went to federal prison for two years before his 2008 release, could not be reached for comment. Fouch's billboard advertising interests at the airport go back to 1981. She partnered with a firm that eventually was acquired by Clear Channel.[233]

---

[233] Paul, "Ex-Airport Manager Claims."

It was a policy started by Jackson that Mr. Corey challenged in federal court, and initially won. Just what did that policy entail?

> In Atlanta, it was the construction of the city's airport almost 25 years ago, and the desire to give minority-owned businesses a hand in obtaining lucrative construction contracts, that caused then-mayor Maynard H. Jackson Jr. to begin the city's first race-based preference program.
>
> At the time Jackson instituted the first set-aside program, less than 1 percent of contracts in Atlanta went to minority-owned businesses. Today, under the leadership of Mayor Bill Campbell, the city has an established goal of committing 35 percent of all contracts to minority contractors.[234]

So since roughly 1974, the city of Atlanta has been creating an artificial class of Black millionaires, at the same time disenfranchising potential entrepreneurs because of the color of their skin. Didn't some God King say we should only judge by the color of one's content? Wasn't Atlanta his hometown too?

Back to the future. The AJC reported on June 4th:

> A federal appeals court tossed out a jury verdict in favor of Corey Airport Services in the company's longrunning dispute with the Atlanta airport and one of its contractors.
>
> The 11th U.S. Circuit Court of Appeals said Monday that Corey's "conspiracy claims" involving an advertising contract it failed to win were too vague.
>
> Corey, which lost the contract in 2002, claimed the city of Atlanta and Hartsfield-Jackson International broke the law by steering the contract to a competitor with political connections, Clear Channel Outdoor Inc. One of its principals, Barbara Fouch, was a longtime friend of the late former Mayor Maynard Jackson.

---

[234] Hanson, "Set-Asides for Insiders Only."

After a federal jury agreed and awarded $17.5 million in damages to Corey, the city last year settled its share with Corey for $3.9 million and admitted no wrongdoing. The appeals court ruling effectively vacates the portion of the damages that were to be paid by Clear Channel and Fouch.[235]

Could this whole incident be headed to the Supreme Court of the United States? Look, the amount of money wasted on just one airport over a near 40-year time span (the money left on the table because of racial cronyism—which blinded the Blacks in charge of Atlanta from actually utilizing the bidding process for garnering the most beneficial and lucrative deals) could have been used in far more realistic manners. Like, the repatriation of Black people from some of the nation's worst public housing in the inner-city of Atlanta . . . the once crime-free and virtually all-White suburbs of Atlanta.

For now.

But the Billy Corey experience (thus far) with the Judicial Branch of the United States is illustrative of just who the government favors, and just who the government wants to promote. Any and all discrimination against White people in the present will be justified on the grounds of past discrimination against Black people (and increasingly every "disadvantaged" group real or made up); and all future discrimination against White people will be justified as merely the logical conclusion of Operation Poetic Justice: what Whitey did to the Amerindians, we now do to you.

An article by Dale Cardwell of the *Neighborhood News* (uh-oh, a North Fulton newspaper!) nailed it when he wrote this:

As for the jury wanting to rectify that corrupted Atlanta bid process, the court added, "The letting of municipal contracts ought not (sic) regularly be the start of a federal case. . . . Governments must have more leeway than that in conducting bid processes for their contracts."

---

[235] Yamanouchi, "Appeals Court Tosses Judgment."

Yes, Atlanta—with its rich history of bid rigging and airport contract corruption, in this court's opinion, needs
MORE "leeway" in conducting bid processes.

It's no small coincidence Atlanta is caught up in another
round of controversy regarding airport contacts. Once again,
the city has awarded millions to connected individuals in
the name of protecting disadvantaged businesses; only for
the public to discover after the fact—the contracts were
awarded to incredibly wealthy, politically connected individuals who fail to meet the disadvantaged standard. Even
more frightening, is the precedent this court's decision HAS
created. . . . What citizen will dare spend $5 million and
eight years fighting for his or your constitutional rights—
when a three judge panel can wipe out a unanimous jury
verdict—delivered by everyday Americans?

God bless Billy Corey, and how he tried to protect us—
from the 11th Circuit Court of Appeals.[236]

Political winds can change quickly; understand that the City of
Atlanta has been run as a post-apartheid South Africa since
Maynard Jackson was sworn in as mayor back in 1974. The
city implemented what became the blueprint for affirmative action programs nationwide Black mayors took over a city and
began hiring only Black people for public positions and insti-
tuting mandatory percentages of contracts to go to minority-
owned firms). Here's what *The New York Times* published in
1989:

Georgia's highest court, relying on a recent United States
Supreme Court decision on affirmative action, today overturned a widely copied program that has guided Atlanta
construction contracts to minority groups.

The State Supreme Court ruled that the program, which
sets a goal of 35 percent minority participation in city-financed construction contracts, failed to meet the standards

---

[236] Cardwell, "Column: Judges Affirm."

of a United States Supreme Court decision in January involving a similar program in Richmond, Va.

Mayor Andrew Young, reacting to the decision, said he would immediately impose a moratorium on letting any new contracts for city construction.

The Georgia court stopped short of saying that such racially based efforts as the program, the Minority Female Business Enterprise plan to broaden participation in city contracts, were unconstitutional and violated the state's own equal protection law. The court's decision read: "Rather, assuming without deciding the M.F.B.E. is constitutional on its face, we apply a strict scrutiny standard."

Using that standard. which was also applied in the Richmond case, the court said that Atlanta officials had failed to produce "convincing evidence" of discrimination to justify the program. They also failed, the court said, to create a program "narrowly tailored" to eliminate the discrimination the officials said had existed.

To many advocates of affirmative action, the decision was as much a blow to such programs as was the United States Supreme Court decision in the Richmond case. Atlanta was termed by one official of the National Association of Minority Contractors as the "granddaddy affirmative action programs."

Atlanta's program has been credited with increasing minority participation in city contracts to more than 35 percent today from less than 1 one percent in 1972. The city's Office of Contract Compliance said that in 1972 members of minority groups held about $40,000 of contracts totaling $29 million. Last year they had contracts for $33 million of a total city construction program of $80 million.

The Gains Made in Atlanta

When it was started in 1973 by Maynard Jackson, the city's first black mayor, it was initially applied to expand Hartsfield International Airport. The airport was competed within the allotted time and under its budget. Goal Is 35% Participation The program sets a goal of 35 percent participation by women, blacks, Hispanic people and Asians on all city-financed projects. Rodney Franklin, the city's chief compliance officer, said that did not mean a quota. He pointed out that goals in participation were waived when it was clear that they could not be reached.[237]

Here's what *The New York Times* would publish in 1996 regarding affirmative action and the Atlanta Olympic Games:

All across America, affirmative action has been chased into retreat by lawmakers and judges. But here in Atlanta, the private corporation that is staging this summer's Olympic Games has awarded almost a third of its $387 million in construction and vending contracts to companies owned primarily by minorities and women.

Experts on affirmative action say such numbers are unheard-of in the private sector. But to city leaders, the commitment to minority participation is a reflection of a political reality so entrenched that it has come to be known as "the Atlanta way."

Twenty-two years ago, after Atlantans elected Maynard H. Jackson Jr. as their first black Mayor, the city pioneered the practice of encouraging joint ventures between white-owned companies and those with minority or female owners. Two decades later, even as such programs elsewhere are being attacked as reverse discrimination, Atlanta's political establishment still embraces affirmative action with enthusiasm.

"Everybody who is a person of color in this country has benefited from affirmative action," said Mayor Bill Campbell, the third black to lead a city that is now 67 percent black. "There's not been anybody who's gotten into a college on their own, nobody who's gotten a job on their own, no one who's prospered as a businessman or businesswoman on their own without affirmative action."

---

[237] Smothers, "Atlanta Affirmative Action Plan."

"The sad truth in this country, the sad truth even in the city of Atlanta, is that without our affirmative-action programs, our minority businesses would wither."

In 1973, the year Mr. Jackson was first elected, a tenth of a percent of the city's contract dollars went to companies with minority and female owners. Last year, the figure was 40 percent, exceeding the goal of 36 percent the city had set by statute. And these companies tend to have far more minority employees than do white-owned companies. (Black-owned companies here get far more business than do those owned by women or other minorities.)[238]

The sad truth is this: even with massive amounts of affirmative action, metro Atlanta (and the city of Atlanta and Fulton County) is still plagued with some of the greatest disparities of wealth between Blacks and Whites in the nation. And this is just a reflection of nature's cruel joke on a world that still doesn't want to laugh at the punchline.

But in the actions of Billy Corey (and subsequent reversal by the 11th Circuit Court of Appeals), those who can see can laugh. This whole system could come crashing down literally overnight.

That's how fragile it is.

---

[238] Sack, "Atlanta Leaders See Racial."

36

A Murder in Midtown:
What Brittney Watts's Murder Symbolizes

July 16th, 2011

You see their faces in newspapers, local news reports, and on the Internet. Collateral damage in the unending civil rights struggle to permanently create Black-Run America (BRA). That's all. You wonder if these poor souls—in their final seconds on earth—grasped what was happening to them, that their death would not become a celebrated textbook martyr moment galvanizing one community and creating unimaginable guilt in another.

That their life was essentially meaningless and their death just another statistic.

I have one friend who was shot by a Black guy on his college campus, an attack that had no motive. I've never been acquainted with someone who would ultimately lose their life at the hand of a Black individual or known someone who lost a close friend the same way. All of this changed last night, when visiting the city too busy to hate, I received a text from a dinner companion who was running late, reading, "One of my friends was killed by a Black guy in Midtown."

Immediately, I thought of all the times I've told people to take precautions in cities like Atlanta, New York City, Chicago, and other places, only to be scoffed at and told that I'm "ignorant" for thinking that way. Well, if ignorance has the ability to keep you alive because you can assess threats and under-stand criminal patterns, so be it.

Atlanta is probably the number one city in the south that young, college-educated White people gravitate to and start their professional careers in. The bars in Midtown, Buckhead, and the Virginia Highlands are basically an extension of the college fraternity and sorority experience, with unbelievably beautiful White girls slutting it up and bar hopping in a city with a distinctively Black criminal problem.

So you'll understand that upon receiving this text last night at one of the trendy restaurants in Buckhead—with White girls slutting it up in short dresses in one of the only safe enclaves of the city and pathetic White guys in Bama Bangs hoping to notch another score on their belt—that I lost my composure.

Here's the story:

Atlanta police released new information Friday evening on the arrest of a security guard charged with killing a woman and wounding two other women in Midtown.

Police announced the arrest of 22-year-old Nkosi Thandiwe shortly after 6 p.m.

According to an APD news release, the suspect released he had been identified by investigators, so he contacted an attorney and later turned himself in.

Police said Thandiwe worked as a security guard in the same building at 1170 Peachtree Street where the three women worked. The building is directly across the street from the parking deck at 14th Street and Crescent Avenue where the shootings took place at around noon.

Thandiwe is being held at the Fulton County Jail on one count of murder and two counts of aggravated assault.

Investigators say Thandiwe ambushed 26-year-old Brittney Watts by opening fire and killing her.

Investigators said one of the surviving victims was shot in the back and the other was shot in the ankle. Both were taken to Grady Memorial Hospital in stable condition.

Police said they believe Thandiwe shot the women as they headed to the parking deck in the Proscenium building.

Police have not released a possible motive for the shoot-ings.[239]

Brittney Watts went to Roswell High School and had a full life ahead of her. As my dinner companions walked into the restau-rant—where a multitude of young White people engaged in pointless banter while consuming copious amounts of drinks all around us—I could see the remnants of tears in her red-dened eyes.

I imagined at that moment that that was the same look so many family members and friends in the City Too Busy to Hate had over the loss of Watts. I realized that those melancholy eyes were the same that Carter Strange's parents had, and the hundreds, thousands, tens of thousands, hundreds of thou-sands of swollen, reddened eyes that people have had in cities all across the country because someone they loved was harmed in a random, senseless altercation with a Black person.

Trying to make sense of the moment, I looked around the restaurant at the tables of happy, complacent White people—all dressed like the former fraternity and sorority members they still aspire to be—and realized that any one of them could have been in Watts's shoes.

Dying for no reason in a parking garage of an Atlanta park-ing garage, shot through the neck at the hands of some Black security guard, Watts's death symbolizes the futility of gentri-fication in the City Too Busy to Hate.

It was a moment like that night that I sometimes wish I could have taken the blue pill so many years ago, and just gone back to talking about the Braves game or discussing the finer points of Harry Potter's latest film battling for the rights of muggles everywhere.

I found a way to not let the reddened eyes of one of Watts' friends impact me: to block them out entirely and drown in a

---

239 Watson, "Triple Shooting Suspect Waives."

sea of booze and sexual hedonism like the rest of the people in the restaurant. But I can't do that. Watts could have been my sister—she could have been your sister—or a cousin or a good friend. Or a daughter.

May the day come when the guilt finally ebbs from our hearts and minds and we no longer feel sorry for the plight of Black people nor make excuses for the criminal nature of a larger percentage of their population. It's not our fault.

37

"Obama's Son" Nkosi Thadiwe Targeted Brittney Watts for Being White

April 10th, 2012

Brian Nichols wanted to start a race war, believing that Black males were being unfairly incarcerated by an evil society bent on maintaining White supremacy. In actuality, it's just Black people's (primarily Black males') predilection for breaking the law that sees them incarcerated in such disproportionate numbers.

It appears that the accused killer of Brittany Watts (who also targeted two other White females) had delusions of racial grandeur similar to those of Nichols:

Channel 2 Action News has learned new information about a possible motive in a deadly midtown shooting from last summer.

Police said a woman was killed and two others injured when a security guard went on a shooting rampage in a parking lot. Channel 2's Dave Huddleston obtained the 43-page lawsuit from the case that was filed in state court April 5. The documents show that race may have played a role in the shootings.

The sound of gunfire echoed off midtown buildings July 15. When it was over, marketing executive Brittany Watts had been shot in the neck and killed. Police said the shooter, security guard Nkosi Thadiwe, took off in Watts's car and fired a gun, randomly shooting two more—Lauren Garcia, who was paralyzed, and Tiffany Ferenczy.

Nine months after the shooting, lawsuits have been filed against the defendant, the security company he worked for, Allied Barton, and the owners of the building where the shooting took place.

They said Thandiwe demonstrated an intensely negative attitude toward another race, which was unnamed. About a month prior to the shooting, Thandiwe had an altercation with a visitor with the parking garage.

Documents state he assailed a visiting courier with racial epithets and had to be physically restrained by company personnel from striking and causing harm to visitors.

Company officials, lawyers and shooting victims declined to comment on the matter.

But attorney Musa Ghanayem, who is unaffiliated with the case, gave his legal perspective.

"I saw where there were a couple of instances prior where they have red flags come up; that Mr. Thandiwe has some issues as a security guard," Ghanayem said.

Thadiwe is still in Fulton County jail. His defense team has asked the court for a mental evaluation. According to documents found before the shooting, there was another act of violence, Huddleston reported.[240]

For those wondering, Thadiwe is a Black man. He looks like Obama's hypothetical son.

Watts is dead and no one cares. The story of the murder of Brittany Watts has been buried in the black hole that is Atlanta in much the same manner as are the continuous assaults on White Georgia Tech students by Black people.

The story of Watts being gunned down hit me hard.

And now, the second battle of Atlanta begins. This time, we wage war with a pen.

Brian Nichols hoped to start a race war, yet this was not covered by the mainstream media. Thadiwe targeted three

---

[240] WSB-TV, "Court Records Show Race."

White girls in Midtown Atlanta because of their race, and the silence of that same MSM (even the Atlanta press), while outrageous, is tragically expected.

The privilege of being White indeed.

Brittany Watts will never have the chance to enjoy being a wife; a mother; a grandmother. How many other voiceless, now lifeless, citizens of Atlanta are in the same position?

She could have been any White girl who grew up in the metro Atlanta area, safe in one of the Whitopias that surround the Black Mecca of America. Moving to Atlanta to start her career and family, her life was taken in a moment of racial hate that doesn't fit the politically correct narrative for a "hate crime" in Black-Run America.

38

The Atlanta School Scandal After a Year:
Chamber of Commerce (a.k.a. Conservatism, Inc.)
Doesn't Want to Know

July 12th, 2012

There's a possibly apocryphal story featuring longtime Coca-Cola president Robert Woodruff—although the direction Atlanta took afterwards seems to confirm it.

In the early 1950s, in a smoke-filled room at the exclusive Piedmont Driving Club (the all-White club for the Atlanta WASP elite that Jay Gatsby couldn't have bought his way into), Woodruff supposedly made an announcement: the Old South was dying. Integration was coming. There was no use resisting the end of segregation, Woodruff supposedly said. Capitalism must be colorblind—to ensure that Atlanta led the way for the "New South."

Looking around the room, he asked that a vote be taken by public show of hands: those for integration, and those opposed.

The men who raised their hands in opposition had their names jotted down by one of Woodruff's Coca-Cola flunkies.

Woodruff's goal from that point forward: to ostracize them— to see that their businesses and commercial endeavors failed.

This story is unconfirmed. But it is indisputable that, for example, Woodruff strong-armed Atlanta's White business community into attending (White) mayor Ivan Allen's banquet in honor of Martin Luther King, Jr. upon King's being awarded the Nobel Peace Prize in 1964. Realizing that if respectable

Southern society didn't attend, the national mainstream media would embarrass Atlanta (and by extension Coca-Cola), Woodruff made it known through his subordinates that he favored the dinner.[241]

Woodruff and Atlanta's White business elite aimed to stay wealthy by protecting the image of the city "too busy to hate"— fostering outside investment and attracting talent to staff the Fortune 500 companies that called the metro area home.

Secure in their upscale economic gated community, they simply did not care how inept and corrupt the Black-ruled city of Atlanta became.

Six decades later, and almost forty years after the election of Atlanta's first Black mayor, the charade continues.

Exactly one year ago, it emerged that the very White Atlanta Chamber of Commerce was complicit in covering up the very Black Atlanta Public Schools (APS) cheating scandal—the systematic falsification of test results that involved teachers, principals, and apparently even APS Superintendent Beverly Hall. Farcically, Hall had been named 2009 National Superintendent of the Year by the American Association of School Administrators' National Conference on Education, largely after being hyped by overeager White business leaders hoping to promote an image of Atlanta that would be inviting to outside investors.

The scandal had been first exposed in *The Atlanta Journal-Constitution* and was finally confirmed in July 2011 by a special investigation ordered by Georgia's then-Governor Sonny Perdue after he rejected the district's own whitewashing report.[242]

Prior to Hall's fall from grace, the Chamber of Commerce in Atlanta had been touting Superintendent Hall as the Superperson that Black children had patiently waited for. White business leaders from Delta Airlines, Georgia Power, GE, UPS,

---

[241] Pendergrast, *For, God, Country, and Coca-Cola*, 282.
[242] Vogell, "Investigation into APS Cheating."

Home Depot, and Coca-Cola all considered Hall a great investment who would help bridge that notorious "racial gap" in
achievement—and, more importantly, continue Woodruff's policy of keeping the pig that is Atlanta's race relations slathered
in lipstick.

In a devastating follow-up story, *The Atlanta Journal-Constitution*'s Alan Judd showed the extraordinary lengths members of the respectable White community went to cover up the
scandal:

> In February 2010, some of Atlanta's top business leaders re-
> alized they had a problem.
>
> For a decade, they had aligned themselves with Beverly
> Hall, the superintendent of Atlanta Public Schools. They
> willingly accepted Hall's story line of rebirth in an urban
> school system. They promoted and sometimes exaggerated
> Hall's achievements—for her benefit and for their own.
>
> State officials, though, were suggesting gains by Atlanta
> schools resulted from widespread cheating. Suddenly, the
> deal between Hall and the business community took on
> Faustian overtones.
>
> The way business leaders responded underscores their
> complicity in creating the façade of success that hid a decade
> of alleged wrongdoing, an examination by *The Atlanta Jour-
> nal-Constitution* shows...
>
> The city's chamber of commerce and another business
> group took control of the district's investigation last year
> into irregularities on state-mandated tests. Executives at
> the Metro Atlanta Chamber set the parameters of the in-
> quiry and largely selected the people who ran it. Later, they
> suggested ways to "finesse" the findings past the governor.
>
> Business leaders published opinion pieces and letters to
> the editor defending Hall before cheating inquiries were
> complete; calls for the superintendent to resign, they said,
> could undermine the district's progress. And just as they
> had lobbied almost a decade earlier to give the superinten-
> dent more autonomy from the Board of Education, this year

they sought new power for the governor to remove recalci-
trant board members.

A memo drafted by a chamber executive on Feb. 15 last
year laid out the hazards that a cheating investigation
might unloose:

"This issue has serious implications—on Dr. Hall's reputation and career, for the principals and administrators who
perhaps let lapses occur in testing procedures, and most importantly for the children who may be missing out on critical
remediation," said the memo, obtained recently by the AJC.

But, the document continued: "It also has implications
on the business community, many of whom . . . are heavy
investors, and on the economic development community
who touts the superintendent and school board's recent
awards as best in the nation."[243]

For more on how the White business community was complicit
in hiding the embarrassingly Black APS scandal, see "How biz
community dealt with APS scandal" by Maria Saporta in *Atlanta Business Chronicle*[244] and left-wing loony John Sugg's
"The 'Atlanta Way' failed a generation of children: The city's
business elite were complicit in Beverly Hall's con" in *Creative
Loafing.*[245]

The enrollment of APS is currently 79 percent Black and 12
percent White. (Needless to say, the sons and daughters of Atlanta's White elite going to private schools like Marist and
Westminster). The teachers, school administrators, and principals behind the cheating scandal were virtually all Black.

Jim Goad commented on *TakiMag*:

"Principal Diane Quisenberry noted that the investigation
seemed to be targeted exclusively at African-American
schools. Principal Carla Pettis suggested the whole kit 'n'

---

[243] Judd, "Major Execs Invested in Hall."
[244] Saporta, "How Biz Community Dealt."
[245] Sugg, "'Atlanta Way' Failed."

caboodle was a cynical front to conceal white folks' racist urge to retake the predominantly black city of Atlanta.

Since they—and not I—were the ones who brought up this culturally touchy subject, I will note that every picture I've seen of every educator named in this report is of African ancestry. And many of the teachers' names—lively handles such as SuJuana, Raqketa, Chynel, Tremelia, Denethia, Lucious, Lashaine, Sheretha, Cernitha, Kwabena, Tiffonia, Lesma, Ketchia, Letrecia, Tabeeka, Cawanna, Lucrelia, and Jamesia—likewise suggest that sub-Saharan genetics are involved. [See the official report, PDF 828 pp.][246]

It was overwhelmingly Atlanta and other majority-Black counties that showed testing irregularities.

But a year after first being reported, the Great Atlanta School Scandal has completely disappeared down the Orwellian Memory Hole.[247] No one has been prosecuted. Twelve of the accused have just been allowed to return to work, provoking former state Attorney General Mike Bowers to say of APS: "They haven't learned a thing."[248]

Meanwhile, *The Atlanta Journal-Constitution* investigated other extreme test score swings in major cities, finding signs of cheating in Baltimore, Dallas, East Saint Louis, Detroit, Los Angeles, Houston, and Mobile.[249] The AJC calls these "urban school systems." But, of course, they are all overwhelmingly Black.

And last month, Birmingham School System (98 percent Black enrollment) was taken over by the state of Alabama because of corruption. Like Atlanta, virtually all the teachers, administrators, and those on the district's governing board are Black.

Nevertheless, the scandal in Atlanta has evoked barely a murmur from those who still expect Superman to appear and

---

246 Goad, "Won't Get Schooled Again."
247 Scott, "Nation's Biggest Cheating Scandal."
248 Rankin, "Special Investigators Question APS."
249 AJC Staff, "Cheating Our Children."

magically save American education—which, curiously, only needs to be saved for Non-Asian Minorities [NAMs]; Whites and Asians are doing just fine.

What the APS scandal teaches us is not that Black children can only close the "racial gap" by cheating or that Black institutions tend to be corrupt. That much was already known.

Instead, what the APS scandal teaches us is this: the descendants of those White elites who signed on to Woodruff's vision of Atlanta, and the White businessmen who moved to the city and run Fortune 500 companies, are irrevocably wedded to a governing philosophy that excuses Black failure and Black wrongdoing in any manifestation.

And the APS scandal further teaches us that this elite will, with calculated malice aforethought, cove up any such Black failure and Black wrongdoing.

These are the people who fund Conservatism, Inc. for the political cover it provides them—which is why no Conservatism, Inc. mouthpiece that I can find has discussed the Atlanta Chamber of Commerce's disgraceful role.

Only one year later, the biggest test cheating scandal in American history can no longer be mentioned—for it is a proof that establishment educational policy, and much of our current social order, is based upon a lie.

But, in the proud tradition of Coca-Cola's Robert Woodruff, we can just cover up this fact and smile. Better yet, have a Coke *and* a smile.

That's the Atlanta Way.

39

Will Both Clayton and DeKalb
County Lose K–12 Accreditation?

December 19th, 2012, VDARE

Remember all those old commercials for LifeCall, where an old woman has fallen to the floor and hilariously quips, "I've fallen and I can't get up?"

This commercial came to mind when reading of the latest trials and tribulations—self-inflicted wounds—befalling both DeKalb and Clayton County in the metro Atlanta area, particularly the K–12 school systems.

Clayton County—home to some of the first Chick-fil-A restaurants and to its founder, Truett Cathy—was 90 percent White back in 1980. Today, the county is 70 percent Black. With these racial changes have come property devaluations, tax base erosion, the shuttering of businesses, and the election of a permanent Black power structure within all levels of government.

Famously, the first Black sheriff in 2006 fired all the White police officers and had them marched out of the main station with snipers positioned on the roof.

As you can imagine, this new Black political elite took over the management of the school system, too. In 2008, Clayton County became the first school system in forty years to lose it accreditation. Schools that were once all White were now al-most exclusively Black.[250]

As the New York Times reported in 2008, five members of the Clayton County Board of Education were terminated. All were Black. The residents who filed the complaint that led to their removal: all White, perhaps worried that further degra-dations to the school systems reputation would harm the prop-erty value of their homes.

Flash forward to 2012. Clayton County is once again poised to lose its accreditation. *The Atlanta Journal-Constitution* re-ported on September 25 that the Southern Association of Col-lege and Schools (SACS)—an accrediting agency that deter-mines the value of a high school diploma to prospective col-leges—sent a letter to the system, warning that the "school board infighting, micromanaging, and grandstanding" could lead to yet another revoking of accreditation.[251]

It should be pointed out that out of 51,348 students enrolled in K–12 in 2008, 70 percent were Black, 16 percent Hispanic and five percent were White. By 2010, the school system was still 70 percent Black, but was 19 percent Hispanic and only four percent White. More troubling: in 2008, 79 percent of the students were eligible for free/reduced lunches; by 2010, that number was 85 percent.

Understanding that the health of the public K–12 school system is one of the primary young families decide to invest in a community, you should understand why a terminally ill school system frightens away both potential homebuyers to Clayton County but also outside capital in the form of desper-ately needed investment in new business.

Clayton County's school board has nine members.[252] Seven are Black, two are White. Dr. Pam Adamson, one of the Whites on the school board, is the board chair, and has appealed to the

[250] Brown, "Georgia School System."
[251] Badertscher, "SACS Sends Warning Letter."
[252] Clayton County Public Schools "About" page

governor of Georgia to step in and remove some of her fellow members before disaster hits the system:

> The chairwoman of the Clayton County school board says the governor may need to intervene and remove some school board members to save the school system from losing accreditation again.
>
> "We've had troubles on the board. We've had troubles for a long time," Chairwoman Pamela Adamson told *The Atlanta Journal-Constitution* Wednesday.
>
> The school system of about 51,000 students lost accreditation in 2008, prompting then-Gov. Sonny Perdue to remove four of the nine school board members for infighting, micromanagement and other governance issues.
>
> Kesha Williams, 18, said she considered leaving the district when it lost accreditation in 2008, but her parents wouldn't move from their house around the corner from the school.
>
> Losing accreditation has the potential to hurt both students and school systems. Graduates' chances at college acceptance—especially out of state—can be diminished when their diplomas are from unaccredited schools. It also can tarnish a community's image, particularly with business prospects, who see a good school system as a quality of life issue for employees.[253]

The perception of Atlanta being a majority Black city with a ring of solidly White suburban counties the outgrowth of White flight—is, well, outdated.

As is the belief in endless opportunity and prosperity within these suburban counties; with the racial changes from majority (almost monochromatic) White to majority Black—or majority-minority—counties like Clayton, Gwinnett, and DeKalb have reverted back the type of communities that White people fled

---

[253] Badertscher, "Clayton School Board Chairwoman."

when Blacks became the majority in Atlanta in the late 1960s and early '70s.

Back in 2004, the AJC published a piece by Kevin Duffy that included this quote:

> In Clayton, blacks also feel that they can "participate in the political process," according to Obie Clayton, chairman of the sociology department at Morehouse College. The County Commission will have two more black members come January, for a total of three, including the new chairman. And seven of the nine school board members next year will be black.[254]

Looking at the state of Clayton County in 2012, it should be painfully obvious the type of "political process" that manifests in a democracy where Black people are the majority.

The lesson of Clayton County's metamorphosis from almost all-White to a permanently declining Black county is simple: once the demographic threshold is past and Blacks can democratically elect their leaders, these individuals will fight exclusively for the majority (i.e., Black) interests.

Or as Detroit's racially contentious Mayor Coleman Young said, "I'm Black first, a Democrat second."

Whites don't want to learn this game. Instead, they'd rather move to another suburb, another all-White county where "the schools are good, property value is high, crime is non-existent, and business is flourishing." The reason such an environment, the unmentionable Whiteness, can never be stated.

Clayton County is, for all intents and purposes, a "sunk cost" that all able White residents are fleeing.

DeKalb County, long pegged as one of top counties in America for Black people, is near that same category.

In a previous chapter, I pointed out that unincorporated of both Fulton and DeKalb were incorporating, in what will hopefully emerge in the next year as a drive for secession and the

---

[254] Duffy, "Blacks flock to Clayton County."

forming of a new county. One of the reasons can be found in a study of the Atlanta Public Schools cheating scandal.

The other? High rates of taxation in the majority White areas by DeKalb and Fulton County government to ensure that millage rates there produce more tax revenue.

Like Clayton, the DeKalb County school system is in danger of losing its accreditation. With a majority Black school board, SACS is now investigating[255] claims of "mismanaged oversight of the system and ignored key financial responsibilities."[256] Attempts to bar the public from meetings of the board have only intensified the fears of parents and questions from SACs.

The DeKalb County K–12 enrollment is 71 percent Black and 10 percent White, though we aren't supposed to mention this fact.

It wasn't that long ago that DeKalb County was almost 90 percent White.

White flight from the county and the school system meant that the Black population of the K–12 DeKalb school system went from 6% to more than 47% between 1969 and 1986. It's at 71% Black now.[257]

White people are free to flee from areas that become "diverse," but that doesn't mean that that area is then from the consequences of diversity.

The metro Atlanta area stands as testament to the folly of the overturning of restrictive covenants. White people, who will abandon the communities and counties they created out of the farmland (a directly result of the Black takeover of Atlanta and Fulton County) of Georgia, and search new pristine land to participating in a rinse and repeat of the same process.

What do they leave behind? In the case of Clayton and DeKalb County, something that we can't mention.

But it ties back to the LifeCall commercial: once White people leave and Black people have assumed political control of a

---

[255] Tagami, "Accreditation Agency to Investigate."
[256] Tagami, "DeKalb school board draws scrutiny."
[257] Education Law, "Freeman v. Pitts."

county, it won't be long before, "help, I've fallen and I can't get up!" is heard.

Or, in the case of the Fayette County School Board, why aren't we in charge yet?

Fayette County's fight to preserve its election system has turned into a costly legal battle that voting rights attorneys say Fayette won't likely win.

The NAACP contends Fayette's at-large voting methods, which means some candidates must run countywide for seats on the county commission and school board, has diluted African-American voting strength.

Fayette's case pits 10 African-American residents against the county's long-held political structure that until recently was set up around militia districts dating to the mid-1800s. The 10 African-Americans—lawyers, pilots, accountants and other longtime residents—aren't the first to try to change Fayette's at-large voting system. There's been a coalition of whites and blacks dating back nearly 20 years that has tried to get the county to move to district voting which they say would be a more equitable system. Fayette is 21 percent African-American.

The case now awaits a federal judge's decision which is not likely to come until next year. The school board, which also was a part of the suit, attempted to settle with the NAACP but that settlement was overturned after the judge learned the county had not agreed to the settlement. The school board is now bound by the outcome in the NAACP's suit against the county.

The NAACP thinks the Fayette system of election is dated.

"The country has now twice elected an African American to serve in the highest office in the land," Ryan Haygood, director of the political participation group of the NAACP Legal Defense Fund in New York. "And yet in a state that is incredibly racially diverse, the Fayette County Commission has dug its heels in and fully committed itself to an electoral scheme that no African American will be elected countywide."

Horgan said the current election method does not discriminate. And he says African-Americans benefit from the decisions of an all-White council.

"Nobody can say how being a black person you're not getting anything," said Horgan, who lives in the north end of Fayette county. "The roads get repaired just as any place in the county. . . . Show me where are you not getting representation?"[258]

An all-White School Board has propelled Fayette County to one of the top school systems in all of America; though that might have something to do with boasting an enrollment of students that once hovered near 90 percent White.

To answer Mr. Hogan's question, though: look to Atlanta Public Schools, DeKalb County, and Clayton County for the type of leadership on the school board and the city council that you get when White people are replaced with Black people.

---

[258] Joyner, "Fayette Spends $225,000 Fighting."

40

Billy Payne, Augusta National, and
the End of the All-Male Golf Club
(Also of Freedom of Association)

August 23rd, 2012

A strange, anti-climactic ending to what once was the most talked about story in golf transpired on Monday: the "glass ceiling" at Augusta National, home of the golfing world's most prestigious event, the Masters, was shattered when two women were finally admitted as members to the exclusive private golf club.

The eunuchs at ESPN erupted into euphoric ecstasy as a horrible reminder of gender discrimination was finally ended, with the announcement that female financier Darla Moore and Conservatism, Inc.'s favorite Black female minority Condoleezza Rice had accepted membership invitations.

Throughout the day, ESPN's never-ending show *Sports Center* proudly boasted about the Iron Curtain keeping women, Title IX, and— ultimately—Progress out of Augusta National. Featured columnist Rick Reilly asserted that this "should have been done 40 years ago."

Oddly, Reilly didn't make this point in any of his *Sports Illustrated* columns (such as *A Three Rings Master*, April 21, 2003) during the 2002–2003 war on Augusta National that feminist Martha Burk and *The New York Times* waged together. At the time, he was dismissive of the whole feminist thing.

As Steve Sailer just noted, this garnered 40 (forty!) news stories, columns, or editorials from The Old Grey Lady denouncing the private club for bigotry, oppression, and persecution. [*The New York Times' Augusta Blog,* By Jack Shafer, *Slate,* Nov. 25, 2002,]

Perhaps it was the me-too "tweet" sent out by Senator John McCain—who told South Carolinians in 2000 he was in favor of the Confederate battle flag, only to apologize for the *faux pas* later—that epitomizes the entire Augusta National fight to remain exclusively male: "Congratulations to Augusta Nat'l for joining the 21st century."

The 21st century, McCain (or his tweet-staffer) apparently believes, will be a cultural Marxist nirvana in which petty bourgeois values like freedom of association will be not merely illegal but pathologized.

Earlier in the 21st century that the former chairman of Augusta National, Hootie Johnson, received a letter from Martha Burk inquiring about admitting women. *Sports Illustrated* reported his famous reply:

"We do not intend to become a trophy in their display case," Johnson wrote of Burk and the National Council of Women's Organizations. "There may well come a day when women will be invited to join our membership, but that timetable will be ours and not at the point of a bayonet."[259]

Master of his Universe, by Alan Shipnuk, April 7, 2003

But Hootie was replaced as chairman in 2006 by Billy Payne, formerly chief executive of the Atlanta Committee for the Olympic Games (ACOG), the man who brought the 1996 Olympics to Atlanta. Ominously, the *New York Times* ran a flattering piece on Payne in 2007, introducing the new chairman of Augusta National as a southern gentleman who would have fit in nicely at the Piedmont Driving Club with long-time Coca-Cola President Robert Woodruff. Reading between the

---

[259] Shipnuck, "Master of His Universe."

lines, you get the feeling that Payne was put in place to apply that bayonet and usher in the progressive 21st century:

> How might Payne handle the membership question?
> [St. Luke's Presbyterian Church Minister Christopher A] Price, who continues to share church services with Payne, said he was not sure how the new chairman might address the membership issue.
> "I'm looking forward to seeing that myself," Price said. "There is an awful lot, the sex and racial issues, women and minorities; it's a very tough thing he's getting into."
> "I think everything Billy does will be a reflection of his integrity, of his faith, and how he understands it."[260]

Interestingly, Payne had earlier unsuccessfully attempted to have both the men's and women's golf event at the 1996 Olympics played at Augusta National (and, paradoxically, bringing gender integration to the club six years before the Burk-*New York Times* blowup).

But Mayors Maynard Jackson and Andrew Young and Black nationalist city council members were upset that Payne would dare suggest the playing of an Olympic sport at a venue where Black people were, once, barred from being members.

The *New York Times* joined in, noting that Augusta's first Black member— Ron Townsend—was only admitted in October 1990. In its account, Billy Payne was on the defensive:

> "Besides, we'll be running the tournaments. When we open up this prestigious course to both sexes and to all races and religious backgrounds, black inner-city kids are going to see blacks, Indians and Asians playing on a course that is so magnificent, so beautiful."
> "They're going to say, 'I don't have to grow up to be 6-foot-10 to play basketball,'" continued Payne, who is white. "They can play golf."

---

260 Hack, "For Payne, Leading Augusta."

The issue has already divided politicians in Georgia—along racial and geographic lines. The Atlanta City Council this week unanimously passed a nonbinding resolution urging the U.S.O.C. and the I.O.C. not to select Augusta as the host course for the Olympic competition. Councilman Bill Campbell, the sponsor of the resolution, called the site "profoundly inappropriate, given the historic lack of any black, Jewish or other minority members."

"Augusta National, by virtually all accounts, had a racially and sexually discriminating membership," said Campbell, who is black.[261]

The result:

Regrets? Billy Payne's had a few, but too few to mention.

The man who has done it his way in bringing the Olympic Games to Atlanta always accentuates the positive. He never publicly expresses regrets about the process of putting on the Olympics.

But Saturday over lunch with a dozen reporters from around the world he admitted his 1996 Olympics experience isn't quite complete.

"It's clear the biggest thing missing here is golf at Augusta," said Payne, president of the Atlanta Committee for the Olympic Games. "I'm sorry about that. It's my biggest personal disappointment."

Losing Olympic golf also was one of the biggest disappointments for Augusta-area residents, many of whom said the whole episode left a bad taste in their mouths for the whole Olympics.

After Atlanta won the rights to host the Olympics the members of Augusta National agreed to allow–their club—normally closed for the summer—to be used as the site of Olympic golf. Payne and the Augusta National even held a joint press conference on Oct. 21, 1992, at the golf club to

---

[261] Bondy, "Augusta: A Dispute Within a Dispute."

announce that golf would return to the Olympics after a 92-year absence.

It seemed a marriage made on Mt. Olympus: The most famous sporting event in the world hosting a golf tournament on one of the most famous golf course in the world.

But members of the Atlanta City Council had not been consulted about the decision to try to play golf in Augusta and they raised objections. They said they were concerned because the Augusta National is a predominantly white club. They also wanted to have the golf tournament held in Atlanta.

ACOG officials tried to smooth things over, but the political squabbling got so intense, not even the persuasive Payne could calm down the Atlanta political leaders. Finally, ACOG decided to not even ask the International Olympic Committee to approve golf as a sport in 1996.

That ended Augusta's Olympic dream. And in the middle of Billy Payne's biggest triumph it still bothers him.[262]

So it shouldn't come as a surprise when Payne announced that Rice and Moore had been extended membership offers to Augusta National. He wanted his legacy to be something other than going against the *New York Times*.

So one of the last remnants of the so-called "culture war" now ends, with Martha Burk getting the last laugh: "Oh my God. We won," she blurted out when contacted by the Associated Press.

Welcome to the 21st Century indeed, Mr. Payne. Your legacy is now firmly cemented as the man who threw open the doors of Augusta National so that Martha Burk could eventually be a guest of Rice for a round of 18—a true representation of progress, equality, and the awesome power of democracy in America.

---

[262] Augusta Chronicle Staff, "Billy Payne Is Teed."

41

Obama, Romney—Who Cares?
Secession Is Returning to America

September 4th, 2012

Mitt Romney is the GOP nominee, and Conservatism, Inc. is jubilant—or, at least, it says it's jubilant.

But what if the upcoming election contest against President Barack Obama just doesn't matter?

What if, regardless of the outcome, the catastrophe that Peter Brimelow anticipated in the final pages of *Alien Nation: Common Sense About America's Immigration Disaster* back in 1995, is already upon us?

Brimelow wrote:

> The contradictions of a society deeply divided as the United States must now inexorably become, as a result of the post-1965 influx, will lead to conflict, repression, and perhaps, ultimately to a threat thought extinct in American politics for more than a hundred years: secession.

If mass immigration was not stopped, Brimelow predicted, "[d]eep into the twenty-first century, American patriots will be fighting to salvage as much as possible from the shipwreck of their great republic. It will be a big wreck, and there will be a lot to salvage."

Mass immigration, of course, has not been stopped. And, right on cue, secession has been showing up—first at the local level. It will become the hot issue during the next administration, regardless of who wins the presidency.

Modern Atlanta, Georgia, is arguably what 250,000 Confederates died to try and prevent: a downtown area controlled by Blacks since the 1970s,[263] with crime, property devaluation, and the unmentionable disadvantages of integrated schools driving Whites ever further out into the suburbs.

This process has been rinsed and repeated again and again, with Clayton, Gwinnett, and DeKalb County going from majority white to majority non-White over the last twenty years, as diversity progressively enriched the once-monolithic White suburbs.

Atlanta's still-predominately White outer suburban counties, as *Atlanta Magazine* happily notes in its August 2012 issue, are set to become majority-minority in the coming years, ushering in another era of peace and tranquility. These suburbs are currently full of transplants from all over America who merely want a safe community for their children to prosper in, an increasingly tough—and expensive—aspiration.[264]

Perhaps it's fate: the region where the Civil War reached its fratricidal climax could provide the blueprint for what Brimelow suggested was Americans' future—fighting, in this case through secession, to salvage something from the wreck.

Note that, although White flight has created disastrous traffic problems for those who must commute to the city for work, a proposal that would have raised $7.2 billion in new taxes over a 10-year period to deal with congestion was voted down nearly 3-1 on the 10-county metro Atlanta on July 31.[265]

Why? The leftist editors of *Sprawl City: Race, Politics, and Planning in Atlanta* outlined their view in their chapter "Dismantling Transportation Apartheid":

[263] Sailer, Steve. "Diversity vs. Efficiency: The Olympic Moral: Articles."
[264] *Atlanta Magazine*, "View from the Brain Trust."
[265] Hart, "Voters Reject Transportation Tax."

Transportation equity is not a new concept nor is it a new goal. It has long been a goal of the modern civil rights movement. Many poor people and people of color, who are concentrated in central cities, are demanding better transportation that will take them to the job-rich suburbs. Ideally, it would be better if jobs were closer to the inner-city residents' homes. However, few urban-core neighborhoods have experienced an economic revitalization that can rival the current jobs in the suburbs.

Really? Why is that? Note also that, finally tired of pulling up stakes and running for the next suburb every ten years, the primarily White areas of northern Fulton and DeKalb County are laying the groundwork for secession.

Sandy Springs successfully incorporated in 2005. Others have followed suit. Most recently, the citizens of Brookhaven approved cityhood on July 31.

USA Today published a vitriolic article prior to the July 31 vote that inadvertently contained some truth:

Cityhood is a contentious issue in metropolitan Atlanta, one rooted in and shaped by politics and race. Wealthier, largely white communities on the city's north side, which watched for years as their tax dollars were spent in poorer, mostly minority areas elsewhere in the two counties, had sought for years to break away and incorporate as cities with more local control.

But with Democrats wielding power in the statehouse and the governor's office, those efforts were rebuffed for years. "It used to be considered local legislation," says William Boone, [Email him] a political scientist at Clark Atlanta University here. [*VDARE*.com note: *a black political scientist—at a black university.*]

"The majority forces in the legislature would go along with the local legislators."

That all changed after the elections of 2002 and 2004, when Republicans—who tend to be white and from suburban or rural districts—gained control of the Legislature and the governorship and promptly passed laws allowing the creation of new cities.

Sandy Springs, which had been trying to incorporate since the 1970s, was the first new city, in 2005. The other four soon followed.

The majority-white new cities *absorbed lucrative commercial areas* [Emphasis added] that had been vital revenue producers in the two counties, which have African-American leadership, Boone says. "It's a definite trend in the metro area," he says. "It's picked up momentum. Pretty soon what you could have is a county like Fulton or DeKalb not having enough revenues to support those still in it."[266]

"Absorbed lucrative commercial areas that are vital revenue producers"? That's as ridiculous a claim as President Obama telling small business owners that they didn't build their business, the government did.

The highest property valuations in both Fulton and DeKalb County are in the Whitest areas. A significant portion of economic activity and tax revenue for the primarily Black county governments is generated there. Thus, the onus of providing the bulk of both economic activity and tax revenues falls on the White homeowners in both Fulton and DeKalb, with increased rates hitting each county hard.[267]

There's a reason the tallest building in the South, the Bank of America Tower located on south Fulton in the heart of downtown Atlanta, sold for only $235 million in 2012, whereas it sold for $436 million six years prior: corporations are abandoning downtown Atlanta, because unmentionable Black dysfunction drives away investment.

---

266 Copeland, "Georgia Scraps over Creation."
267 Hunt, "How DeKalb Wound Up."

In contrast, in predominately White north Fulton, the King and Queen Towers hit the market in April of 2012 and are expected to go for $375 million.[268]

The reason: White people in Sandy Springs, Dunwoody, Johns Creek, and Milton are capable of building and sustaining thriving businesses and residential areas. But minorities in places like Clayton County and DeKalb County have demonstrably proved incapable of maintaining the economy after White flight.

In 2010, as the secession movements got underway, state Sen. Vincent Fort, a Black Atlanta Democrat, was quoted as saying

It sends a message when you say the hometown of Dr. Martin Luther King is going to be split apart in a kind of latter-day secessionist movement.[269]

Yeah, it sure does send a message.

Subsequently, Senator Fort filed suit to stop the White taxpaying serfs from leaving primarily Black south Fulton. The argument: the new emerging White cities were a violation of Black people's civil rights—basically meaning that affluent White people were responsible for providing the tax revenue for Black people to have lucrative government jobs and pensions for all eternity.[270]

Surprisingly, *The New York Times* has run an article praising Sandy Springs for creating an efficient, streamlined and privatized government with few employees, a healthy balance sheet, and, more importantly, accountability to its citizens:

Critics contend that the town is a white-flight suburb that has essentially seceded from Fulton County, a 70-mile-long stretch that includes many poor and largely African-American areas, most of them in Atlanta and points south.

---

[268] Suggs, "Atlanta's Royal Couple Apparently."
[269] McCaffrey, "Atlanta's White Suburbs Seek."
[270] Leslie, "Lawsuit Seeks Dissolution of Dunwoody."

The champions of Sandy Springs counter that they still send plenty of tax dollars to the county and that race had nothing to do with the decision to incorporate. (The town's minority population is now 30 percent and growing, they note.) Leaders here say they had simply grown tired of the municipal service offered by Fulton County.

"We make no apologies for being more affluent than other parts of the metro area," says Eva Galambos, the mayor of Sandy Springs. And what does she make of the attitude of the town's detractors? "Pure envy," she says.[271]

Galambos is right. In fact, she should go further: it *is* about race—but about performance, not prejudice.

Another example: the affluent, wealthy, and extremely White Ballantyne area of Charlotte, North Carolina (which is growing increasingly non-White and poor) is considering secession. The plan to break was unveiled on June 14.

What if—what if, the "city too busy to hate" is supplying a glimpse of the future?

We have already reached the point that Brimelow predicted: The formation of White (a.k.a. American) enclaves has begun.

---

[271] Segal, "Georgia Town Takes."

42

The Black Gold Rush in the Black Mecca Ends

May 24th, 2012

Gold rushes end once the resource that attracted people to the area has been exhausted. Infrastructure that was quickly built to accommodate the influx of people instantly loses value once the economy that momentarily was based upon intense speculation collapses.

Once all of the gold has been successfully procured during a "rush," the once booming town brimming with those hoping to strike it rich dies overnight. The primary engine for driving economic activity has ceased to produce, leaving ghost town where prosperity once seemed endless.

Bodie, California represents one of these ghost towns, a city where all economic activity and growth was connected to mining for gold; once the gold was gone, the city died.

The Black Mecca of Atlanta has represented a Black "gold rush" since 1973, when Maynard Jackson was elected mayor of the city and implemented massive affirmative action policies to enrich Black entrepreneurs who were required by city law to get 35 percent of city contracts.

It was Mayor Jackson, who in an article for *Ebony* published in December 1980 bragged that he held a figurative gun to the White business community over the exclusion of Black involvement with the construction of what would become the world's busiest airport:

So when Mayor Maynard Jackson had the audacity to insist that he would let crab grass grow on the site selected for the airport unless Blacks were given a "fair" share of the mammoth project, some of his critics began to wonder if he were in control of himself.

"You know, I never said anything publicly, but I thought Mayor Jackson was asking for too much," confesses one Black Atlanta businessman who eventually reaped nearly $1 million from the airport project because of the mayor's refusal to back down. "I mean, here Maynard was telling these white people—I mean, big industries and financial giants like Hertz and the airlines—that if Blacks didn't get at least 25 percent of the action, there would be no airport, or they (the big businesses) would not be permitted to be a part of it. Let's face it, you hear about affirmative action and all that stuff, but whoever heard of it working? Who ever heard of anyone trying to make it work? I was prepared to settle for whatever I could get, to make about $60,000 or $70,000, but thanks to the mayor I ended up with much more."

(Mayor Jackson. "The word minority should not mean women. Women are an oppressed group, but they are not a minority; they are over 51 percent of the population. Minorities and women, as separate oppressed groups, must have affirmative action. But the word minority, by definition, design and inclination, cannot include White women. When I insisted on minority participation, I meant the inclusion of Afro-Americans. And I wasn't talking about excluding anyone; my objective was to include everyone because it's the right thing to do."[272]

Not exactly free, uninhibited markets? Government manipulation of the bidding process to ensure equality instead favored Black businesses owners and minority-majority owned firms started with the construction of Hartsfield International Airport, but in continued in every facet of contracting with the city of Atlanta (and Fulton County).

---

[272] Berry, "The Airport that Maynard Built."

More to the point, public jobs in Atlanta (both Fulton County, the city of Atlanta, and MARTA) became almost entirely Black, with every department funded by tax dollars headed and staffed—from the water board, sanitation, the courts, and voting boards—by Black people. Whites need not apply for these jobs (or other non-Blacks), as a vice, a stranglehold has been placed upon public employment in the Black Mecca, the surest way to create a semblance of a Black middle class (just look at Prince George's County for further evidence) in Atlanta.

But it's all artificial. The wealth of the Black middle class is nothing more than an illusion, manifested by hyper affirmative action in government contracting and a reliance on public employment that the private sector (not even companies like Coca-Cola can employ enough Blacks) can't replicate.

The Atlanta Paradox, edited by David Sjoquist, writes this about Black reliance on the public sector for employment:

> Along with the denial that African Americans exhibit ethnic solidarity, it is popular to deny that the government sector can serve as a valid economic asset for creating business linkages. The public sector is seen as siphoning off black talent that could have gone toward business development or achieved influence in private-sector labor markets. However, first, the public sector clearly has been the source of the greatest accumulation of saving among African Americans which could be invested in business development. . . . African American presence as mayors and significant city administrators was a major factor in increased ability of African American owned businesses to become large enough no longer to be classified as primarily self-employment. The importance of the use of municipal political power to engender large-scale stable employment among other American ethnic groups is well documented.[273]

---

[273] Sjoquist, *Atlanta Paradox*, 204.

We already know that Black reliance on government jobs to create a middle class is not just relegated to Atlanta, but standard operating procedure by federal, state, and local governments nationwide.

As evidenced by the almost non-existent Black entrepreneurship or small business ownership (economic activity of any legitimate kind) in once-thriving Rockdale and Clayton Counties, the visible Black hand of economics is beginning to catch up with the "city too busy to hate."

NPR noted in 2011 that the Black middle class in Atlanta was drying up, with government contracting eroding that Blacks had come to rely on so heavily because the odds were stacked in their favor (as opposed to unencumbered free markets that weren't manipulated by Black-controlled government to favor Blacks):

> Atlanta is a city where civil rights leaders are the namesakes of thoroughfares the way presidents and signers of the Declaration of Independence are in most other cities. There are boulevards named not just for Martin Luther King Jr. and former Atlanta Mayor Andrew Young, but also for civil rights leaders Joseph Lowery and Ralph David Abernathy. Last year, Raymond Street was renamed SNCC Way, after the Student Nonviolent Coordinating Committee.
>
> But no place in Atlanta embodies the progression from the civil rights movement to political empowerment to economic development quite like the Hartsfield-Jackson Atlanta International Airport. The airport is named after the city's first African-American mayor, Maynard Jackson, who negotiated a unique deal for its construction.
>
> "That airport was constructed with a mandate of having at least 25 percent of all of the subcontracting opportunities going to minorities and women," says Thomas "Danny" Boston, a Georgia Tech economist who studies minority businesses. "First time anything like that happened in the country."

It was a kind of New Deal for blacks in Atlanta, and it grew into many other deals, including mandated set-asides for African-American and other minority contractors and subcontractors.

But the deals also made minority business disproportionately dependent on public sector work. Now, the shrinking of the public sector is having a disastrous effect on many African-American business owners, including electrical subcontractor Melvin Griffin.

Griffin's business depended heavily on public contracts for things like installing stoplights with red-light cameras. Now he gets less work and, in turn, he gives less work.

"Employees are down quite a bit," he says. "Right now, I'm only working about three people. Couple guys, I just told them don't worry about calling me because I really got no work for them."[274]

So, what do we mean by Black gold rush? Blacks have been flocking to the Black Mecca since Mayor Jackson established unprecedented statues that favored Black people in garnering city contracts. *The Wall Street Journal* reported that this trend has only increased since the dawn of the new millennium.[275]

USA Today reported that the suburban population of metro Atlanta is exploding, fueled by Black migration to the once pure Whitopia's surrounding the "city too busy to hate":

Atlanta itself has actually grown whiter in the past decade while its suburbs have gotten blacker, according to Frey's analysis. Atlanta's population in 1990 was 67% black and 30% white; the suburbs were 71% white and 25% African American. By the end of the decade, non-Hispanic whites made up 39% of the city and 53% of the suburbs while blacks were 51% of the city and 31% of the suburbs.[276]

---

274 Siegel, "Black Atlantans Struggle to Stay."
275 Martin and McWhirter, "Number of Blacks, Hispanics."
276 Copeland, "Georgia's Black Population Outgrows."

What does all of this mean? That the Black Gold Rush is over. Ghost towns are coming to metro Atlanta. *The Atlanta Journal-Constitution* reports that half of metro Atlanta mortgages are now underwater (worth less than what is owed):

> More than half of homeowners with a mortgage in metro Atlanta owe more than the house is worth, a new report says.
>
> Their negative equity will slow a real estate recovery as some homeowners who would like to sell and move are "trapped in their homes," because they cannot afford to sell at a loss, said Zillow's chief economist Stan Humphries. It also makes foreclosure more likely if the mortgagee loses a job or hits other economic shocks, he said.
>
> Zillow, the online real estate data and search firm, analyzed 35 million mortgages, including 778,870 in 22 metro Atlanta counties, to conclude 55 percent of mortgages here were in the negative range. That far exceeds the national average of 31 percent. Humphries pointed out that despite the high numbers, only 8 percent of metro Atlantans were delinquent on paying.
>
> Employed homeowners who plan to stay in their homes long-term are not bothered as much by the "paper losses," he said, which makes the situation less dire.[277]

Property valuations are directly tied to the standard of living created and sustained in a community. As metro Atlanta gets Blacker, each community is negatively affected with higher crime rates, business closings, and a drop in the quality of the schools (directly correlated to the majority race of the students enrolled in the school system).

Black property values are significantly less than White (or any other race) in Atlanta—and nationwide.

With metro Atlanta getting Blacker—the allure of the Black Mecca and being part of the Black middle class that was 100

---

percent a manipulation of the free market by Black elected officials and Black cronyism [278]—and property values falling
counties that go majority Black (Clayton and DeKalb County),
tax revenue begins to drop dramatically, immediately requiring austerity measures to be implemented:

> Fiscal 2011, which starts July 1, is already a rotten apple on
> the teacher's desk.
>
> The avalanche began when DeKalb County school offi-
> cials said last month that the system would be short $88
> million in its 2011 budget. Since then, so many other shoes
> have dropped, it's starting to look like a Rack Room out
> there.
>
> On Thursday, Cobb County schools said their shortfall
> would approach $100 million. On Friday, Gwinnett County
> schools gave the same report: $100 million short. Clayton
> County said it will be nearly $63 million in the hole; and
> Atlanta, $47 million. Fulton County has said its shortfall
> could reach $120 million.
>
> DeKalb now says its gap could hit $115 million. Those
> systems alone are facing total cuts of more than a half-bil-
> lion dollars. [279]

Fayette County, Gwinnett, DeKalb, Clayton . . . as each metro
Atlanta county sees an increase in its Black population, the
ability for each county to raise tax revenues to pay for teachers
and improve infrastructure declines.

The Black Mecca is underwater. The manipulation of the
free market by Black radicals—and by a compliant Connected
Capitalism of the Disingenuous White Liberal establishment
in Atlanta—has created an unstable system. It's a black hole
from which no matter will be able to escape.

The Gold Rush is over. Ghost towns will now start popping
up all over the metro Atlanta area, with Black people unable

[278] Downey, "DeKalb must take."
[279] Staples and Fox, "Metro Schools to Slash."

to create or sustain any of the local economies they take over as White residents flee the encroaching Black Undertow.

The White citizens of metro Atlanta have two choices. The first is to move to North Fulton (Alpharetta) and secede from Fulton County and immediately become of the richest counties in all of America, or forever be taxed to support the lecherous South Fulton area of predominately Black residents who reside on tax dollars and public employment to subsist. The second choice is to leave Atlanta and never look back.

Regardless of what choice is made, a substantial part of metro Atlanta will eventually look like Bodie, California (go to Union Station Mall in Union City to see the truth of this statement), a reminder that the free market can't be manipulated without devastating consequences.

A reminder that the Visible Black Hand of Economics will always appear.

Because policies were enacted that attracted largely Black people (whose labor couldn't demand the same salaries in cities they left) to the Black Mecca to strike it rich—based solely on their race—the whole region is now in serious financial trouble. Atlanta was overwhelmed. The burden of employment of these Black people fell directly on the sustaining of affirmative action policies that run counter the laws of economics.

43

"The Worse, the Better":
What the Story of Ivan Allen III Tells
Us About Romney and Obama

November 5th, 2012

There are those who believe in a strategy of "the worse, the better," believing that some magic concoction of one part financial collapse, two parts hyperinflation, and three shots of racial violence will somehow awaken White people (the historic majority population of America) to the dangers they face.

That these same White people have already abandoned Detroit to Black rule—and know full well the deathblow this action served to the civilization they created and sustained there—and numerous other cities to the same fate doesn't seem to register as a "the worse, the better" scenario.

But the death of major American cities and their takeover by a Black political machine that works to consolidate Black control of the city (putting an iron grip on public jobs and diverting lucrative contracts to a certain percentage of minority contractors/suppliers) has happened across the nation. Worse, White people in places like Birmingham, Memphis, Baltimore, and Atlanta not only fled these cities, but have acclimated themselves to Black political control.

It was reading Gary M. Pomerantz's *Where Peachtree Meets Sweet Auburn: A Saga of Race and Family* that, to me, the notion of "the worse, the better" lost all applicability to our current situation.

Pomerantz book tells the story of two influential Atlanta families: one that produced Ivan Allen, Jr., the White mayor of Atlanta who capitulated control of the city to Black rule, and Maynard Jackson, the first Black mayor of Atlanta, who took that political control and turned it into a weapon to enrich Blacks.

The Disingenuous White Liberals (DWL) in Atlanta would applaud Allen, Jr. as a racial progressive for his surrendering the city to Black rule. They would cherish Jackson (and his legacy) as a bulwark of change who ushered in an era of stability and economic growth.

Allen's son, Ivan Allen III, was president of the Atlanta Chamber of Commerce when Jackson was elected mayor. He would plead with White business owners—whose investments downtown were seeing significant losses as the lethal combination of Black political control and White flight occurred—to get behind Jackson and accept Black control of the city:

> "It will do no good to wait for a white knight on a silver charger to rescue us from reality," he said. "The challenge, indeed the absolute necessity, will be or us to establish better communications and to obtain more, not less, input into the decision making process as it now exists."
>
> To those who would sit and carp and complain because things aren't as they were, I say that things will never as they were for change is constant."[280]

His successors on the Atlanta Chamber of Commerce would be instrumental in covering up the almost all-Black Atlanta Public Schools cheating fiasco, an act that symbolizes what happens when White commercial interests are usurped by Black political control: never give credence to White racists claims that Blacks are incapable of self-government.

Ivan Allen III wasn't his father, nor did he allow his father's legacy as a racial progressive who saved Atlanta from the fate

---

[280] Pomerantz, *Where Peachtree Meets Sweet Auburn*, 456.

of Birmingham by peacefully paving the way for Black political control to write his ticket to a life of DWL luxury. It should be noted that Ivan Allen, Jr.'s great legacy is his name is attached to the Ivan Allen, Jr. Prize for Social Courage, which "is awarded in honor of Ivan Allen, Jr. who was a pivotal leader during America's struggle for racial integration during the 1960s. As mayor of Atlanta, he risked his place in society, his political future, and ultimately his life to testify before Congress in support of what became the Civil Rights Act of 1964." There is no glory in what Ivan Allen, Jr. did, though his act of presiding over the capitulation of power to Black-Run America (BRA) will be honored in perpetuity.

Ivan Allen III would commit suicide in 1992; the son of one of Atlanta's most distinguished White Anglo-Saxon Protestant (WASP) families—who had been considered a potential "White knight" by the Black establishment that might try and take City Hall back at some point—would remain silent about the legacy of his family:

> In an interview conducted the year before his death, Ivan III was asked about his famous name. "I really don't want to talk about that," he said. His reason: "Because I never have."
>
> "What did Ivan mean by that?" the old mayor (Ivan Allen Jr., one of the last white mayors of Atlanta) asked when his son's response was related to him months after the funeral.
>
> Searching for his own answers, Ivan Jr. came to believe that the city—and its people—had refused to let his son escape its clutches.[281]

It should be known that back in the 1970s, when Atlanta was experiencing White flight and nearly becoming a city that was 75 percent Black, close friends of Ivan Allen, Jr. asked him of his son's political aspirations. Would he dare be a Great White Hope who stood as the White establishments champion in the

---

[281] Ibid., 524.

face of a future dominated by Black political control? "No," he said, "[t]here is no way to defeat the Black vote. I don't care how liberal or well respected or what name you carry, it's not going to get you in office. No White man is going to run [and win] against the Black ticket."[282]

This admission from the man who was instrumental in paving the road for Black control of the city of Atlanta . . . is telling of the power of Black solidarity and, more importantly, the realization that what you individually do to uplift Black people, they will always turn on you when the favors stop.

In 2009, when it appeared that the Black vise on City Hall in Atlanta might come to an end, the Black Leadership Forum published a memo that argued Black people should unite around a single candidate to ensure control of the city went uninterrupted.[283]

But it is an anecdote from 1981, found in *Where Peachtree Meets Sweet Auburn*, that the reality of what Black-Run America (BRA) has done to White people—and those hoping for a "the worse, the better" scenario—came crashing home.

A runoff for Maynard Jackson's vacant "mayors" seat was to be held, with the Black Andrew Young only a few percentage points ahead of White challenger Sidney Marcus. With Black people hovering around 70 percent of the city's population, Marcus would need some Black support to win, and these Black supporters were spreading

> falsehoods about Young. Something had to be done, and he decided (Jackson), to make certain that black Atlantans understood the necessity for a Young victory.
>
> In his most heavy-handed, racially inflammatory speech as mayor . . . Maynard Jr. told a predominantly black audience at the Butler Street YMCA . . . that any black supporting Marcus was a victim of self-hatred. He likened their condition to that of the freed slaves who, following the issuance

[282] Ibid., 450.
[283] Galloway, "Memo that's about to shake."

of Lincoln's Emancipation Proclamation, asked to be returned to their masters.

"We are beginning to see shuffling and grinning around the camp of our opponent by a few of our [black former] allies in the struggle. . . ." These surfacing Negro voices we are hearing from our own community are the voices of the new selfishites . . . which are rooted in a shameful part of American history that has forced some Afro-Americans into the corner of racism [which] creates an anger and self-hatred that are awesome in their destructive power.[284]

Carrying 89 percent of the Black vote, Young would win the runoff (Marcus would carry 90 percent of the White vote). Jackson's speech had the effect of galvanizing the Black community to use their numeric majority and vote in their candidate:

For one more time as mayor, Maynard Jr. had played the aggressor's role, and at considerable personal risk. He cared deeply about preserving the political power of Atlanta's black elite. Had Andy Young been defeated in the runoff, "it would have said that the black community had not learned anything about politics," recalls Michael Lomax, the Jackson protégé and Fulton County commissioner, "and that wasn't the case. This was a very sophisticated black community."[285]

Puts the whole Black Leadership Forum "memo" from 2009 into perspective, doesn't it?

At some point, Black America must be told no instead of being constantly rewarded for their repeated failures in public office. Maynard Jackson was a horrible mayor for Atlanta, though he did enrich his Black allies as the mayor of Black Atlanta. The same can be said of any Black mayor, Black congressman, or, yes, Black president.

---

[284] Pomerantz, *Where Peachtree Meets Sweet Auburn*, 487–8.
[285] Ibid., 489.

They are good for their constituents by merely being Black and being elected to office. That's why maintaining control of Atlanta is so important to Black people, and why, once the power is finally broken, the symbolizing of this act will be earth-shattering, or ideology-shattering.

One day, the tragic truth of Ivan Allen III will be told, but it is not my place to tell this story. It is my place to tell you that the son of the man who was tasked with handing over power of the city of Atlanta to a half-century of Black rule never basked in the glorious DWL light this act would have garnered him.

He never even wanted to talk about it. Perhaps he knew that Whites would become acclimated to Black political control, the leadership caste satiated with this scenario as long as their investments weren't harmed in the process. Meanwhile, the Black leadership caste understood the importance of winning elections: to ensure that racial socialism remained unimpeded.

"The worse, the better." No. We have already watched as our major cities have become the breeding ground for crime and corruption. Although Black people have destroyed property value in places like Detroit, Birmingham, St. Louis, Baltimore, Gary, Rochester, Memphis, and Atlanta, it is unsafe for White people to dare venture into these areas—purchasing cheap property in the process—knowing that their children would be minorities in public schools that are nothing more than day-cares for the Black kids.

It's time White people tell Black people no. That's what a Mitt Romney victory on November 6 means. It has to start somewhere. Why not with the repudiation of the first Black President of the United States?

After all, "the worse, the better" didn't work, even with the sacrifice of Detroit, Birmingham, and Memphis. Even with South Africa and Rhodesia.

44

Where the Sidewalk Ends

November 4th, 2012

It's well-documented that once Black people took over political control of Atlanta, White people evacuated the city (well,
and the fact they had a healthy and correct view of Black crime)
and created thriving suburbs. Then, Black people followed the
prosperity Whites had created in the suburban counties, eventually importing the very Black lifestyle (crime, mayhem, misery, and their children, who bring down the quality of the pupils at public schools) that Whites had tried to flee.

Take for instance this story from south Atlanta (an area
that is overwhelmingly Black), which illustrates why White
people are suspicious of Black neighbors:

Atlanta police were investigating a double-shooting early
Saturday that left a 2-year-old dead and her infant brother
hospitalized.

The shooting took place around 1:40 a.m. when someone
fired at least two bullets through the bottom of the door of a
red-brick house in south Atlanta, authorities said.

The bullets struck Ty-Teyanna Motley and her one-year-
old brother, Isaiah, who were sleeping with their grandmother in a sofa bed behind the door, said Charlie Howard,
the victims' uncle.

Ty-Teyanna was rushed to Grady Memorial Hospital,
where she was pronounced dead. The boy was taken to Children's Healthcare of Atlanta at Egleston. Police said he was

stable but in critical condition. His uncle said he suffered a bullet wound near his spine.

"We never had any problems with anybody," Howard said.

"Whoever did that was a coward. My niece was only 2 years old. If they had a problem, they should just tell us."

Howard was in the basement of the home sleeping with his family when the bullets shattered the silence. He rushed upstairs and found his nephew screaming and soaked in blood. His niece was unresponsive.

Police said they had no leads but said the incident did not appear to be the result of a drive-by shooting. They asked the community for tips, but many of the neighbors who gathered around the house Saturday morning could offer little help.[286]

The tragic shooting death of two-year-old Ty-Teyanna in south Atlanta (south Fulton County, an almost entirely Black area) is a reminder of the reason property values (and a lack of commercial investment) in the area is so low:

> The breadth of Atlanta's epic housing collapse unfolds block by block in the cluster of historic neighborhoods just west of Turner Field.
>
> In some areas, it's possible to walk down entire blocks and see nothing but boarded up or fenced off properties, the owners having long since abandoned them to weeds—and thieves. Many of the properties, rehabbed before the housing market's collapse in 2007, have been plundered for plumbing fixtures, wiring, doors and windows.
>
> Atlanta code enforcement officers do almost daily battle with squatters occupying properties illegally, or attempting, often futilely, to convince occupants to clean trash collecting in yards.[287]

---

[286] Bluestein and Steward, "2-Year-Old Killed."
[287] Trubey and Grantham, "Housing Still a Crisis."

The joys of an all-Black community, where social trust and capital are but a dream. The free market has accurately captured the value of property in an all-Black area, and it isn't pretty:

> LaShawn Hoffman's nonprofit in southwest Atlanta can renovate a vacant home for a new buyer in a couple of months. Vandals and thieves can strip out anything of value and render the house uninhabitable in just a couple of hours.
>
> Neighborhoods across metro Atlanta are struggling to rebound from the real estate crisis. But few face the hurdles found in the working class communities south and west of downtown.
>
> Atlanta code enforcement officers regularly respond to complaints of squatters occupying properties illegally, or attempt, often futilely, to convince occupants to clean trash collecting in yards.
>
> Vacant and abandoned properties have attracted drug dealers, prostitutes and squatters. Those renovated for new buyers are often plundered before they can go on the market.
>
> The general lawlessness is a major reason some in-town neighborhoods have failed to rebound from the housing market's collapse despite their proximity to downtown, the Atlanta Beltline and neighborhood parks. It's also a daily affront to the residents who've decided to tough it out or can't leave.
>
> "Having children walking by vacant and abandoned houses that are open and [they can] witness any kind of illicit activity that might be going on is a huge concern," said Hoffman, CEO of the Pittsburgh Community Improvement Association.
>
> Hoffman's group has been attempting to rehabilitate vacant houses in Pittsburgh, where as many as 45 percent of the community's 1,800 residences are vacant.
>
> But some days, Hoffman feels the effort moves one step forward for every two steps back.

In 2009, the Coalition for the Preservation of Pittsburgh (PCIA) bought a two-story home with a double front porch on Humphries Street. Although the group secured the property with steel shields over the windows and doors, one door, on a second story porch, was left unprotected.

Since 2009, violent and property crimes have hit residents of neighborhoods like Pittsburgh, West End and Adair Park about two to three times more frequently than the city overall, according Atlanta police statistics. Pittsburgh's hollowed-out streets have seen nearly four times more burglaries and aggravated assaults as the city overall.[288]

Adair Park and West End were once nice, White working-class communities. That changed with White flight in the 1950s, as the neighborhoods devolved into representing the character of the its majority occupants (Blacks). Property value plummeted with the change to a majority-Black community. Pittsburgh was founded as a Black working-class suburb, but over time became just another reminder of what Black people can collectively create: low property value and blight.

When Black people had the ability to move into White neighborhoods in the 1950s (when the first Black family moved into Adair Park), the White exodus began, and an immediate drop in property value occurred. More importantly, with White flight went the job creators.

In the book *Atlanta Paradox*, edited by David. L. Sjoquist, we learn:

Ronald H. Bayor notes that blacks had historically been confined to a small geographic area. With the end of legal housing segregation, the black population began to decentralize. While blacks increased throughout the MSA, the growth was concentrated largely in areas adjacent to existing concentrations of blacks, namely, south DeKalb county and south Fulton County, just beyond the city of Atlanta. As

---

[288] Trubey and Grantham, "Unsafe Streets Stifle Housing."

blacks moved into these area, white fled. The result of these dynamics is that better than 65 percent of the jobs are located in the northern half of the region, while more than 71 percent of the blacks are located in the southern half of the region. Furthermore, the poor are housed in the city (71 percent of the area's poor are there).

Evidence suggest a spatial mismatch between the residential locations of poor blacks and the locations of available jobs, and the large number of female-headed households residing within the city suggests a significant welfare-dependent population that may be untouched by the economic growth in the region.[289]

Ah, sociology jargon from the entrenched Disingenuous White Liberal (DWL) caste in academia. Basically, what the attempted creation of a "spatial mismatch" theory illustrates is the visible Black hand of economics. White people create jobs in areas where it is conducive to creating a thriving business (i.e., White areas).

As south Fulton went exclusively Black, businesses closed up shop leaving a commercial void that the new majority couldn't fill—a void that they never filled. South Fulton is located in what is known as inside the Perimeter; much of north Fulton is located outside the Perimeter. The Midas Touch followed Whites wherever they went, with Kevin M. Kruse's *White Flight: Atlanta and the Making of Modern Conservatism (Politics and Society in Twentieth-Century America)* reminding us:

Between 1963 and 1972, for instance, Atlanta's share of retail sales in the metropolitan area fell from 66 to 44 percent, with the share of the once-booming central business district (CBD) bottoming out at just 7 percent. Jobs followed the general pattern. . . . If old-guard members of the business

---

[289] Sjoquist, *Atlanta Paradox*, 3.

elite, such as Coca-Cola and Georgia Power, had not remained fiercely loyal to downtown Atlanta, the decline
would have been even more pronounced.

With the Perimeter region emerging as a new economic
hub, Atlanta's businesses abandoned downtown. Back in
1960, central Atlanta had contained roughly 90 percent of
the region's office space; by 1980, it held only 42 percent; by
1999, just 13 percent.[290]

Gentrification is the only hope for south Fulton. The only hope
for property value growth is with the removal of the Black population from Adair Park, West End, and Pittsburgh. With a
White population, crime levels would drop to the levels found
in north Fulton. More importantly, businesses would immediately flock to the area, knowing that their investment wouldn't
require 24/7 armed guards and bars on the windows and doors.

It's really that simple.

Black dysfunction must no longer be tolerated.

---

[290] Kruse, *White Flight*, 243–5.

45

Until "CPT" Ends:
"Swear Allegiance to the Flag, Whatever Flag They Offer"

November 7th, 2012

In reading the autobiography of Ivan Allen, Jr., one of the leading members of the White Anglo-Saxon Protestant (WASP) establishment of Atlanta who engineered and orchestrated the eventual takeover of city by Black people, one story stuck out as absolutely nailing the current zeitgeist we've lived under almost fifty years.

No, it's not that he was one of the mayors who testified before Congress on behalf of the Civil Rights Act. No, it's not that he earnestly believed that Atlanta's "pragmatic White business power structure" would negotiate a peaceful and amicable to impending Black rule; it's a quote from MLK to Allen that cuts to the heart of Black-Run America (BRA).

Recall that in 1964, Martin Luther King, Jr. was awarded the Nobel Peace Prize, and that Coca-Cola and leading White liberals in Atlanta strong-armed reluctant White businessmen in the city to attend an integrated dinner in his honor.

Ivan Allen, Jr. is a traitor, whose story is a microcosm of the many capitulations and surrenders that occurred across the nation as pampered White leaders ceded power to the hydra of White liberals and Black leaders, but one anecdote from the dinner for King:

When we got back to Atlanta, [J. Paul] Austin (president of Coca-Cola) called a meeting of two dozen prominent white business leaders one night at the Piedmont Driving Club. There was general agreement at the meeting that there should be a biracial dinner, and that they would support it. I don't you could say there was overwhelming, enthusiastic endorsement for the planned dinner. They were for it primarily on pragmatic grounds: that it would look bad for Atlanta's image if we did *not* honor Dr. King.[291]

King would arrive late to the posh dinner, which was being held in his honor:

He had arrived late for dinner, and I remember his leaning over and apologizing to me.
"I forgot what time we were on," he said with a grin.
"How's that?" I said.
"Eastern Standard Time, CST or CPT."
"CPT?"
"Colored People's Time," he said. "It always takes us longer to get where we're going."[292]

Why tell this story? Why concentrate on Atlanta? Because, like all of America, the city too busy to hate has been on "Colored People's Time" since 1963.

1963 was the year that Disingenuous White Liberals (DWLs) officially won, using the control of news dissemination to paint the events of Birmingham, Alabama as the most egregious acts of racism and White supremacy imaginable.

That Birmingham has floundered under Black political control is not up for debate; the glorious overthrow of White rule was accomplished! That's what matters.

"Colored People's Time" has been the official time measurement since 1963, with White people holding themselves back to ensure that Black people can keep up (think any type of

[291] Ivan and Hemphill, *Mayor: Notes on the Sixties*, 97–9.
[292] Ibid., 99.

state-sponsored affirmative action bill, diversity initiative, or education agenda to close the racial gap in achievement). White America was forced to adjust its trajectory to "CPT" or face the consequences of having every city with a Black population forever be held hostage by the fear of a sudden riot.

I hold no illusions that Mitt Romney is nothing more than a tool of Conservatism, Inc., but his victory over Barack Obama in the race for White House will be viewed as a symbolic repudiation of Black by . . . Black people.

Nevertheless, "CPT" will continue to be the official time table for all of Western civilization until, like Captain James Hook, we dare smash this evil clock once and for all.

Perhaps on this night, lyrics from a 1980s song are needed to remind people of the struggle that lays ahead and why a different form of pragmatism (outside of the WASP elites' pragmatic surrender of America) is needed:

Swear allegiance to the flag
Whatever flag they offer
Never hint at what you really feel
Teach the children quietly
For some day sons and daughters
Will rise up and fight while we stood still

All of the Western world lives under the tyranny of "CPT." To break free from this tyranny and move forward, ending "CPT" might mean looking backward.

Never forget that White America owes Black America only the truth. With a Mitt Romney victory—and the rejection of Obama—the dissemination of truth, however insignificant it might seem, begins.

Bibliography

11 Alive Staff. "Atlanta Symphony thinks two Cobb high school choruses 'not diverse enough.'" *11 Alive*, August 15, 2012. https://tinyurl.com/3r6xys6c.

ABC. "Forbes: Atlanta traffic the worst in America." *Atlanta Business Chronicle*, May 1, 2008. https://tinyurl.com/55u8rf27.

ABC. "Zillow: Atlanta Home Prices Dropped 13% in 2011." *Atlanta Business Chronicle*, February 9, 2012. https://tinyurl.com/57ymtumf.

ABC News. "Remembering Dr. Eugenia 'Jeanne' Calle." ABC News, February 19, 2009. https://tinyurl.com/2fupseb8.

Adams, Sharon C. "No Jobs Near?" *Atlanta Tribune: The Magazine*, October 2006. https://tinyurl.com/3h3yf458.

Adenekan, Shola. "Maynard Jackson: First African American Mayor of Atlanta, Georgia." *The New Black Magazine*. Accessed November 8, 2023. http://www.thenewblackmagazine.com/view.aspx?index=516.

AJC. "Dekalb Under the Gun Raise Taxes or Make Dire Cuts Including Closing Beloved Fernbank." *The Atlanta Journal-Constitution*, May 25, 2012.

AJC. "Cheating Our Children: List of Cities That Show High Probability of Cheating in Schools." *The Atlanta Journal-Constitution*, March 27, 2012. https://tinyurl.com/5e3k6j9f.

AJC. "Face of Gwinnett's Leadership Slowly Changing." *The Atlanta Journal-Constitution*, August 22, 2011.

AJC. "Grandmother Grazed with Shotgun Pellet as She Fights off Home Invaders." *The Atlanta Journal-Constitution*, June 15, 2012. https://tinyurl.com/5bjyjx89.

AJC. "Racial shifts speak volumes, And metro Atlanta will have to listen." *The Atlanta Journal-Constitution*, March 9, 2006.

Applebome, Peter. "Atlanta's Olympic Park Plan Reveals the Complications of Urban Renewal." *The New York Times*, December 19, 1993. https://tinyurl.com/mwes3cwz.

Allen, Frederick. *Secret Formula: How Brilliant Marketing and Relentless Salesmanship Made Coca-Cola the Best-known Product in the World*. New York, NY: HarperBusiness, 1994.

Allen, Frederick. *Atlanta Rising: The Invention of an International City, 1946–1996*. Atlanta: Longstreet Press, 1996.

Allen, Ivan, and Paul Hemphill. *Mayor: Notes on the Sixties*. New York: Simon and Schuster, 1971.

Allen, Jonathan, and John Bresnahan. "Ethics Cases Raise Racial Questions." *Politico*, August 2, 2010. https://tinyurl.com/hv6n2fpu.

Anderson, Virginia. "The Lessons of Memorial Drive: The Once-Booming Avenue That Connected the City and Suburbs Fell on Hard Times. Those Pushing for Its Revival Say the Changes That Have Befallen the Road Tell Us a Lot About Managing Growth." *The Atlanta Journal-Constitution*, May 25, 1998.

Arrington, Marvin S. "Judge: Whites, Step Aside." Interview by Michel Martin. *Tell Me More*, NPR, April 14, 2008. Audio, 13:39. https://tinyurl.com/2s3wwdky.

Arrington, Marvin S. *Making My Mark: The Story of a Man Who Wouldn't Stay in His Place*. Macon, Ga.: Mercer University Press, 2008.

Associated Press. "Atlanta secession effort raises race issues." *MSNBC*, January 7, 2010. https://tinyurl.com/bd8kxbah.

Associated Press. "Georgia Sheriff Fires Workers, but Then a Judge Intervenes." *The New York Times*, January 5, 2005. https://tinyurl.com/4pvt9tm3.

Associated Press Staff. "Jury Says Official's Mass Firing Of Whites Was Racially Based." *The Washington Post*, March 31, 2005. https://tinyurl.com/mx6v3tbj.

Atlanta Magazine. "View from the Brain Trust." *Atlanta Magazine*. Accessed November 13, 2023. https://tinyurl.com/yhr7vb2x.

Atlanta Public Schools. "What Does Grady Have to Offer?" PowerPoint Presentation, Grady High School, February 22, 2011. https://tinyurl.com/384bev53.

Augusta Chronicle Staff. "Billy Payne Is Teed off over Olympic Golf." *The Augusta Chronicle*, August 4, 1996. https://tinyurl.com/4zw5wbmd.

Badertscher, Nancy. "Clayton School Board Chairwoman Says Governor May Need to Step In." *The Atlanta Journal-Constitution*, September 26, 2012. https://tinyurl.com/khed9kme.

Badertscher, Nancy. "SACS Sends Warning Letter to Clayton Schools." *The Atlanta Journal-Constitution*, September 25, 2012. https://tinyurl.com/bdhna8md.

Badertscher, Nancy. "State: No plans to take over N. Atlanta High." *The Atlanta Journal-Constitution*, October 10, 2012. https://tinyurl.com/ys33j4fc.

Barancik, Scott. "Chicken with a Conscience." *Tampa Bay Times*, Last modified September 3, 2005. https://tinyurl.com/evd9w8zr.

Bauerlein, Mark. *Negrophobia: A Race Riot in Atlanta, 1906*. San Francisco, Calif.: Encounter Books, 2001.

Bauerlein, Valerie. "Race Enters Atlanta Mayoral Vote." *The Wall Street Journal*, August 28, 2009. https://tinyurl.com/ebmdymdw.

Bayor, Ronald H. *Race and the Shaping of Twentieth-Century Atlanta*. Chapel Hill, NC.: University of North Carolina Press, 1996.

Beauregard, Daniel. "DeKalb Schools improvement slower than other systems on CRCT." *The Champion Newspaper*, July 20, 2011. https://tinyurl.com/yp63bkdv.

Bennett, D.L. "Atlanta water, sewer rates among nation's highest." *The Atlanta Journal-Constitution*, October 5, 2009. https://tinyurl.com/5bsrrccb.

Bernstein, Andrea, Nancy Solomon, Laura Yuen, and Casey Miner. "Back of the Bus: Mass transit, race and inequality." Transportation Nation, Accessed November 8, 2023. https://project.wnyc.org/backofthebus/.

Berry, Bill. "The Airport that Maynard Built: Blacks reap bonanza at world's biggest airport." *Ebony*, December 1980.

Beverly, Cal. "2010 Census: Minorities Gain in Fayette." *The Citizen*, March 23, 2011. https://tinyurl.com/599rvdu3.

Bibb, Porter. *Ted Turner: It Ain't as Easy as It Looks*. Boulder, Colo.: Johnson Books, 1997.

Blanding, Michael. *The Coke Machine: The Dirty Truth Behind the World's Favorite Soft Drink*. New York: Avery, 2010.

Blatt, Shane. "Atlanta Property Taxes: Gwinnett Is Foreclosure Central in Metro." *The Atlanta Journal-Constitution*, Last modified December 27, 2010. https://tinyurl.com/4rb3fdfn.

Bloch, Matthew, Jason DeParle, Matthew Ericson, and Robert Gebeloff. "Food Stamp Usage Across the Country." *The New York Times*, 2009. https://tinyurl.com/5bf2m7pb.

Bluestein, Greg. "Firm: Georgia Foreclosure Rate Tops in U.S. for May." *The Atlanta Journal-Constitution*, June 15, 2012. https://tinyurl.com/35bpy8aa.

Bluestein, Greg. "Letters: Courthouse gunman angry at justice system." *The San Diego Union-Tribune*, March 27, 2011. https://tinyurl.com/4yffdahk.

Bluestein, Greg, and Christopher Steward. "2-Year-Old Killed, 1-Year-Old Shot in South Atlanta." *The Atlanta Journal-Constitution*, November 3, 2012. https://tinyurl.com/2av8crwy.

Boger, John Charles, and Judith Welch Wegner. *Race, Poverty, and American Cities*. Chapel Hill: University of North Carolina Press, 1996.

Bondy, Filip. "Augusta: A Dispute Within a Dispute." *The New York Times*, November 21, 1992. https://tinyurl.com/2vyecj4f.

Boone, Christian. "Horde of teens attack, rob MARTA passengers." The Atlanta Journal-Constitution, April 20, 2011. https://tinyurl.com/53k96578.

Boone, Christian. "Parents Turn in Suspect in Cabbagetown Kidnapping, Robbery." The Atlanta Journal-Constitution, July 13, 2012. https://tinyurl.com/2s47u77b.

Boone, Christian. "Suspect in Standard Bar Killing May Soon Leave Jail." The Atlanta Journal-Constitution, May 10, 2012. https://tinyurl.com/5branup3.

Boston, Thomas D. *Affirmative Action and Black Entrepreneurship*. London: Routledge, 1999.

Brandos, Wendy. "Out of Step with the Times? 'A Man in Full' Tom Wolfe." CNN, November 23, 1998. https://tinyurl.com/y5s6jdsv.

Bresnahan, John. "Racial Disparity: All Active Ethics Probes Focus on Black Lawmakers." Politico, Last modified November 3, 2009. https://tinyurl.com/mw8s2cur.

Briggs, James. "Young Calls for Suspending Liens Tied to Unpaid Water Bills." *Baltimore Business Journal*, March 5, 2012. https://tinyurl.com/3s9nmy8r.

Brimelow, Peter. "Another Case of Collusion?" MarketWatch, September 29, 2008. https://www.marketwatch.com/story/wall-street-washington-collusion.

Brown, Robbie. "A Georgia School System Loses Its Accreditation." *The New York Times*, August 28, 2008. https://tinyurl.com/3hh4x84y.

Bullard, Robert D., Glenn S. Johnson, and Angel O. Torres. *Sprawl City: Race, Politics, and Planning in Atlanta.* Washington, D.C.: Island Press, 2000.

Bullard, Robert D. *The Black Metropolis in the Twenty-first Century: Race, Power, and Politics of Place.* Lanham: Rowman & Littlefield Publishers, 2007.

Cardinale, Matthew. "Clayton County Votes in Favor of Joining MARTA, What Next?" *Atlanta Progressive News,* January 16, 2011. https://tinyurl.com/y8zfvmt7.

Cardwell, Dale. "Column: Judges Affirm: You Have No Individual Protection." *Neighbor Newspapers,* June 14, 2012. https://tinyurl.com/25faeumx.

Cathy, S. Truett. *Eat Mor Chikin: Inspire More People.* Decatur, GA: Looking Glass Books, 2002.

Cathy, S. Truett. *How Did You Do It, Truett?: A Recipe for Success.* Decatur, Ga.: Looking Glass Books, 2007.

Cathy, S. Truett. *It's Easier to Succeed Than to Fail.* Nashville: Oliver-Nelson, 1989.

Cathy, S. Truett. *Wealth: Is It Worth It?* Decatur, Ga.: Looking Glass Books, 2011.

Clemmons, Jeff. *Rich's: A Southern Institution.* United States: History Press, 2012.

CNN Money. "Best Places to Live 2009." CNN Money, August 2009. http://money.cnn.com/magazines/moneymag/bplive/2009/top100/.

Coca-Cola. "Our Progress." The Coca-Cola Company, Accessed April 30, 2012. https://tinyurl.com/2py7waes.

Colburn, David R., and Jeffrey S. Adler. *African-American Mayors: Race, Politics, and the American City.* Urbana: University of Illinois Press, 2001.

Cook, Rhonda. "Hill Wins Another Term as Clayton County Sheriff." *The Atlanta Journal-Constitution,* August 22, 2012. https://tinyurl.com/cnpb3bt5.

Copeland, Larry. "Black Youths Learn to Make the Right Moves." *USA Today,* June 15, 2004. https://tinyurl.com/4xac2srx.

Copeland, Larry. "Georgia's Black Population Outgrows Other Minorities in State Georgia's Black Population Outgrows Other Minorities in State." *USA Today,* Last modified March 17, 2011. https://tinyurl.com/3fvhznaz.

Copeland, Larry. "Georgia Scraps over Creation of New, Mostly White Cities." *USA Today,* July 29, 2012. https://tinyurl.com/y93aekve.

Daley, Richard M., and Bruce Katz. "Atlanta Can Flourish in Global Economy." *Brookings,* April 22, 2013. https://tinyurl.com/3n646vf7.

Darnell, Emma. Interview by Jackie Shearer. Blackside, Inc., Washington University Libraries, Film and Media Archive, Henry Hampton Collection, October 27, 1988. https://tinyurl.com/duenn2s4.

Dettlinger, Chet, and Jeff Prugh. *The List.* Atlanta: Philmay Enterprises, 1983.

Douglas, John E., and Mark Olshaker. *Mindhunter: Inside the FBI's Elite Serial Crime Unit.* New York: Scribner, 1995.

DeKalb County School Watch, "Dropout Crisis Is Statewide Problem." DeKalb County School Watch, August 19, 2009. https://tinyurl.com/2k7yzvk3.

Dewan, Shaila. "Georgia: Award in Reverse Discrimination Suit." *The New York Times*, April 1, 2010. https://tinyurl.com/bdhspkp3.

Dewan, Shaila. "Gentrification Changing Face of New Atlanta." *The New York Times*, March 11, 2006. https://tinyurl.com/2y8krwjm.

Dixon, Bruce. "Atlanta Leads Nation in Child Poverty." *The Black Commentator*, Accessed November 9, 2023. https://tinyurl.com/mryjz3hu.

Downey, Maureen. "DeKalb must take an unflinching look at cronyism." *The Atlanta Journal-Constitution*, May 6, 2012. https://tinyurl.com/2bs7ukrn.

Downey, Maureen. "NAEP science: Scores rise across country and in Georgia. But few kids are at top level." *The Atlanta Journal-Constitution*, May 10, 2012. https://tinyurl.com/bdhkz5xj.

Duffy, Kevin. "Blacks flock to Clayton County: The Southside area now has the highest percentage of African-American residents in metro Atlanta." *The Atlanta Journal-Constitution*, September 7, 2004.

Edelstein, Ken. "A New Mixed-Income Village for Downtown Atlanta." *The New York Times*, November 24, 1996. https://tinyurl.com/2s35ra9n.

Education Law. "Freeman v. Pitts." Education Law, February 6, 2012. https://tinyurl.com/y2u9s4jn.

Edwards, Johnny. "Battle Brews over Proposal to Send North Fulton Money South." *The Atlanta Journal-Constitution*, October 5, 2011. https://tinyurl.com/5649b3zn.

Edwards, Johnny. "County Official Asked to Stop Insulting North Fulton." *The Atlanta Journal-Constitution*, May 8, 2012. https://tinyurl.com/bkrc274n.

Edwards, Johnny. "Jury: Fulton Discriminated against White, Male Job Applicant." *The Atlanta Journal-Constitution*, August 30, 2012. https://tinyurl.com/cufx4kwr.

Edwards, Johnny. "Marta Bill Blasted as Racist, Divisive." *The Atlanta Journal-Constitution*, March 8, 2012. https://tinyurl.com/4wbdjtvm.

Eisinger, Peter K.. *The Politics of Displacement: Racial and Ethnic Transition in Three American Cities*. New York: Academic Press, 1980.

Elliott, Charles Newton. *"Mr. Anonymous," Robert W. Woodruff of Coca-Cola*. Atlanta: Cherokee Pub. Co., 1982.

Farber, Henry. "Race colors Sandy Springs' future" *The Atlanta Journal-Constitution*, June 26, 2005.

Farnham, Alan. "Bank of America Tower Foreclosed, Sells for Half Price." ABC News, February 8, 2012. https://tinyurl.com/5n8y66ny.

Feagans, Brian. "'White Flight' in Gwinnett?" Free Republic, November 15, 2005. https://freerepublic.com/focus/f-news/1522570/posts.

Find Good School. "Fayette County High School Fayetteville GA." Find Good School, July 2014. https://tinyurl.com/ucymk34c.

Frampton, Will. "DeKalb County schools: Falling property values to blame for budget deficit." CBS Atlanta, May 30, 2012. https://tinyurl.com/3849v56j.

Freeman, David B. *Carved in Stone: The History of Stone Mountain*. Macon, Ga.: Mercer University Press, 1997.

Gallery at South DeKalb. "Mall Information." The Gallery at South DeKalb, Accessed August 26, 2012. https://tinyurl.com/yx6rk2uh.

Galloway, Jim. "House GOP Leader: 'My Goal Is to End Fulton County.'" *The Atlanta Journal-Constitution*, May 17, 2012. https://tinyurl.com/3tduryc5.

Galloway, Jim. "The memo that's about to shake the Atlanta mayor's race." *The Atlanta Journal-Constitution*, August 27, 2009. https://tinyurl.com/6brsjxbc.

Galloway, Jim. "Trust and the transportation sales tax." *The Atlanta Journal-Constitution*, June 30, 2012. https://tinyurl.com/yckvnp6k.

Georgia Tech Enterprise Innovation Institute. "Clayton County Community Needs Data Fact Sheet." Georgia Tech, August 4, 2010. https://tinyurl.com/2bw98prr.

Goad, Jim. "Blight of the Living Dead." *Taki's Magazine*, January 2, 2012. https://www.takimag.com/article/blight_of_the_living_dead/.

Goad, Jim. "Won't Get Schooled Again." *Taki's Magazine*, July 11, 2011. https://www.takimag.com/article/wont_get_schooled_again/.

Godshalk, David Fort. *Veiled Visions: The 1906 Atlanta Race Riot and the Reshaping of American Race Relations.* Chapel Hill: University of North Carolina Press, 2005.

Goodman, Josh. "Will Immigration Turn Gwinnett County Blue?" Governing, December 11, 2009. https://tinyurl.com/muvvbs4w.

Gottfried, Paul. "Chick-Fil-A Eats Crow." *Taki's Magazine*, July 29, 2012. https://tinyurl.com/mw3xwwe.

Gray, Justin. "Clayton County Food Stamp Snafu Angers Many." *My Fox Atlanta*, August 10, 2011. https://tinyurl.com/2p8b959d.

Greising, David. *I'd Like the World to Buy a Coke: The Life and Leadership of Roberto Goizueta.* New York: Wiley, 1998.

Goldberger, Paul. "Atlanta Is Burning." *The New York Times*, June 23, 1996. https://tinyurl.com/34zvjfbc.

Hack, Damon. "For Payne, Leading Augusta National Is Another Solemn Mission." *The New York Times*, April 3, 2007. https://tinyurl.com/2nrzw8ry.

Haines, Errin. "NAACP Suit: Fayette County Disenfranchising Blacks." *Associated Press*, August 10, 2011. https://tinyurl.com/n94ds2m3.

Haines, Errin. "Slim win for mayor shows battered black electorate." *The San Diego Union-Tribune*, December 4, 2009. https://tinyurl.com/et79u85s.

Hairston, Julia. "Black activists change vote tactics: Demographics, computers bring new political reality." *The Atlanta Journal-Constitution*, July14, 2001.

Hampton, Henry, Steve Fayer, and Sarah Flynn. *Voices of Freedom: An Oral History of the Civil Rights Movement from the 1950s Through the 1980s.* New York: Bantam Books, 1990.

Hanson, Gayle M.B. "Set-Asides for Insiders Only - Atlanta and San Francisco's Problems with Affirmative Action." Insight on the News, October 18, 1999. https://tinyurl.com/k6wcadtj.

Harrison, Eric. "Mountain of Racist History Casts Shadow on Olympics: Games: Atlanta wants the world to see a harmonious city. But anger has flared over flag and other issues." *Los Angeles Times*, July 19, 1995. https://www.latimes.com/archives/la-xpm-1995-07-19-mn-25619-story.html.

Hart, Ariel. "Mass Transit: A Must-Have or a No-Win?" *The Atlanta Journal-Constitution*, January 17, 2012. https://tinyurl.com/zb9fdw9y.

Hart, Ariel. "Public 'in the Dark' on T-SPLOST $1B." *The Atlanta Journal-Constitution*, July 2, 2012. https://tinyurl.com/4b6x3jtv/

Hart, Ariel. "Voters Reject Transportation Tax." *The Atlanta Journal-Constitution*, August 1, 2012. https://tinyurl.com/ye27mvuc.

Hays, Constance L. *The Real Thing: Truth and Power at the Coca-Cola Company.* New York: Random House, 2004.

Headley, Bernard D. *The Atlanta Youth Murders and the Politics of Race.* Carbondale: Southern Illinois University Press, 1998.

Henry, Scott. "The chinks in Shirley's armor." *Creative Loafing Atlanta,* May 28, 2008. https://tinyurl.com/4akvuttu.

Hinton, Matt. "Grieving New Mexico safety hauled off plane, booked for baggy pants." *Yahoo! Rivals,* June 16, 2011. https://tinyurl.com/32betmvx.

Holmes, R. *Maynard Jackson: A Biography.* Miami: Barnhardt & Ashe Pub., 2009.

Hong, Christopher. "Gunmen Rob, Kidnap Man from Cabbagetown Home." *The Atlanta Journal-Constitution,* July 5, 2012. https://tinyurl.com/2wfs2tsc.

Hood, Gregory. "The End of an Illusion." *American Renaissance,* June 8, 2012. https://www.amren.com/commentary/2012/06/the-end-of-an-illusion/.

Hornsby, Alton. *Black Power in Dixie: A Political History of African Americans in Atlanta.* Gainesville: University Press of Florida, 2009.

Howerton, Jason. "NBC/WSJ Poll Shows Romney Support Among Blacks at Zero Percent - Should It Be Taken Seriously?" *The Blaze,* August 21, 2012. https://tinyurl.com/ykzcjkvn.

HuffPost Media, "Ed Schultz: Neal Boortz, Right Wing Radio Using 'Racist And Violent Rhetoric' (VIDEO)." *The Huffington Post,* August 16, 2011. https://tinyurl.com/2wzk7asb.

Hunt, April. "How DeKalb Wound Up with 26% Tax Rate Hike." *The Atlanta Journal-Constitution,* July 14, 2011. https://tinyurl.com/479ehxre.

Husock, Howard. "Atlanta's Public-Housing Revolution." *City Journal,* Autumn 2010. https://tinyurl.com/4bctpbpf.

Husock, Howard. "Reinventing Public Housing." *The Washington Times,* November 8, 2010. https://tinyurl.com/nhjjpcr6.

Isdell, Edward Neville, and David Beasley. *Inside Coca-Cola: A CEO's Life Story of Building the World's Most Popular Brand.* New York: St. Martin's Press, 2011.

Jacoby, Tamar. *Someone Else's House: America's Unfinished Struggle for Integration.* New York: Free Press, 1998.

Johnson, Eleana L. "Graduation Rates Amongst African American Male Students in Georgia." *Yahoo!,* September 29, 2010 https://tinyurl.com/27er9vpk.

Joyner, Tammy. "Fayette Spends $225,000 Fighting Election Changes." *The Atlanta Journal-Constitution,* November 30, 2012. https://tinyurl.com/ju8p2278.

Joyner, Tammy. "Housing Crisis Reaches Full Boil in East Point; 62 Injured." *The Atlanta Journal-Constitution,* August 12, 2010. https://tinyurl.com/4n6dtbz6.

Joyner, Tammy. "Riverdale named Georgia's most affordable housing market." *The Atlanta Journal-Constitution,* June 16, 2011. https://tinyurl.com/32dtt7sb.

Judd, Alan. "Major Execs Invested in Hall." *The Atlanta Journal-Constitution,* July 17, 2011. https://tinyurl.com/2wjat2p6.

Keating, Larry. *Atlanta: Race, Class, and Urban Expansion.* Philadelphia: Temple University Press, 2001.

Kellogg, Rachel. "Lawmakers Still Optimistic about Milton County." *Neighbor Newspapers*, May 9, 2012. https://tinyurl.com/yvu234ec.

Kersey, Paul. "Robert Putnam, The Detroit Corollary, And The Slamming-Shut Of The American Mind." *VDARE*, June 11, 2012. https://tinyurl.com/mr23b4yj.

King, Mike. "Blacks leaders concerned about losing power." *The Atlanta Journal-Constitution*, June 2007.

Koeppel, Fredric. "Couple's findings link crime in Memphis to Section 8 voucher renters." *The Commercial Appeal*, September 11, 2008. https://tinyurl.com/452dmpfx.

Kovach, Bill, and Glenn McCutchen, eds. *The Color of Money: Home Mortgage Lending Practices Discriminate Against Blacks*. Report by The Atlanta Journal and The Atlanta Constitution, 1988. https://tinyurl.com/2wwb44a7.

Kruse, Kevin Michael. *White Flight: Atlanta and the Making of Modern Conservatism*. Princeton, N.J.: Princeton University Press, 2005.

Kusmer, Kenneth L., and Joe William Trotter. *African American Urban History Since World War II*. Chicago: The University of Chicago Press, 2009.

Lacey, Peter. "Atlanta Games." *Chief Executive Magazine*, April 1, 1992. https://tinyurl.com/zcsj52cw.

Lacoss, Michelle. "The Olympic Class: The Politics Behind the 1996 Atlanta Centennial Olympic Games." Georgia State University (Spring 2010): 6. https://scholarworks.gsu.edu/univ_lib_ura/6.

Lenskyj, Helen. *Inside the Olympic Industry: Power, Politics, and Activism*. Albany: State University of New York Press, 2000.

Leslie, Katie. "Lawsuit Seeks Dissolution of Dunwoody, Sandy Springs, Johns Creek, Milton, Chattahoochee Hills." *The Atlanta Journal-Constitution*, March 29, 2011. https://tinyurl.com/4w33nkdy.

Lohr, Kathy. "Atlanta Housing Demolition Sparks Outcry." NPR, March 10, 2008. https://www.npr.org/templates/story/story.php?storyId=87964901.

Mallard, Jack. *The Atlanta Child Murders: The Night Stalker*. Charleston, SC: Booksurge Llc, 2009.

Marin, Rick. "Can Manhood Survive the Recession?" *Newsweek*, April 17, 2011. https://www.newsweek.com/can-manhood-survive-recession-66607.

Markallwood. "Crowd in East Point Waiting for Housing Vouchers Gets Rowdy." *Hot*, August 11, 2010. https://tinyurl.com/4b7r6wwm.

Martin, Timothy W, and Cameron McWhirter. "Number of Blacks, Hispanics Increases in South." *The Wall Street Journal*, March 18, 2011. https://tinyurl.com/25cs9rc7.

Matteucci, Megan. "Civil Rights Complaint Filed Against DeKalb Schools." *The Atlanta Journal-Constitution*, March 3, 2010. https://tinyurl.com/4p7kv5ez.

McCaffrey, Shannon. "Atlanta's White Suburbs Seek Split from County." *The Seattle Times*, January 7, 2010. https://tinyurl.com/3n8d57mn.

McCosh, John. "MARTA calls on marketers for image aid; Can soft drinks fill empty seats?" *The Atlanta Journal-Constitution*, February 11, 2001.

Morris, Mike, and Tim Eberly. "Police: 'Brazen' Suspect Returned to Scene of Midtown Slaying Atlanta Man, 22, Charged with Murder, Met Calle by Chance While Viewing Condos." *The Atlanta Journal-Constitution*, February 19, 2009. http://www.amnation.com/vfr/archives/012551.html.

Mui, Ylan Q. "Americans Saw Wealth Plummet 40 Percent from 2007 to 2010, Federal Reserve Says." *The Washington Post*, June 11, 2012. https://tinyurl.com/4x2rwxre.

Murray, Mark. "NBC/WSJ Poll: Heading into Conventions, Obama Has Four-Point Lead." NBC, August 21, 2012. https://tinyurl.com/mrs8nfz3.

MyFoxAtlanta Staff. "Chaos As Crowd Waits for Section 8 Housing Assistance." *My Fox Atlanta*, August 11, 2010. https://tinyurl.com/4s6vhyk7.

Nasser, Haya E. "Minorities Make Choice to Live with Their Own." *USA Today*, July 8, 2001. https://tinyurl.com/2k5x5zb2.

Neely, Frank Henry. *Rich's, A Southern Institution Since 1867*. New York: Newcomen Society in North America, 1960.

Nelms, Ben. "Census: Fayette Getting Grayer, Numbers of Households with Kids Drops." *The Citizen*, July 11, 2012. https://tinyurl.com/5c6x5bpu.

Nelms, Ben. "Female Resident Shot in PTC Home Invasion." *The Citizen*, July 4, 2012. https://tinyurl.com/54d2fbys.

News Wire Report Staff. "University of Georgia Professor Receives $505,000 Grant for Study of African-American Adolescents' Development in Atlanta Suburb." *Diverse*, November 7, 2005. https://tinyurl.com/69earh9u.

Nifong, Christina. "Atlanta's New Transit Chief." *The Christian Science Monitor*, January 27, 1998. https://www.csmonitor.com/1998/0127/012798.us.us.6.html.

NYT. "Atlanta's Mayor Defies Threat to End Affirmative Action." *The New York Times*, July 16, 1999. https://tinyurl.com/79znv992.

Orfield, Gary, and Carole Ashkinaze. *The Closing Door: Conservative Policy and Black Opportunity*. Chicago: University of Chicago Press, 1991.

Paul, Péralte C. "Ex-Airport Manager Claims Mayoral Cronyism Influenced Contract." *The Atlanta Journal-Constitution*, July 19, 2010. https://tinyurl.com/55usmhdy.

Paul, Péralte. "Jonathan Redding Sentenced to Life for Shooting Death of Grant Park Bartender." East Atlanta, GA Patch, March 14, 2011. https://patch.com/georgia/eastatlanta/guilty-2.

PBS. "The Keys to the Kingdom Transcript." PBS, August 23, 2006. https://tinyurl.com/27u45cr8.

Pendered, David. "Gwinnett County's Dramatic Demographic Shift Illustrates Question: 'Who Are We?'" SaportaReport, September 5, 2012. https://tinyurl.com/mvtwtmwb.

Pendergrast, Mark. *For God, Country, and Coca-Cola: The Definitive History of the Great American Soft Drink and the Company That Makes It.* 2nd ed. New York: Basic Books, 2000.

Penn Museum. "The Gordian Knot." University of Pennsylvania, Accessed March 16, 2014. https://tinyurl.com/5dn29t7d.

Poinsett, Alex. "Atlanta's Winning Fight Against Black-on-Black Crime." *Ebony*, June 1976.

Pomerantz, Gary. *Where Peachtree Meets Sweet Auburn: The Saga of Two Families and the Making of Atlanta*. New York: Scribner, 1996.

Porter, Oliver W. *Creating the New City of Sandy Springs: The 21st Century Paradigm: Private Industry*. Bloomington, IN: AuthorHouse, 2006.

Quinn, Christopher. "Half of Metro Atlanta Mortgages Underwater." *The Atlanta Journal-Constitution*, May 24, 2012. https://tinyurl.com/43n3u7ne.

Quinn, Christopher. "Home Sales up as Prices Plummet." *The Atlanta Journal-Constitution*, June 10, 2012. https://tinyurl.com/5zasmy7u.

Quinn, Christopher, and Katie Leslie. "Atlanta home price index at 16-year low." *The Atlanta Journal-Constitution*, April 24, 2012. https://tinyurl.com/ycyuwxh6.

Rankin, Bill. "$2 Million Verdict Sought in DeKalb Discrimination Case." *The Atlanta Journal-Constitution*, March 31, 2010. https://tinyurl.com/nvsw8yzy.

Rankin, Bill. "Court Denies Selective Prosecution Claim." *The Atlanta Journal-Constitution*, March 17, 2011. https://tinyurl.com/34d9hjzu.

Rankin, Bill. "Special Investigators Question APS Teachers' Reinstatements." *The Atlanta Journal-Constitution*, July 1, 2012. https://tinyurl.com/23p754p8.

Reid, S.A. "Judge Arrington wants to turn drug dealers around." *The Atlanta Journal-Constitution*, May 21, 2008. https://tinyurl.com/49mdjn3s.

Richwine, Jason. "The Myth of Racial Disparities in Public School Funding." The Heritage Foundation, April 20, 2011. https://tinyurl.com/yu5fjax5.

Rubin, Jennifer. "The King and Spalding Plot Thickens." *The Washington Post*, April 26, 2011. https://tinyurl.com/y25u9j8r.

Russell, Dale. "City minority contracts investigated." *My Fox Atlanta*, May 3, 2012. https://tinyurl.com/bdcvrdwk.

Rutheiser, Charles. *Imagineering Atlanta: The Politics of Place in the City of Dreams*. London: Verso, 1996.

Sack, Kevin. "Atlanta Leaders See Racial Goals as Olympic Ideal." *The New York Times*, June 10, 1996. https://tinyurl.com/2e8t99hw.

Sack, Kevin. "Birthplace of Klan Chooses a Black Mayor." *The New York Times*, November 22, 1997. https://tinyurl.com/ytwteerz.

Sailer, Steve. "Diversity vs. Efficiency: The Olympic Moral: Articles." *VDARE*, March 20, 2002. https://tinyurl.com/bdd4w2e8.

Saporta, Maria. "How Biz Community Dealt with APS Scandal." *Atlanta Business Chronicle*, July 15, 2011. https://tinyurl.com/bddfwu5t.

Sarrio, Jamie. "N. Atlanta High teacher quits, rips racism claim." *The Atlanta Journal-Constitution*, October 13, 2012. https://tinyurl.com/yc7947d5.

Sarrio, Jamie. "N. Atlanta High's poor performance startles some." *The Atlanta Journal-Constitution*, October 11, 2012. https://tinyurl.com/bdd6bs5t.

Schmidt, William E. "Racial Roadblock Seen in Atlanta Transit System." *The New York Times*, July 22, 1987. https://tinyurl.com/ywh5hm37.

Schmitt, Angie. "In Tight Times for Transit Budgets, FTA Warns Agencies Not to Discriminate." *Streetsblog Capitol Hill*, March 15, 2011. https://tinyurl.com/5n7pcnr9.

Schneider, Craig. "Blacks, Hispanics Lead Metro Population Growth." *The Atlanta Journal-Constitution*, March 18, 2011. https://tinyurl.com/565b3c2x.

Schneider, Craig, Katie Leslie, and Marcus K. Garner. "Census data show gap closes between city, suburbs." *The Atlanta Journal-Constitution*, December 15, 2010. https://tinyurl.com/3kacbvaa.

Scott, Jeffry. "Great divide lurks beneath Fulton's SAT success." *The Atlanta Journal-Constitution*, September 29, 2012. https://tinyurl.com/yh53ftd2.

Scott, Jeffry, and Jamie Sarrio. "In emails Atlanta Public Schools board members disagree how to investigate allegations of racism at North

Atlanta." *The Atlanta Journal-Constitution*, October 16, 2012. https://tinyurl.com/4dv966wk.

Scott, Rose. "The Nation's Biggest Cheating Scandal a Year Later, Questions Still Remain." *WABE*, July 5, 2017. https://tinyurl.com/y6ctcp7n.

Segal, David. "A Georgia Town Takes the People's Business Private." *The New York Times*, June 23, 2012. https://tinyurl.com/t4vz6fhv.

Seidl, Jonathan M. "Are You Ready to Hear Barack Obama's New Ad Targeting Blacks?" *The Blaze*, June 12, 2012. https://tinyurl.com/2yyfv3we.

Severson, Kim. "Stars Flock to Atlanta, Reshaping a Center of Black Culture." *The New York Times*, November 25, 2011. https://tinyurl.com/ymt37em6.

Shaw, Michelle E. "Atlanta property taxes: Foreclosures, frustration define Clayton's market." *The Atlanta Journal-Constitution*, December 20, 2010. https://tinyurl.com/4wxp85xh.

Shear, Michael D., and John Schwartz. "Law Firm Won't Defend Marriage Act." *The New York Times*, April 25, 2011. https://tinyurl.com/kdwr52ew.

Sheinin, Aaron G. "Shifting Population Could Help Democrats in Georgia." *The Atlanta Journal-Constitution*, September 2, 2012. https://tinyurl.com/msrznj7t.

Shipnuck, Alan. "Master of His Universe." *Sports Illustrated*, August 7, 2003. https://tinyurl.com/54fyse8a.

Sibley, Celestine. *Dear Store: An Affectionate Portrait of Rich's*. Garden City, N.Y.: Doubleday, 1967.

Sierra Club. "Ten Most Sprawl-Threatened Large Cities: Number One: Atlanta." *1998 Sierra Club Sprawl Report: 30 Most Sprawl-Threatened Cities*, June 20, 2005. https://tinyurl.com/5b3u3xt2.

Siegel, Robert. "Black Atlantans Struggle to Stay in the Middle Class." *NPR*, December 8, 2011. https://tinyurl.com/yrdtfwxe.

Sjoquist, David L. *The Atlanta Paradox*. New York: Russell Sage Foundation, 2000.

Sing, Bill. "Coca-Cola Acts to Cut All Ties with S. Africa." *Los Angeles Times*, September 18, 1986. https://tinyurl.com/8at32vkk.

Small, Byron E. "Foreclosed for $235M: Bank of America Plaza." *Atlanta Business Chronicle*, February 10, 2010. https://tinyurl.com/4f2bxv3u.

Smith, Brittany. "More Businesses Than Ever Rated 'Gay-Friendly.'" The Christian Post, November 21, 2011. https://tinyurl.com/5n92935a.

Smothers, Ronald. "Atlanta Affirmative Action Plan Is Upset." *The New York Times*, March 3, 1989. https://tinyurl.com/2p8rdwrp.

Stafford, Leon. "Chick-Fil-A Says 'Appreciation Day' Sets Record." *The Atlanta Journal-Constitution*, August 2, 2012. https://tinyurl.com/yc6a8st8.

Stafford, Leon, and Janel Davis. "Minority populations make strides in metro Atlanta demographics." *The Atlanta Journal-Constitution*, June 16, 2010. https://tinyurl.com/nvyaefva.

Staples, Gracie Bonds. "The Honorable 'Was A Thug Now A Judge' Tell Black Folks To Straighten Up And Fly Right…" *The Atlanta Journal-Constitution*, April 24, 2008. https://tinyurl.com/fnxpvcz9.

Staples, Stacey B, and Patrick Fox. "Metro Schools to Slash Again." *The Atlanta Journal-Constitution*, March 14, 2010. https://tinyurl.com/yr4m4wsk.

Stewart, Nikita. "In a Pocket of Prince William." *The Washington Post*, April 12, 2006. https://tinyurl.com/yna4ta66.

Stirgus, Eric. "Is Atlanta Drowning in the Nation's Highest Water Bills?" *PolitiFact*, September 23, 2011. https://tinyurl.com/mp86bmsb.

Stirgus, Eric. "Outstanding Water Bills Reach $811,011." *The Atlanta Journal-Constitution*, September 30, 2009. https://tinyurl.com/ms7t7rab.

Stix, Nicholas. "Could Atlanta Property Crime Rise 147%, While Violent Crime Remained Flat?" *Nicholas Stix Uncensored*, April 14, 2012. https://tinyurl.com/5xcnxjtz.

Stix, Nicholas. "Never Too Busy to Hate: Affirmative Action Criminal Justice in Atlanta: Articles." *VDARE*, June 30, 2012. https://tinyurl.com/5jzvwchz.

Stone, Clarence N. *Regime Politics: Governing Atlanta, 1946–1988*. Lawrence, Kan.: University Press of Kansas, 1989.

Sugg, John F. "The 'Atlanta Way' Failed a Generation of Children." *Creative Loafing*, July 20, 2011. https://tinyurl.com/3v6djv4v.

Suggs, Ernie. "Atlanta's Royal Couple Apparently on the Market." *The Atlanta Journal-Constitution*, April 19, 2012. https://tinyurl.com/bde5zfdu.

Tagami, Ty. "Accreditation Agency to Investigate Allegations of School Board Mismanagement." *The Atlanta Journal-Constitution*, September 18, 2012. https://tinyurl.com/4x4jnw9s.

Tagami, Ty. "DeKalb school board draws scrutiny." *The Atlanta Journal-Constitution*, August 30, 2012. https://tinyurl.com/532tyejh.

Tagami, Ty. "DeKalb schools cuts could include Fernbank Science Center." *The Atlanta Journal-Constitution*, May 25, 2012. https://tinyurl.com/mr4b9ctp.

Taylor, Kristinn. "Valerie Jarrett: Blacks Should Support Obama for Sharp Reduction in Crack Cocaine Sentencing." Free Republic, June 26, 2012. https://freerepublic.com/focus/f-news/2899824/posts.

Thomas, Oliver. "Basic Reason Gwinnett Has Prospered Is Its Proximity to Atlanta and Hartsfield." *The Atlanta Journal-Constitution*, September 15, 1985.

Toppo, Greg. "Schools try to pull out of science slump." *USA Today*, May 8, 2012. https://tinyurl.com/4h99byfw.

Torpy, Bill. "Greenbriar Mall Boosters Hope for Its Survival." *The Atlanta Journal-Constitution*, December 21, 2009. https://tinyurl.com/bddd9cem.

Torres, Kristina. "More kids stick with Buckhead schools." *The Atlanta Journal-Constitution*, March 15, 2010. https://tinyurl.com/mr3tpype.

Trubey, Jeffery S. "Bank of America Plaza Becomes Atlanta's Priciest Repo." *The Atlanta Journal-Constitution*, February 8, 2012. https://tinyurl.com/3vt7zwtu.

Trubey, Jeffery S, and Russell Grantham. "Housing Still a Crisis in Southwest Atlanta." *The Atlanta Journal-Constitution*, October 28, 2012. https://tinyurl.com/36kr5fp9.

Trubey, Jeffery S, and Russell Grantham. "Unsafe Streets Stifle Housing Rebound in Southwest Atlanta." *The Atlanta Journal-Constitution,* October 29, 2012. https://tinyurl.com/4s7j23rz.

Turknett, Jenny. "Chick-Fil-A Closes One of Its Oldest Mall Stores." Access Atlanta, January 24, 2012. https://tinyurl.com/m8u7x5tw.

US News. "Fayette County." *US News*, June 2013. https://tinyurl.com/yc3466wh.

USA Today. "Civil Rights Museum Location Finalized in Atlanta." *USA Today*, September 29, 2008. https://tinyurl.com/msjys598.

Visser, Steve. "Audit: MARTA spends $50M too much, should privatize some functions." *The Atlanta Journal-Constitution*, September 24, 2012. https://tinyurl.com/msputurw.

Visser, Steve. "Union leaders say MARTA audit unfairly targets workers." *The Atlanta Journal-Constitution*, October 16, 2012. https://tinyurl.com/4n4p3hcj.

Vogell, Heather. "Investigation into APS Cheating Finds Unethical Behavior across Every Level." *The Atlanta Journal-Constitution*, July 2011. https://tinyurl.com/2djmc6dr.

Walker, Andre. "The NAACP Places Race Ahead of Student Achievement in Fayette County." Georgia Unfiltered, January 26, 2012. https://tinyurl.com/hntxar83.

Wallace, Hunter. "Atlanta: The Color of Crime." *Occidental Dissent*, May 5, 2012. https://occidentaldissent.com/2012/05/05/atlanta-the-color-of-crime/.

Wallace, Hunter. "National Chick-Fil-A Appreciation Day Strikes a Nerve in Alabama." Occidental Dissent, August 2, 2012. https://tinyurl.com/2mzffb8e.

Watson, Bernard. "Triple Shooting Suspect Waives First Appearance." CBS Atlanta, July 15, 2011. https://tinyurl.com/4umjrc7a.

Webley, Kayla. "Controversial Chicken: Chick-Fil-A's Gay Rights Rumble." *Time*, January 31, 2011. https://tinyurl.com/mr28434x.

Wheatley, Thomas. "Buckhead secession movement gains steam -and gets heated." *Creative Loafing*, September 12, 2008. https://tinyurl.com/2fk6ee23.

Wheatley, Thomas. "Cover Story: Clayton County's Tribulations." *Creative Loafing*, July 23, 2008. https://tinyurl.com/3jkuf2dh.

Whitaker, Charles. "Is Atlanta the New Black Mecca? With Its Affordable Housing, Livable Pace and Reputation for Encouraging Entrepreneurship, Atlanta Is the 'Go to' City for Enterprising African-Americans." Ebony, March 2002. https://tinyurl.com/5dfs2kms.

White, Jeremy, Robert Gebeloff, Ford Fessenden, Archie Tse, and Alan Mclean. "The Geography of Government Benefits." *The New York Times*, February 11, 2012. https://tinyurl.com/3tthhfkp.

Wiese, Andrew. *Places of Their Own: African American Suburbanization in the Twentieth Century.* Chicago: University of Chicago Press, 2004.

Williams, Christian. *Lead, Follow or Get Out of the Way: The Story of Ted Turner.* New York, N.Y.: Times Books, 1981.

Willis, Winston A.. *Challenging U.S. Apartheid: Atlanta and Black Struggles for Human Rights, 1960–1977.* Durham: Duke University Press, 2006.

Winter, Greg. "Coca-Cola Settles Racial Bias Case." *The New York Times*, November 17, 2000. https://tinyurl.com/2tnppdfx.

Within the Black Community. "Dekalb County Ga Sees Fewer 'Street Pirate Killings' in 2010." Within the Black Community Blogspot, January 17, 2010. https://tinyurl.com/b9hkrsrn.

WND Staff. "Atlanta's tax hike bankrolls racial discrimination." WND, July 27, 2012. https://tinyurl.com/bdjhdjxz.

WND Staff. "Taxpayer Smackdown 'Wave of the Future'?" WND, August 4, 2012. https://www.wnd.com/2012/08/taxpayer-smackdown-wave-of-the-future/.

Wolfe, Tom. *A Man in Full: A Novel.* New York: Farrar, Straus and Giroux, 1998.

WSB-TV. "Atlanta Implements Curfew for Teens." *WSB-TV*, May 31, 2011. https://tinyurl.com/48xr9j8u.

WSB-TV. "City Of Atlanta Accountable For $8 Million In Unpaid Water." *WSB-TV Atlanta*, May 30, 2008. https://tinyurl.com/2rbje4n7.

WSB-TV. "Court Records Show Race May Be Motive in Shooting Rampage." *WSB-TV*, April 9, 2012. https://tinyurl.com/bdesxxb2.

WSB-TV. "Delta Employees Attacked On MARTA Train." *WSB-TV Atlanta*, April 20, 2011. https://tinyurl.com/yc86yh6z.

WSB-TV. "Judge Orders Whites Out Of Atlanta Court." *WSB-TV Atlanta*, March 28, 2008. https://tinyurl.com/bdfpufmz.

Yahoo Voices. "Is Atlanta's Gentrification Creating Crime Wave?" Yahoo Voices, 2012.

Yamanouchi, Kelly. "Appeals Court Tosses Judgment in Airport Case." *The Atlanta Journal-Constitution*, June 4, 2012. https://tinyurl.com/5ebjsdad.

Yarbrough, C. Richard. *And They Call Them Games: An Inside View of the 1996 Olympics.* Macon, Ga.: Mercer University Press, 2000.

Young, Andrew. *A Way Out of No Way: The Spiritual Memoirs of Andrew Young.* Nashville: T. Nelson Publishers, 1994.

Young, Andrew. *An Easy Burden: The Civil Rights Movement and the Transformation of America.* New York: HarperCollins Publishers, 1996.

Zamost, Scott, and Kyra Phillips. "Skyrocketing Water Bills Mystify, Anger Residents." *CNN*, March 2, 2011. https://tinyurl.com/ycy22ras.

ENJOYED THIS BOOK?

TO READ MORE, VISIT US AT

ANTELOPEHILLPUBLISHING.COM

www.ingramcontent.com/pod-product-compliance
Lightning Source LLC
Chambersburg PA
CBHW020431130626
46549CB00001B/90